Chomsky and Me

Chomsky and Me

A Memoir

Bev Boisseau Stohl

OR Books

New York • London

Published by OR Books, New York and London
Visit our website at www.orbooks.com

© 2023 by Beverly Boisseau Stohl

All rights information: rights@orbooks.com

The drawings by Michel Gondry on pages 49 and 268 are reproduced here by the kind
permission of the artist. The page from Jeffrey Wilson's graphic novel *The Instinct for
Cooperation* is reproduced here with his kind permission.

Cataloging-in-Publication Data:
A catalog record for this book is available from the Library of Congress.
A catalogue record for this book is available from the British Library.

ISBN: 978-1-68219-377-8 (paperback)
ISBN: 978-1-68219-380-8 (e-book)

Designed and typeset by Hiatt & Dragon, San Francisco, Calif.
Cover photo by R. Paul Boisseau.

For my parents: Charlotte, my biggest cheerleader,
and Ray Boisseau, who reminded me to do my best.

For my most excellent son, Jay,
and for Laura, my favorite poet.

For Roxy, my work Prozac, our comic relief.
We forgive you for stealing our food.

And for Noam.

Bev, the world is getting so ridiculous that the only way to deal with it is by laughing. "Laughter through tears," as it's called in the Yiddish tradition that Morris and I are carefully grooming you in. —Noam Chomsky

Be kind, for every person you meet is fighting their own battle too. —Fortune cookie

Contents

Author's Note

After a decade managing Noam Chomsky's work life, I recognized the continuum along which he lived—from deadly serious and dry to funny, and most surprisingly, playful. As if guided by something larger, I was compelled to scribble memories on sticky pads and napkins, and to text ideas and quotes to my phone. At red lights I jotted cryptic words on gas receipts. After amassing hundreds of these notes, I had no choice but to find common denominators and begin to tell these stories. In 2012 I posted the first essay on my blog (bevstohl. blogspot.com), the jumping off point for this book. Noam never wanted to be the center of attention, but when he read some of my stories and encouraged me to keep writing, I did. Although my initial plan was to simply publish a series of essays, it became clear over time that it was important to tell the whole story, including my own.

To the best of my ability, I wrote accurate representations of conversations and memories, changing some names and identifying characteristics when appropriate. Any oversights or missteps are entirely of my own unintentional doing.

PART I

What Is This Place, and How (and Why) Have I Landed Here?

1

My Kind of Sufi– Awakenings: Late 2012

You are inside every kindness.—Rumi

At work, I checked our morning schedule: a student discussing her linguistics research, a crew filming a documentary on the expanding carbon bubble, and a journalist writing about the US elections. I had a habit of holding my breath while concentrating, and I caught myself swaying with dizziness throughout the day, steadying myself with deep breaths. A half-hour before our last appointment, noted on our schedule as *"Meeting with Sufi L. to discuss oppressed Sindh people, 30 minutes,"* I looked up to see him, a middle-aged man with dark curly hair hanging his coat on our coat rack. Our office assistant, Glenn, ushered him back out to the hallway, where two mesh chairs near an emergency exit made up our waiting area.

The scene reminded me of a *Saturday Night Live* TV skit where God enters a waiting room and the receptionist asks, "And you would be … ?" "God." "And you would be here to talk about … ?" "Eternity." The receptionist tells him, "Have a seat with the others. He's running late." I worried that asking people to make an about-face and wait outside was discourteous, but our minuscule entryway was at the hub of our office suite. I didn't know how far Sufi L. had traveled, nor did I get how ironic it was that I had been reminded of that particular sketch.

When I asked him in, a young woman rose to join us, just as Noam created a logjam in the doorway, uttering a quick hello with a wave and a promise to return soon. To me he was Noam, but to most of the world he was Noam Chomsky, renowned linguist, US media and social critic, political activist, cognitive scientist, and author. Roxy, my cocker spaniel and our usual greeter, slept on her cozy bed under my desk during the commotion. At ten, she was beginning to lose her hearing.

Sufi L. introduced the woman, his student, by name, then introduced himself as "Sufi." When I took his hand, or he took mine, something unexpected coursed through me. I felt a slow fall into a sense of peace, and for a moment it took some effort to keep my knees from buckling. He had gotten my attention.

Sufi's eyes, like black almonds, drew me in, and I got it. He was indeed a *Sufi*, as in the practice of Sufism, which was, to my limited knowledge, a spiritual mysticism. Holding his hand, I felt serenity, nothingness. Nothingness except that he was clean-shaven. I would have expected a Sufi to have a beard. Everyone has told me to breathe more, beginning with the nurse who put me in an oxygen tent as a four-pound newborn. And it was the first thing Sufi—*my* Sufi (if only for this brief moment)—told me.

Noam met with presidents, activists, prime ministers, and ambassadors. He had discussions with mathematicians, mill workers, priests, physicists, teachers, and performers. These were *his* people. *My*, or more accurately *our*, people were those whose correspondence, a few dozen of the thousand communications we received each week, he asked me to intercept, either because I could better answer their logistical, factual, or lecture-related questions, or to keep him from drowning in the loquaciousness.

Most of the more persistent writers were bright and well-meaning souls convinced that they could organize their own agenda if only they had his help. He would often hand me a letter and say, "Acknowledge that we've read it, and tell them I'm inundated. Be sure to be kind." In this way, they became *our*/*my* people. It had been a while since I'd spent real time with one of *his*, like this Sufi.

"The energy around you is calm," I said as I led them into Noam's office, where they remained standing to take in the photographs, posters, and walls of books.

His student nodded. "I've been working with him for only a week, and I have felt this too." Sufi's smile had the pureness of a newborn baby's. I'm a lousy meditator, a busy, thinking meditator, but in his presence, I could have listened to the silence.

"Can you feel my frenetic energy?" I asked.

"Yes, I can." Sufi wasn't mincing words. "You need to breathe more." There it was—again. I hadn't mastered the art of breathing *while* thinking. "Breathe, and stay awake. Be aware of what happens between the breaths. That is where all of life and death is." I wanted to sit in a candlelit room and talk for hours with this man, my Sufi.

I filled two cups with water, and returned to get our visitors settled. When I handed Sufi a cup, he said, "We feel it in here."

"What do you feel?" I asked, handing the other cup to his student.

"We feel truth. Truth and goodness." Sufi found my eyes, his face softening. "This is your bliss. You were born to do this work." His words felt powerful and true, but also confusing. I didn't want to pierce his spiritual aura with my self-conscious questioning, but I had to ask.

"Do you mean I was born to work *here*, in this office, with Professor Chomsky?"

"Yes," he said, smiling at his student. What did he know that I didn't? I had often asked myself why I'd chosen to stay when it wasn't my plan. I liked my job, and at times I loved it, but to say I was *born* to do it, that it was my *bliss*, was a whole other thing.

"When you look back on your time here, there will be no regrets," he said. Had he somehow heard my doubts about the choices I'd made? Had I fallen into a pot of spiritual gold, or into a pile of something quite different? I tried to separate truth from magical thinking in my life, but I wanted to believe him. I needed reassurance that I was spending my days in a meaningful way, because even now, almost two decades after taking this job with the intention of moving on, I questioned my decision to spend my days furthering someone else's agenda. Had I sold out, kidding myself in the name of ego, or laziness, into thinking that managing his office and "helping greatness," as some put it, was enough? *Was* this what I was born to do, or could I have better reached my potential as a therapist, as I had planned?

When the topic shifted to compassion, my responsible self felt a nagging pull. Had I stolen one of Noam's people? It was more borrowing than stealing, a benefit of my job, I reasoned. Still, I couldn't shake the feeling that I had broken one of the Ten Commandments, loosely translated as: *Thou shalt not covet thy boss's Sufi.* After fifteen minutes it crossed my mind to check the hallway to see if he had been captured, but the selfish part of me stayed put. I needed my time with this Sufi. I'd earned him.

"I showed up unannounced at your door several years ago and asked if I could come in and shake Noam's hand. You didn't hesitate. You let me do it, and it was wonderful. I ran in, shook his hand, and thanked him for all of his good work, and I left."

"So I was kind to you? I always try to be kind, but some days it's difficult."

"Don't *try* to be kind. When you *try* to be kind, it isn't real. You *are* kind."

Since I like to believe that we are *all* basically kind, I decided to assume he meant that *I*, Noam Chomsky's unintended student and assistant, was kind. As Sufi looked over at his student, a memory I had carried for most of my life came to me. Noam was always challenging me to solve puzzles. Since it wasn't every day I had a personal audience with a Sufi, I asked him if I could share something with him, something that felt like a personal, internal puzzle. He agreed.

"When I was little, I knew for certain that I would someday know a man who knew the big questions and answers about the world. He wasn't the God I had learned about, but a real man. Seven years after I took this job (I know because I wrote it down), I woke from a

Noam standing with Sufi, and wearing Sufi's gift of a robe and hat.

dead sleep with a revelation. "It's Noam. Noam is the person I knew I'd meet."

"This is an awakening, literally," Sufi said, nodding as if my story was neither unusual nor surprising. "We must always be aware of our awakenings."

He was demonstrating his breathing meditation when Noam returned, apologizing for his lateness. The spell ended for me there, beginning in earnest, I suppose, for Sufi and his student. I made quick introductions to save our schedule. Before leaving, I glanced back to see Sufi's body bent forward as he offered Noam a long, low bow, hands clasped at his chest. I closed the door latch softly into the strike plate, feeling grateful to bear humble witness to a deeply personal moment. I would have loved to sit in on their meeting, but that wasn't how it worked. Plus, our in-boxes were growing, I had a trip schedule to complete, and *his* people, and a few of mine, were waiting for replies.

Forty minutes later I knocked and opened Noam's door. He was wearing an orange and pink hat with tiny reflective shapes sewn into the material. A maroon and white cotton shawl with decorative multicolored edging was draped over him, both gifts from Sufi. His student took a few last photos, Noam and Sufi's hands on one another's shoulders.

As I walked them out Sufi asked, "May I have my picture taken with you?" I usually found being photographed with visitors awkward, but I felt at home as we stood together like old friends. Roxy surfaced from beneath my desk and ambled over to us, looking up at Sufi as his student snapped the photo. I tried to be mindful—no, I *was* mindful—when Roxy greeted people on campus. As it was occurring to me that Sufi might not like dogs, she scratched at his pant leg. I was mortified and I apologized as I lifted Roxy up, but his response put me at ease. "They are our brothers and sisters." Seeing her close up, Sufi and his student marveled at her human-like brown eyes, which I had always thought had the look of an old soul. I took in a ragged breath when he bent his head down and kissed the soft, curly fur on the back of her neck. My Sufi had blessed my dog. And my dizziness was gone. Once they left, Noam, still dressed in hat and robe, asked, "Do you like my gifts from the saint?" There was some truth in his words.

Sufi kept in touch with us, which made him one of *our* people. He wrote again three years later to ask for another statement following the death of his brother, political activist Dr. Anwar Laghari, murdered during the local Sindh province elections in Pakistan. When I handed Noam the statement to sign, he said, "This is a statement for your Sufi." Then he sighed, narrowed his eyes, and signed.

2

An Offer I Could Have Refused

Torches ... and trepidations.

The first time I didn't meet Noam Chomsky was in 1992, when a TV news channel asked him to interview me about my ability to talk backward. He said no. I would like to believe he was away, or that he hadn't gotten the message. Now I know that he had probably brushed off the request, preferring to stick to serious issues. Linguist Steven Pinker took the assignment and determined that our skill was not a sign of linguistic brilliance, but simply a trick, like "juggling lit torches from a unicycle" (which I have to admit is on my bucket list). I said "our" because I learned on the day of the interview that my son, Jay, then a college student, could also talk backward.

The second time I didn't meet Noam Chomsky was a year later, when I was interviewed in his office in Building 20, a decrepit MIT radiation lab and research building, by his longtime colleague and friend Morris Halle, for the position of Chomsky's assistant.

During my first two years of part-time studies at Lesley College, I'd held an MIT staff position. I assumed that finding a job a couple of levels lower would allow me time and energy to finish a joint degree in counseling psychology, so I could work as a psychotherapist. My colleague Jamie Young, Professor Chomsky's assistant before becoming Linguistics and Philosophy (L&P) administrative officer (AO), was looking for a new assistant for Chomsky. I had heard his name but knew little about him—except that he was so tightly scheduled that Jamie and a professor were handling his job search.

I met with Jamie, who at the time was still arranging his office and travel schedules. When she opened the door to the Chomsky/ Halle suite, I had an immediate sense of falling into another world, as if she had pushed on a concealed latch and revealed a hidden MIT. Posters of Palestine and East Timor and political artwork beyond my worldview covered the walls. This was a different milieu than that of the MIT I had come to know over fourteen years, ten of them as graduate program administrator in a world of exams, grade sheets, and stressed-out students handing in theses against a deadline. It was a world of casual chats with Civil Engineering Professor Herbert Einstein, Albert's great nephew, and economics commentator Paul Krugman, both sweet, likeable men. (Noam later found a valuable resource in Krugman's *New York Times* articles.)

I wanted to run, not walk, back to overseeing grad student requirements, offering ginger ale when they were sick, and a hug when they were anxious, reminding them that most everyone graduated in the end. I was a therapist to the core, for God's sake.

Jamie introduced me next to Professor Morris Halle, whom she called "the godfather of our suite." Morris, my height, and balding in the manner of a newly hatched bird, oversaw everything. Large, square wire-rimmed glasses framed his round face, and he wore a casual striped dress shirt. Jamie left us. The playfulness in his smile as we shook hands belied my first impression. He asked me to call him Morris.

"So, Beverly …" I made a mental note to ask him to call me Bev, although I liked the way he said my name, *Be-ver-ly*, one clear syllable at a time, hovering around the "r" with an accent I couldn't place. I could live with that for a while. "Our office is a busy place. You will not be here to develop a friendly relationship with Chomsky." He was talking like the job was mine. "Managing his office and coordinating his travel schedules is not a warm and fuzzy position." Morris laughed as he said this, and then added, loudly, "Do you know what I'm getting at?" I did *not*, but I nodded, to show I was listening.

Morris warned in clear and concise English, "Beverly, I want to be sure that your psychology background doesn't make you too gentle in handling the more difficult personalities you will encounter here." I could see that he liked the sounds of words.

I pictured myself being spun around in an ancient office chair by a pushy stranger insisting that I find him a slot on Chomsky's packed schedule. It seemed like an outrageous thought at the time, but as I look back I recall some intense incidents in that office that would fall into the "did that really happen?" category.

"Some of Professor Chomsky's secretaries, for instance, had problems asserting themselves with journalists, who can be manipulative." His use of the term "secretary" hit a nerve. I had held higher positions at MIT, I had hired and fired people while covering for an AO. I had served on committees. I had been around the MIT block. Morris either hadn't gotten the memo that this search was for an *administrative assistant*, or, at seventy, he wasn't changing his vocabulary. What was I stepping into? My mind's eye held a cartoon image of the last assistant running down the creaky wood-floored hallway screeching, arms madly waving, then clasping palms together and diving through the cracked glass pane of the wonky second-floor window. I clasped my own hands together as if the act of doing so would keep my lips closed and my thoughts to myself. I didn't have to accept this job if they did offer it to me.

"When Jamie worked as Chomsky's secretary, someone who couldn't get his way accused her of having ..."—he spoke the last two words deeply, with an upward stress, raising a fist in emphasis—"a *steely impersonality*." I was far from steely. I could be assertive when needed, but I liked to joke, I liked to hug. "Do you see where I am going with this, Beverly?" he asked, spitting on me a little bit in his enthusiasm.

"I think I'm getting it," I said, my smile turning into a glaze of affable panic. Flashing inside my head in bright red lights were the words "fight or flight." I didn't run.

"Are you familiar with *Manufacturing Consent*?" he asked. I didn't know whether it was a book or a video, or if he simply meant the term itself, so I said no.

Morris looked pleased with my reply, as if by not knowing, I had passed a test. He had one last thing to tell me. Over the years I would come to see that his way of looking at things was true to his straight-shooting personality. "Pretend that you have an *on-off* switch. The *off* position is for corresponding, planning Chomsky's lectures, travel, meetings, and interviews. The *on* position is activated for those who try to take advantage of the good nature of our office; those who refuse to take *No* for an answer." Again he lifted his fist and laughed. "For those situations, you turn on your steely imper-sonality!" His habit of laughing and talking at once was infectious, and this time I laughed with him. I was beginning to like him, and if he found this funny, I could heed his caveats with a grain of salt. He left to talk with Jamie, and soon I was in her office again. Plenty of groupies were interested in the job, but she and Morris preferred someone who was not a Chomsky fanatic, and so would not be distracted by his notoriety. They were convinced that would be me. I had trepidations about the inner workings of World Chomsky, but I accepted. After all, I would work on my master's degree and move on in a few years.

The plan for Chomsky and me to meet in ten days had the feel of an arranged marriage. "He is an expert on language studies, but he's like Ralph Nader," my brother Paul, a graduate of MIT's physics doc-toral program and my personal Google before Google was a thing, told me. I knew Nader was an activist focusing on environmentalism and consumer protection, and I learned from pamphlets Jamie had handed me that Chomsky was a whole other story: a supporter of human rights and a critic of US foreign policy and the media. His linguistics work was highlighted in the departmental catalogue, along with terms like "universal grammar" and "language acquisition."

Described by many as the world's most vehement crusader for social and political change, his concern about people being killed by enemy bombs was only the start. I had been too young and naïve to march in Vietnam War protests, and was relatively ignorant about our government in those days; I knew little about corporate bedfellows, foreign policy, the World Court, the UN, or guerrilla warfare. What if my deficient political background disappointed him? If we didn't like one another, would they ship me back to my home in Watertown, or would we stick it out to see if we could get along?

Building 20: An MIT Time Capsule

On my first day, Jamie showed me to a gray metal desk from the 1950s, where I could settle in and familiarize myself with the office. Unlike the posters and photos I had noticed the day of my interview, this suite of offices had tumbled back in time. To a collector, the place was a gold mine. Even shoddy replicas of the ancient metal desks and sturdy coat racks, bookcases, and oversized metal-and-leather swivel chairs would now fetch a high price at a vintage store. My father would have looked around and said, "They don't make them like this anymore, ya know." One had to look beyond the gray-white dust covering the chairs, lamps, barrister bookcases, and picture frames, but the only thing needed to complete the retro look was Fred Flintstone's bird-beak record player.

I walked next door to get my office keys from Jamie and heard her on the phone with Carol Chomsky. I felt uneasy listening as Jamie explained that she couldn't foresee every possible scenario when Noam traveled. In this case, he had needed a special key to get back into a hotel after midnight, so was essentially locked out until he found someone to let him in. Overhearing their conversation, I was intimidated. Looking back, I know Carol wasn't as fear-worthy as I'd imagined. Over time I would understand and empathize with her; she was being protective, trying to circumvent future issues.

For some reason, the department's mailboxes were located inside our suite, near my desk. During my first two hours, a dozen people—

professors, staff, and students—came in to retrieve mail. How would these interruptions play out for me? Would they be distractions, opportunities to say hello to my future good buddies, or would the traffic fade to background noise? Soon I saw an immediate, maybe larger problem. Folks picking up mail stood around laughing. The laughing strangers didn't seem to notice me working six feet away, so it was anything but funny to me. On Thursdays the same couple of people wandered in for their mail ten minutes before Noam's 2 pm lecture, hoping, I'm sure, to walk to the classroom with him.

One of the first conversations I had was with Philosophy Professor Sylvain Bromberger, Morris's best friend, who also laughed when he talked. Department head Wayne O'Neil, an expert in second-language acquisition, had cultivated a cheerful, convivial atmosphere at the department.

I now had the key to a room down the hall housing old furniture and office equipment, as well as Professor Chomsky's library, and I took a break to check it out. When I unlocked the door, the musky smells of ink, old paper, and cardboard brought me back to the used schoolbooks of my youth covered in brown grocery bag paper. I saw books, thin and thick, with gray, black, white, and colored spines, some classics, and some, I would later learn, written by colleagues, friends, and students. Newspapers, magazines, theses, and periodicals overflowed shelves. Bulging boxes lined the floor's edges. The books he had authored, by then more than sixty according to my notes, filled long shelves. Translations in myriad languages abutted the English versions. More shelves held books, journals, and periodicals for which he had written an article, chapter, foreword, or introduction.

This treasure trove housed his favorite books, including some rare volumes by Marx and others. Walls of file cabinets held papers, correspondence, articles, reprints, and interviews. Scores of half-open bins and boxes held who-knew-what. I learned years later that someone had borrowed a book draft, and then sold it. Really?

I moved along the wall to check out his bibliography. The first book on the uppermost shelf was a thin paperback published in 1951. I picked it up to examine it, hoping to discover more about my new boss. I would like to say that the first thought I had when I held what turned out to be his master's thesis, "Morphophonemics of Modern Hebrew," was, "I would love to read this." Not the case. The cover of the thin, army-green volume raised goose bumps across skin—my unfortunate version of fingernails on a blackboard. I put it back and read one alarming book title after another at the other end of the collection: *Towards a New Cold War* (1982); *The Race to Destruction* (1986); *The Culture of Terrorism* (1988); *What Uncle Sam Really Wants* (1992). Jamie had suggested I take any book with three or more copies to begin my own collection. I pulled out the *Uncle Sam* book to start, since it appeared less forbidding and more readable to this Chomsky newbie. Plus, its cover was deliciously smooth.

I slid two large boxes of books toward the wall to free up a path near the doorway. The title printed on the front was *Year 501: The Conquest Continues* (Boston: South End Press). I remember thinking, "Why does he have forty copies of this book?" I realized at that point that I clearly knew nothing of the Chomsky operation. (This turned out to be an understatement.) He would later reveal a fond childhood memory of collecting stacks of fascinating books at his local library and taking them home to devour them. He had always been surrounded by books.

Professor Chomsky and I would be introduced the next day, on my second day of work. He would meet with folks on a schedule Jamie had arranged, a task I would soon take over. His Fridays were filled with appointments as well. On Thursdays he would arrive shortly before his 2 pm workshop. He worked from home Mondays and Wednesdays.

I looked at my notes on navigating the DOS-based email system. The bulk of his correspondence came by postal mail then (envelopes, stamps), but he was starting to get as many as a whopping thirty emails a day, each requiring five steps before reaching his home computer, an hour-long process at the end of each day.

Building 20, watercolor by Anne Marie Sobin.

Since Noam wouldn't have a computer in his office until years later, he wrote letters at home using an antiquated word processing program called Final Word, which I had to learn so I could correct and print his letters and articles. His son Harry had set it up for him as a young teen in the late 1970s. Noam liked to tell the story of Carol calling Harry's school to pull him out of class under the guise of a "family emergency" when Noam hit a snafu. Harry never worried when the principal came to get him; he knew his father had probably hit the wrong series of keys again. I recently found my original notes on Final Word, and they look like this:

C:\OldFiles\fw
C:\Shared\fw
C:\WINNT\Profiles\fw

Building 20 was put up in 1942 as a temporary structure for radiation research during World War II, to be torn down at war's end. Yet here it stood, or *leaned*, nearing collapse. Wood shingles had cracked and fallen during our scorching summers and icy winters, and the whitewashed walls had faded to gray. Each time the door to our suite flew open, a knob-sized hole in the wall poured a layer of white powder onto the floor. Asbestos dust, we later learned. This was my new home.

3

Meeting Noam Chomsky and Getting to Know His MIT World

What if we didn't like each other?

The knob hit the wall. Startled, I looked up to see a slim, nice-looking man in his mid sixties standing by the mailboxes. Mailboxes—ugh, I was used to an assistant bringing mail to me and had forgotten to put the day's mail on his desk. He was about five foot ten with longish white-gray hair, square wire-rimmed glasses, and a chiseled face. He wore a gray crewneck sweater over a blue denim shirt and blue jeans rolled up to expose beige walking shoes and sensible white socks. He held a briefcase in each hand—one heavy blue canvas, the other worn brown leather with the letters "NC" stamped in faded gold at the top—a good indication that this was my new boss.

Sighing, he pulled a thick pile of papers out of the brown briefcase. "Backup," he said, plunking them onto my desk, expecting me to understand. He looked up, appearing to notice that I was not his usual assistant, and introduced himself simply as "Noam." I stood to shake his outstretched hand and watched him do something I would see a thousand times more: a subtle shift as Noam Chomsky's mind joined his body from a faraway place and he arrived in full. "Hi, Professor Chomsky. I'm Bev Stohl. It must be strange to meet your new assistant for the first time," I said, referring, I guess, to his not having interviewed me. It was too late to start over, and fainting would have made a bad first impression, so I stood there, looking at him.

To my relief, he spoke again. "You can call me Noam. I have full confidence in Jamie and Morris. If they chose you for the job, I'm sure we'll make a great team." He tilted his head upward, looking good-humored and delighted when he said this. His wide smile emanated from his mouth to his eyes, multidimensional behind thick lenses. When he rifled through the mail he had plucked from his box, I watched his face change again, a lifted eyebrow, a sideways tilt of his head, a furrowing of his brow. Then he disappeared into his office. Meeting him for the first time, I thought, "Maybe I won't have to be shipped back home. And what's the big deal about working for Noam Chomsky?"

My learning curve those first two years (1993–95) was steep. Like Dorothy landing in Oz, my eyes had to adjust to a world more colorful and intricate, but also darker, than that of my previous MIT years. Familiarizing myself with the contents of my desk, I found a file labeled "Nutcases." Leafing through, I wondered again what the hell I was getting myself into. It held letters from radio talk show hosts looking for outrageous entertainment rather than informative conversation, as evidenced by a scrawled "No Interviews!!" across the pages.

I found a few senseless, rambling letters from one person, and threatening missives from another. One woman forwarded messages received through a filling implanted by "a dentist in cahoots with the FBI." My heart ached to consider some of their stories. I remember sitting there considering the reasons that people tormented by delusions so often quoted CIA and FBI conspiracies, and why people on the fringes contacted people of authority, celebrity, or perceived higher power. Were they looking for a father figure, a leader, a motivator, or acknowledgment of their own self-inflation? I recall a letter asking Noam whether I was a CIA plant. The p.s. read: *If you don't reply, I'll read between the lines.* Two sane students told me later that they had also suspected I was a secret informant. (As far as I know, I was not.) I finally replaced the Nutcase file, relieved not to find myself, maybe dubbed "backward-talking-lady," among the pages.

I met, one by one, more of his core group of linguistics colleagues. From my newbie vantage point, the linguistics side of things seemed innocuous, but also murky. I could define phonology and syntax, but knew little more about linguistics. Standing outside Noam's office, I'd overheard him asking an advisee, "Can you say in Icelandic: *There have many men baked cakes?*" These peculiar discussions made me wonder what it was linguists *did*. Years later, I still wasn't sure.

An early task I took over from Jamie was sending a monthly schedule of public talks to a growing email list. Noam wasn't wild about the web, and would in time ask me to stop announcing his talks. Years later, in 2010, I would enter his office to end a meeting with Tim Berners-Lee, the World Wide Web's inventor, as he voiced his disappointment that the web wasn't what he had imagined. When he turned to include me, I asked him what he'd had in mind. He had envisioned a more generalized, widespread vehicle, he said—not a major site for shopping or quickly spreading bogus information. I said, maybe to prove the web's worth, that I researched articles and facts for Noam, and that shopping online saved time and cut down on air pollution. Luckily, he didn't chase me out.

The list of anti-war, anti-nuclear, environmental, and energy organizations writing to Noam was long indeed. I saw from a letter that MOBE had organized an anti–Vietnam War demonstration in Washington, DC, in October of 1967, which Noam had attended with Howard Zinn, a political historian, author, playwright, and friend I had come to know. It would take time to learn all the players—people, groups, and terminology.

Carol Chomsky was proving to be formidable; at times she would write me with a set of directives differing from Noam's. Noam would agree to take part in a panel discussion, but Carol would insist we keep away from panels. I tried talking with Noam about my confusion, but he seemed to want to stay out of it, so I brought my concerns to Morris, who reminded me that Noam was my boss, not Carol. I liked and respected Carol, and eventually took Morris's advice and learned to straddle the line between them. Over time, Carol came to trust me, and we worked well together.

By the end of my second year, I had met most of the Chomsky clan, including Judith (also called Judy) Brown Chomsky, human rights lawyer and human being extraordinaire, who was married to Noam's older brother, David, a medical doctor. Judy helped me manage my intimidation at the larger-than-life Chomsky family, grounding me with her humor and realness. To help me grasp the guiding principles of the Chomskys, she told me that Noam's mother, Elsie Simonofsky Chomsky, was known to ask Noam, David, and friends, without a hint of affability, "What have you accomplished since I last saw you?"

Navigating my strange new world, the phrase *manufacturing consent* continued to surface in different contexts, which confused me. I saw it was the title of a book, *Manufacturing Consent: The Political Economy of the Mass Media*, written by Noam and Ed Herman in 1988, and that filmmakers Mark Achbar and Peter Wintonik had produced the documentary *Manufacturing Consent: Noam Chomsky and the Media*, four years later. In the 1980s, Daniel Ellsberg of *Pentagon Papers* fame had opened my eyes at an MIT lecture by pointing to covert crimes carried out by the US. For instance, weapons supplied by the US had killed American troops, and anyone leaving the US had an FBI file.

Watching the documentary, I began to understand why people had such admiration for Chomsky's dedication to peace and social justice. I felt my own twinge of hero worship as my knowledge of world politics grew to include conflicts and people I had known little about, like public intellectuals Howard Zinn, Palestinian professor Edward Said, and Israeli professor and Holocaust survivor Israel Shahak. A year into my initiation, I wondered at the need for a police detail for a Chomsky-Said-Shahak event on Jewish fundamentalism.

I knew very little then about the Israel-Palestine conflict, the apparent reason behind the police presence.

A string of unreliable temp workers led Jamie to hire a permanent assistant for me. Super-efficient Linda quickly bonded with Morris, calling out an exaggerated, deep-voiced "Hullo, Morris!" each morning. I'd mimic her, to which Morris replied, "Hullo, Bev! Hullo, Linder!" His pronunciation of her name, he later explained, called out to his work on the "intrusive R." That's Boston for you—borrowing R's from the places they should be and adding them where they shouldn't.

It became quickly apparent that working for Noam Chomsky was not going to be any easier than my higher-level job, and I wished I had taken a longer break before taking it on. I had been going nonstop since I was seventeen.

At Seventeen

Words, beans, and hairspray linger over a life-changing decision.

I gripped the edge of the kitchen table, feeling the certain and solid mass of the brown maple, then pushed the fingerprint-smudged salt and pepper shakers next to one another at the table's center, as if organizing them would make things right. The faint smell of my father's morning eggs and Boston baked beans wafted through the room, mingling with the scent of my mother's Aqua Net hairspray.

"A little baby never hurt anyone," my mother said. Danny nodded.

I turned to look outside the kitchen window of our seven-room Cape Cod–style home. My boyfriend Danny and I had just washed my mother's red and white 1970 Pontiac Le Mans, and it gleamed in the driveway in counterpoint to the limp August landscape. We were drying it off when she had overheard us talking and came out and confronted us in her usual, indirect way.

"Is whatever the two of you are talking about something that might keep Beverly from finishing high school?" I preferred to be called Bev, but this was no time to remind her. She had named me Beverly after her sister, and I would remain Beverly in her eyes, the same eyes looking pointedly into Danny's now.

We redeployed our threesome inside to the kitchen, our silent passage providing fleeting relief from some inescapable conclusion. My father was at work. I don't know where my brothers Ron and Paul, or our little sister, Denise, were. That afternoon, there were only three of us in my world—four, counting the baby.

Revealing her sensitive side was never easy for her, so I was startled when she asked, "Now, what *are* we going to do?"—suggesting that I would no longer be alone in this. Danny, six foot two and handsome, felt like home to me, but he was a nonconformist—an untrustworthy eighteen-year-old who broke conventional rules and lived by his own. knew, sitting there, that I couldn't marry him. Nor could I do this alone.

I was a quiet, obedient kid, a straight-A honors student through my teens. In my senior class of over 800 students, three pregnant classmates planned to marry. Two others, also honors students, left for months, returning childless, their experiences seemingly erased. Could I wonder about my child for the rest of my life? The answer was no, but would keeping the baby be a selfish choice?

My father, Raymond (Ray) Paul Boisseau, Sr., was a tough, athletic guy who'd enlisted in the Marines at seventeen during World War II. After the war he worked as a top salesman for a business delivering packaged foods and household goods to people's homes, a prehistoric Amazon. He had a second job as a shoe salesman, and later worked alongside lawyers as a union arbitrator, an unlikely job for a man without a high school diploma, but possible in the days of the American Dream.

My mother, Charlotte (Segien) Boisseau, quit high school at seventeen to marry my father. She worked as a waitress to pay for our orthodontia and an above-ground swimming pool. Her significant tips (some, she said, from hungry Mafia) would also supplement Paul's MIT financial aid package. In her fifties she co-taught at Waltham High School, where her students, high-risk teens on the verge of dropping out or doing jail time, fondly dubbed her "Mrs. B." A slight woman at five foot five, she handled bullies with fearless bravado. When threatened by a switchblade-brandishing student, she matched his indecent language with some of her own to prove her muscle. She saved another from self-harm. Earning her GED at sixty, she taught and tutored for another decade, cheering her students at graduation.

They parented through trial and error, undervaluing their own intelligence even while mastering crossword puzzles, devouring history books, and working at careers above their education level, surprised when we excelled at school. Christmas mornings held the magical, fairy-tale moments my parents had missed, as our small living room swelled with barely affordable piles of presents. As a kid, I wondered if they knew us as individuals, but looking back on those enchanted Christmases, I realize that my poetry books and Singer sewing machine, Paul's circuit board kit and battery-operated robot, Ron's athletic gear, and Denise's musical instruments were thoughtful, fitting gifts for the people we would grow to be. We three younger kids learned a sense of *joie de vivre* from Ron, an athlete, jokester, writer, and pop music fanatic.

Thinking back at all of this, I knew there was only one real choice I—any of us—could live with. Being a mother scared the hell out of me, but giving my baby up for adoption felt unfathomable.

"Of course we'll keep the baby," I said. The words, sounding as if they had been spoken by an older, more capable version of myself, floated above us in the room, mingling with the beans and the hairspray, lingering there, as if offering me one last opportunity to snatch them back. I barely knew who I was in the world.

Danny laughed. My mother all but applauded with relief.

Courage and desperation pushed me to voice my fears. "What about my life?" I whispered. "This will change everything."

"It'll be fun," Danny said.

"I'll help you," my mother said.

College would have to wait. On February 9, on my parents' twenty-fifth wedding anniversary, Jay was born. Debbie, my close and loyal friend, was godmother. My grandfather Charlie, a Polish-Russian immigrant, played guitar and harmonica at his baptism. When Debbie left for the Boston Art Institute in the fall, and Danny drifted in and out chasing his dreams, I saw the enormity of my situation. The choices I made from then on followed a trajectory that would never have been launched had I, barely grown myself, not become pregnant at seventeen. I threw myself into guitar and piano classes, quilting, and car repair. Psychology and writing classes at Boston College filled a void while I figured out how to move forward.

When Jay was six, I followed my brother Paul to MIT, where I worked part time to be home in the afternoons. By the time Jay was twenty-one, I was working full time as a graduate program administrator at MIT, taking classes and writing research papers at night toward a bachelor of science degree in psychology, and sending care packages to UMass Amherst, where he was in the business program. He and I had traveled around Utah and Colorado in 1992, between college semesters. When Danny called to check in, our talks were profound, with philosophical musings that helped me heal from the trauma he'd helped create in my life. Now in my late thirties, I was ready to work more seriously toward a master's degree in psychology—so I chose to take the "easier" MIT job with Noam.

4

The Unabomber, Rage, and
Bad Religion: 1995–1996

Morris's advice comes to life and Bev gets down
on a dusty floor to gather cool Mom points.

During the Unabomber's campaign, I joked with Noam that we should give each piece of mail a vigorous shake to listen for loose parts, but he warned me to take the situation seriously, since he could indeed be targeted. I nevertheless thought the chances of that were slim—until a large suitcase arrived sealed in packing tape and addressed to "Professor Chomsky" with no return address. After an hour of alarm, campus police took it away, though they found its contents innocuous.

However, when we learned that some bomb recipients had worked with Kaczynski in the past, Noam warned me to forward even vaguely threatening mail to campus police. In 1996 Ted Kaczynski's brother turned him in, and Noam's writings were found taped to his cabin walls. They had briefly crossed paths at Berkeley in the mid sixties, when Noam was visiting faculty, a fact he revealed to me when an FBI agent questioned me, looking for ties between Noam and Ted. I suppose Noam had kept this quiet as a way to protect me. A decade later, a friend of Kaczynski's activist mother asked Noam to call her on her eighty-ninth birthday. During the call, I was witness to Noam's empathy and kindness.

As a master's degree requirement, I toured a long-term care facility for people who had suffered traumatic head injuries. There I saw two siblings injured in a car accident as teens, one comatose, the other unable to talk or feed himself. I sat with the nurse manager afterward, in tears, and took an indefinite leave from school. I was over forty now, and my internal clock was ticking. My time with Noam was to have been temporary, and as I leaned more toward changing my trajectory away from psych studies, I worried that this glorified secretarial job would define who I was. I eventually came to see that MIT was filled with administrators working for the benefits while their "real" creative lives happened beyond the Institute. But forty hours a week was a lot of time to be spending away from one's real life.

Remembering the fun Paul and I had as teens building a stereo component cabinet, I studied woodworking and built bookcases, benches, and Adirondack chairs in my spare time. This was my meditation, offering the satisfaction of a finished product I could handle, sit on, or give away. It was a relief to move back into the creativity that lit me up, and was about who I was.

With my mind off psychology studies, my days with Noam and Morris took on more depth. Politically savvy punk and rock musicians wrote regularly. Noam's letter thanking musician Jello Biafra, founding member of a political punk band called The Dead Kennedys, for a gift of audiotapes got my attention. I knew his name from Jay, now twenty-four. Who could forget a name like Jello Biafra? I hoped Jay would be as impressed as I was to hear that he had contacted Noam.

Noam wrote: "Dear Jello Biafra: Many thanks for the tapes … though to be honest, I have to say that finding a moment to listen to tapes is a luxury I rarely have."

I told Noam that this proved that there wasn't always room for Jello. He had no reaction to my pun on the well-known commercial due to his limited internal pop-culture library. My exposure to the broadminded artists of Jay's favorite bands, and to the politics of my own favorites, like Joan Baez and Harry Belafonte, whose names crossed my desk on petitions and letters of appeal, was exciting. I was beginning to embrace the atmosphere of our office, and of Building 20 as a whole. Linda left us to attend grad school. The agency temps we hired to replace her were disasters, and I finally hired a permanent part-time assistant, the sharp-witted Sheila. Signing her emails "Helena Handbasket," she brought buoyancy to our days, and I was relieved to have a new bantering partner. Her presence, along with my growing familiarity with my job, allowed me to lift my head up and look around. Students sat in an oak chair five feet from my desk waiting to meet with Noam, their bodies fidgeting, pencils tapping, eyes darting. Later, they emerged red-faced, waving a quick goodbye before sprinting out. What was going on in there? Years later, I asked a few ex-students what their meetings with Noam had been like. A reply from Raj Singh, associate professor of cognitive science at Carleton University, is typical:

> The way I remember [this one meeting], he was commenting on a draft of a paper I was working on that would become part of my dissertation. It felt to me like each time he turned a page he had a new barrage of criticisms—flaws in the logic, counterexamples, obvious (to a mind like his) ways I could have stated things better ... I was trembling, probably sweating, embarrassed that I had wasted his time yet deeply honored and humbled that I was sitting there getting the beating of my life. When it finally came to an end, he looked at me with that warm, grandfatherly smile and said something like, "Looks pretty good to me." I am sure he meant it. The paper later appeared in *Natural Language Semantics*.

I saw that students were Noam's number one priority, but he could be tough. When Laura and I visited one of her work colleagues, her husband, who had been an MIT student, lamented, "My only non-A grade was in Chomsky's class." In a card I handed him, Noam wrote, "Dear Steve, I hereby change your B grade to an A. Noam Chomsky." We learned that her husband opened the card and screamed with delight.

On another front, Larissa MacFarquhar turned out to be the kind
of journalist Morris had warned me about. After interviewing Carol
and Noam in their home, she would write an article, "The Devil's
Accountant," for the *New Yorker* in 2003, which portrayed Noam as a
classroom bully. It was hard for an outsider to see what most students
came to understand. Noam used the Socratic method, a practice of
argumentative dialogue meant to stimulate critical thinking. Carol
never again opened their home to a journalist.

Guitarist Tom Morello, a former member of Rage Against the
Machine, wrote us again soon after the letter from Jello Biafra. Noam
agreed to do an interview with him on national radio. I felt once
again like a proud mama, not only because Jay's favorite groups in
the late 1980s were Bad Religion and Rage Against the Machine,
but also because Tom called me "Mom" afterward. Years later, Tom
performed on Pete Seeger's 90th birthday DVD: one of Jay's heroes
paired with one of mine. Cool.

In an investigative conversation with Greg Graffin, lead sing-
er-songwriter for Bad Religion (meaning that I had chatted long
enough to impress Jay with details), I learned that the band had
released Noam's political commentary as a single in 1991. Once I'd
set up the interview Greg had called to request, I told him that Jay
was a fan. I shrugged off any guilt about my harmless bartering when
Greg sent him tickets *and* backstage passes to their upcoming gig at
Denver's Paramount Theater, a two-hour drive from Vail, where Jay
was living.

I asked Noam one afternoon if he remembered the Bad Religion
interview. "I do. In fact, I think we have copies of that record somewhere," he said. I wouldn't have guessed he would recall the recording, nor that he would remember the interview's association with
Bad Religion. After all, when I had asked him about a CD I'd found
with his interview with the English rock band Chumbawamba, he'd
had no idea what I was talking about.

During a break I went off to his library, hoping to excavate the
45's from the scores of dusty boxes, returning briefly over the week

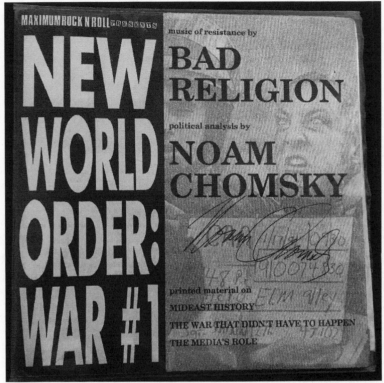

Cover of Bad Religion's 45, "New World Order: War #1."

to uncover article drafts, plaques, mugs, dictation machines, tapes, and old posters announcing talks on the Middle East and Central America—but no records. I cheered when I reached into a box the second week and found, under a pile of class notes, six copies of the seven-inch vinyl record titled *New World Order: War #1*. When I handed Noam three Bad Religion paper jacket covers to sign, he asked, "What are these?" His eyes glazed over with even a brief explanation when he wasn't connected to a subject, so I kept it short and moved on, as he apparently had.

I found Wayne O'Neil in the front office, wearing one of his signature Filene's Basement finds, this one a loose, straight-bottomed shirt decorated with large bowling pins. I handed him a copy of *Powers and Prospects* and said I knew the author if he wanted it signed. He turned into Morris's office, his robust laugh ringing in his wake, bringing Noam out of hiding. When any combination of Noam and Morris, Sylvain, Wayne, Louis Kampf, and Jay Keyser congregated, their laughter was a balm. I told Wayne on his way out about the Bad Religion 45 and Jello Biafra's request, and learned that he too had a Dead Kennedys connection. He left briefly, returning with a promise to share that story one day as he handed me a tape of one song by The Horsies, titled "Noam Chomsky."

Meanwhile, I continued my unintentional education at work, honing my ability to speak loudly and carry a small stick. Gene Searchinger came with his crew to interview Noam for his *Language Series* project. Working at my computer, I heard some commotion and looked up to see two men attempting to nudge Noam's green recliner chair through his narrow doorway. I jumped up and insisted they stop and instead move it aside for the shoot. My reaction surprised them, but they complied. I hadn't known I'd felt this strongly about our office, and our stuff, including Noam's class preparation chair. Later I watched their first DVD and learned some basics about linguistics, like "why does an English-speaking child instinctively say, 'red ball,' and not 'ball red?'" Talking about this with Noam, correcting myself when I used "me" instead of "I" in a sentence, he pointed out that a young child is not incorrect when saying "my friend and me."

5

Leaving Building 20

Bev's wish for a universal sign language; a woman's dream
leads to the resurrection of the Wampanoag language.

By 1997 we had no choice but to prepare to leave Building 20 before
the building threw us out on its own. Preparing to vacate for asbestos removal and demolition, I packed up from the top drawer of
Noam's gray desk an ancient collection of business cards from the
BBC, the CBC, the Chinese, Korean, and Japanese press, photogra-
phers, professors, and others. Boxes of paper clips and staples bore
"cents" price tags from the University Stationery Store, a Central
Square fixture since 1929, the year Noam was taking his first steps
and probably beginning to read.

I emptied the dented side drawer where he had rested his feet for
decades during phone interviews on US foreign policy, the current
war, the Israel-Palestine conflict, the new administration, the latest
language theory. Thus, the dent. I'd tucked boxes of saltines and Fig
Newton cookies into an adjacent drawer when he needed a snack. I
cleared his desktop with ambivalence. I was unable to toss years of
history into the trash, so laid things in a box: his sturdy white mug,
reconfigured paper clips, an open box of thick, white chalk, and a
handful of Noam-made paper springs. He tore narrow strips of paper
and rolled them into springs during phone interviews—the more
intense the interview, the tighter the spring. I'd seen him reading a

book while twirling springs during a few slow interviews; he said he was listening in for key words and phrases calling for a response.

Cleaning out his desk brought me back to a scene in my son's bedroom after he left for college. It was time to toss some old toys and outgrown clothing. An hour in, a garbage bag drooped with three gym socks, green-tinted lawn-mowing sneakers, and a worn quilt he dragged around during an energy crisis in the early 1980s, when he insisted I keep the heat low. I blew my nose and glanced down at a huge pink snake Jay had won at a carnival during one of Danny's rare visits, now coiled in my lap.

A jar filled with Noam's paper springs and paper clips.

I closed Noam's desk drawers and gave email a last check so I could head home. Ken Hale, a professor who focused on endangered and previously unstudied languages, appeared in my doorway, his silver belt buckle beckoning his rodeo days. I told him Noam wasn't in.

"I've actually come to see you, Bev. I heard you've studied sign language." I told him I wasn't proficient, but that I had studied and performed it, and had taught beginners.

"I'm having trouble understanding sign language concepts," he said. Was Ken Hale, a once-in-a-generation language master who spoke Navajo so well that a blind Navajo woman believed he was a native speaker, asking me to help him puzzle out a language? I shared what I knew. When I asked him about my wish for a universal sign language, he explained how various sign languages had properties of the languages of the countries where they were spoken, so a universal sign language might not be possible, though at least he didn't say *impossible*.

I never joined the study group he had invited me to, but I did meet his student Jessie Little Doe Baird when she and filmmaker Ann Makepeace interviewed Noam for a documentary about Jessie and Ken's project. In recurring dreams, elders had spoken to Jessie in a foreign tongue, their voices strangely both familiar and not. Words garnered from her dreams provided a starting point for what grew into the Wampanoag Language Reclamation Project. By some coincidence, when I told my friend Lorraine about this project, she revealed that the title examiners office in Plymouth, where she worked, had on display an old title they believed to be a Wampanoag document. I passed it onto Jessie and Ann, who confirmed that it was in fact written in the Wampanoag language.

A centuries-old prophecy predicting that the language would be spoken again in the seventh generation proved true when Jessie's daughter, Mae, became a native speaker from birth. I was surprised that something so outside of science—elders' voices spoken in recurring dreams—had been taken seriously at MIT. Jessie received a MacArthur award for her work. Witnessing projects like Jessie's was like sitting in the front row of a Disney ride. I never knew which way my seat would swivel, what my in-house theater would reveal this time.

Superheroes and Kleptomaniacs Among Us

Losses, gains, and a few surprises—one about Noam's childhood.

We had barely settled into our new offices above Rebecca's Café in Kendall Square when my private world was shaken. In late October I took my father, the man who had taught me to swim, with whom I had played cards and word games and snuggled up to during scary movies, to an emergency room with breathing issues. The tobacco industry, a major culprit, had hooked him into smoking three packs of cigarettes a day. He died of a heart attack a few days later, as I watched helplessly. Noam was traveling, but seeing Morris at the wake was a comfort. The small surprises of my workdays helped ease my loss. Super Barrio Gómez, a Mexican celebrity—most Mexican kids owned a Super Barrio action figure—advocating for tenant and squatter rights against unscrupulous landlords, requested a meeting. I felt a flicker of magical, whimsical joy, and some internal muscle, when he showed up in costume, as I had half-seriously requested. Some days as Chomsky's assistant were more fun than others.

Following up on an interview request, I wrote Rage Against the Machine member Zack de la Rocha, the band's former front man and songwriter, "Professor Chomsky has agreed to an interview. Can I ask a favor? My son loves Rage and would like to meet you." I'm almost positive I didn't say he could interview Noam only if he agreed to meet with Jay, who was now twenty-seven and had returned home from Vail. When Zack said yes, I poked another notch in my cool mother belt on the shoulders of Noam, who was happy to share his visitor.

More than five years in, Noam, Morris, Sheila, and I had become a solid, well-oiled foursome. Our relationships were evolving. A 1998 article in the *MIT Tech Talk* paper announced a surprise "web-schrift"—notes and memories written on a website—celebrating Noam's seventieth birthday. The article described my trying to explain the birthday card and notebooks on his desk inscribed with the names of 2,000 people from MIT Press, *Z Magazine*, and others. The article quoted my observation that it was hard for Noam to take in that he was making a difference. I had warned Carol that the surprise hadn't sunk in. Noam's note to me that night proved that even as a kid he wasn't focused on himself:

Sorry I couldn't understand the hints I now understand you were dropping all day. When I got home, Carol asked me about the surprise. What surprise? After hysterical laughter, she led me through it ... and I finally understood what the file of names and gift-wrapped package were all about—and realized, after emerging from the fog, that's what you were trying to get me to understand. Takes work. In the genes, I think. When I was a kid, my mother had a surprise party for my birthday every year. I never figured it out, was always surprised—genuinely ... I can imagine—or probably can't—the effort that went into all of this, and really appreciate the sentiment that lies behind it.

When Sheila left for Colorado in early 1998 to finish her graduate studies, we hired Glenn, who had filled in for her the previous year. Tall and thin with surprising muscle, a great singing voice, and an even temperament, he kept me grounded, and we found ways to make our office more manageable. Rule number one: never schedule two film crews in a row. With a few unavoidable exceptions, we stuck to it.

Over time I'd come to enjoy Noam and Morris's friends and colleagues. Wayne came by in late 1999 and handed me a bag: "For you, to wear in the new century."

"Your bowling pin shirt! It's a signature 'Wayneswear' item [Jamie and I had named his clothing line]. I can't take this," I said insincerely, taking it from him. I would wear it for luck, to allay fears that a technical calamity would cripple systems worldwide at the start of the new millennium. Once that proved untrue, I returned to my tradition of infusing more play into our days. Being my father's daughter, I called Noam out on a typo when he promised he was dringing enough water. I asked him to teach me to dring. When he requested that I "Roder the Bowman book," I wrote, "Noam, I'm not sure what's entailed in rodering a book."

He wrote, "Surprised you never heard of rordering books. Maybe it means figuring out how to get them at half-price, or to follow Abbie Hoffman's advice when he wrote a book called *Steal This Book*."

I have a strong memory attached to any book-stealing reference. A colorful Cape Cod acquaintance of Noam's visited twice yearly to fill us in on the latest covert actions according to his brother, allegedly a government official—and to beg free books. Noam always agreed to donate books for libraries, fundraisers, or a needy friend. One day after I loaded his bag, he asked, "Can I have one more book? It would help me feel better about my bankruptcy." I wondered whether he planned to sell the books. He then told me, "You know, Bev, I'm a master klepto. I could have three books under my jacket without you ever knowing." What was I supposed to do with that? I gave the bookshelves a visual scan. Noam's master's thesis was in place, and I saw no observable gaps in our collection of out-of-print books. I did, by way of a slightly prolonged hug and lots of patting, scan his clothing for projections before he left, relieved that he didn't ask for a date afterward.

By early 2000 I was spending time with Laura, a psychiatric nurse. Her playful energy buoyed me, softening my strong-willed edges. In early September of 2001 we made plans to move in together the next spring. I had been with Noam and Morris eight years, and Jay was in a serious relationship. Noam and I were tempering our workdays with playful banter, though he could send a clear, even abrupt, signal when it was time to flip into professional mode, as if the world had knocked on his skull to remind him that serious work was at hand. This was the case on September 11, 2001, when everyday business, and everyday life, came to an ominous standstill.

•••

After the terrorist attacks on the Pentagon and the World Trade Center on September 11, 2001, we fielded constant requests for interviews. Noam took overseas calls into the early morning hours for weeks, until we held interviews to ten minutes so we could accommodate even more of them. I saw a recurring pattern as Noam reported that however horrific the 9/11 events were, most people were unaware of even worse worldwide atrocities, like that on September 11, 1973, when the US overthrew the democratic government of Salvador Allende in Chile in a military coup. Most people in the US, including me, knew little or nothing about this earlier 9/11. Noam's post 9/11 lectures, ranging from linguistics to

Ann Farmer, Noam, Bev, and Laura Gimby, at Google.

the Palestinian Intifada, from America's war on terror to a world
without war, continued for years.

Trying to Move Ahead

When I celebrated 25 years at MIT, they gave me a rocking chair.
My productivity dropped by 50 percent. —from Bev's standup routine

Weeks after 9/11, Ken Hale died of cancer at only sixty-seven. At
his memorial, I met an ex-student and his close friend, Ann Farmer,
for the first time. I told Ann about Ken's difficulty picking up sign
language.

"He couldn't grok sign language," she said, making a tangent
to "parsing" and something about "a horse raced past a barn fell,"
leaving me wondering again what language linguists were speaking.
She clarified. Ken couldn't learn sign language the way he learned
to converse in a few hundred other languages—through intuition.
Visiting the Kendall Square Google suite with Ann, who often stayed
with us when hosting a Google event, was like entering a strange and
colorful world; you could hear the buzz of working brains snacking
on free food. We needed official clearance to enter; I almost remember a thumbprint.

When Laura admired Ann's YouTube jacket, she took it off and
handed it to her. This was not the first time someone had given us

the clothing off their backs. I'd admired shirts, sweaters, t-shirts, hats, and scarves worn by visitors, only to have them handed over. When Noam and Carol traveled to Cuba in 2001, the organizing professor, Mr. M. A. Baby (married to Betty Baby), sent them home with a crisp yellow Cuban shirt for me, just like the one he and his friends wore in the evenings as they sat around smoking cigars. I asked Noam if I could have one of his Cuban cigars to go with it, but he refused, reminding me (knowing I'd never smoked) that smoking was bad for my lungs.

•••

In the summer of 2002 Laura and I moved to Framingham, a forty-minute drive to MIT and to Laura's hospital job. Morris tried to convince me to move back to my Watertown two-family, even mapping a better route to MIT for me. In Framingham, new neighbors helped us build a sprawling deck overlooking a rolling green hill that spilled into the Sudbury River, where we kayaked and canoed. Goodbye, city life.

Work was busy. Pearl Jam's graphic designer asked permission to print Noam's likeness on a skateboard for a series of promotional decks they would name "American Heroes." Noam had replied: "Don't want to sound as though I'm from some newly contacted tribe in the Amazon jungle, but ... I don't know what skateboard decks are." I explained to him that Pearl Jam was an intelligent political band, and that a deck, which became a skateboard when wheels were added, would impress Alaitz, his oldest grandson. Jay loved Pearl Jam and urged me to stress their political significance to Noam. When I did, Noam recalled an article he'd written on Cuba's sovereignty for Pearl Jam's "The Manual For Free Living" newsletter way back. This proved once again that he knew, and remembered, more than he let on. I gave them the OK for the decks. A while later a package arrived. I was ecstatic as I unboxed t-shirts, CDs, and three decks.

Noam had meanwhile begun to say things like, "You have lots of friends in Cleveland. You're a hit in Albuquerque, in Boulder, Turkey, Italy. You should make a world tour." Diemut Strebe, our artist friend, said that I was a legend all over Europe. I knew these moments of sway keeping Noam's gate were illusory and fleeting, but for now I would enjoy the muscle of my position, let it buoy me and boost my self-confidence. I felt a level of excitement at work, since any day could bring a celebrity, a political heavyweight, a prominent author or musician, a well-intended activist. Strolling MIT's halls with him to star-struck stares gave me a kick.

People asked me what it was like to work for Noam Chomsky. When I answered—saying he was a brilliant man, a genius, and an altruistic superhero—I saw the pedestal I had placed him on. I also noticed that I was measuring my worth mostly through the lens of who I was in *his* world, knowing that the pedestal I was on by association with him would in time collapse under me.

Outside Noam's office I continued to focus on woodworking, writing, and stand-up and improvisational comedy. I co-taught an electrical course during MIT's January semester, teaching women simple wiring, outlet installation, and electric repair—things that defined me outside of MIT. By the time we began packing for a move to the Stata Center in late 2003, ten years into my job, I believed more and more that staying with Noam had been a good decision. Although I sometimes wondered what it would have been like to be a professional in my own right, a therapist in a world of therapists.

6

Lost and Found at Stata: 2004

What's silver and brick and defies the laws of gravity?

The first time I saw the plans for the Ray and Maria Stata Center, called simply Stata and pronounced *Stay-tuh*, it looked like a row of silver cylinders exploding onto a red brick floor, shards of brick splitting aluminum, silver rising from brick, reptilian teeth cutting through glass. That night I told Laura I would be working in a building made of toppled stacks of huge crooked cans—a brand new funhouse for smart people. By March of 2004, our new offices were finally inhabitable. Noam's roughly square corner office was wrapped into a turret of the Dreyfoos Tower, nestled down a short hallway from mine, next to Morris's. His desk faced a large window showcasing a panorama of Boston's skyline, a deliberate effect by architect Frank Gehry. But the office had issues, big ones if you were prone to vertigo, as Noam was.

In the back of the building an expansive stairway led to several structures, one resembling an enormous wedge of yellow cartoon cheese, another a silver train engine out of a children's storybook. A white aluminum multistory orb called The Sail was meant to represent sailboats scooting along the nearby Charles River, a nod to Gehry's love of sailing. The building's design with its few right angles was meant to provide a nontraditional, creativity-sparking environ-

Noam Chomsky and Bertrand Russell, Stata Center.

ment. Years before, when Building 20's offices were repainted, Noam glared at the clean walls each morning as if he had a score to settle with them. One night he wrote his usual evening note to me about the next day's business, adding, "Make sure you scrape off bits of paint when you can. We don't want to lose our image." How would he stomach the ultra-modern Stata Center?

We'd been together for eleven years, long enough for me to develop a sixth sense about him, so when the phone rang on his first day at Stata, I knew he was lost.

"Noam?"

"Uh, Bev ..."

"You're lost, aren't you?"

His trademark sigh blew through my end of the receiver. "Yes, how did you guess? I'm calling from a library area on the eighth floor ..." I heard voices, then a brief silence. "I'm in CSAIL, in the Gates Tower. Your friend Maria says hi."

"Well, you're in the right building," I reassured him, imagining that he missed the dilapidated, asbestos-laden Building 20, which reflected life's imperfections and was more fitting with his politics and worldview. He had joked that MIT's administration kept its rabble-rousing professors hidden away there.

"You took the wrong set of elevators. Go back down to the first floor, to the open area—this is Student Street ..." Imagining him waiting for a key piece of information, his brows knitting as I meandered toward my point, I reined in my tendency to wordiness. "Return to the first floor. I'll find you."

I rushed to the elevator and pressed "1." For months I'd organized our new space, refilling floor-to-ceiling shelves with his books by Jacobson, Wittgenstein, Marx. Copies of the books he had authored and their translations, arranged chronologically, filled walls of similar bookcases near Glenn's desk. Noam's master's thesis, "Morphophonemics of Modern Hebrew," was the cornerstone on the top shelf on the lefthand side of the room. *Hegemony or Survival*, his newest book, was shelved on the other side of the room. His published books by my count neared ninety. Six long empty shelves beckoned future crises, future truths.

Noam's larger-than-life black-and-white poster of philosopher and activist Bertrand Russell had been torn in the move, but a tenacious member of the Bertrand Russell Society sent another, which I'd had mounted on foam core. On the bookcase below the poster was a Russell quote, cut from our old poster:

Three passions, simple but overwhelmingly strong, have governed my life: the longing for love, the search for knowledge, and unbearable pity for the suffering of mankind.

Noam had told me that this quote mirrored many of his own sentiments. Russell's logical and philosophical work, and his dedication to serious issues—resulting in his doing jail time during World War I—inspired him. The poster, with Russell's sober expression, had provided the backdrop for thousands of photo ops since Noam appointed me amateur resident photographer early on. I joked that no matter how often I had snapped Bertrand's picture, he never cracked a smile, and no matter how fancy the camera or phone they handed me, most people left with a nice enough photo, and a close-up of my finger.

A few years before, a young man had written to ask Noam just before a trip: "What role does love play in your work? What keeps you going after 40-plus years as an activist-intellectual?"

Noam wrote me: "Too much for me. Can you switch to your (authorized) role as a barefaced liar, and write him that I didn't pick up email before leaving (mostly true). Then copy the great quote from Bertrand Russell and tell him that's been on my office wall for thirty years, and might have some bearing on his question."

On the same bookcase, a Sandinista doll stood beside a quote by Archbishop Oscar Romero: *To educate is to create a critical spirit and not just transfer knowledge.* A print depicting the Grim Reaper standing over the heads of Romero and the other slain priests hung on a nearby wall. Noam was known to ask visitors if they understood its meaning. Some did. Noam told me that Romero was the first of more than six Jesuit priests murdered in El Salvador in 1980 as he celebrated a mass.

A framed print of three bronzed and faceless men holding shovels and picks hung on an adjacent wall. I admired it until Noam told me the story of the miners and their families. That story haunted me enough that I expunged it from my mind for years, until I asked him to fill in the details. I made eye contact with it only by mistake; I could bear only so much heartache in a day. Across the room I had leaned the poster of a blue mailing envelope against a slanted post on a file cabinet, the *Palestine* address canceled out by a row of red stars, with "Return to Sender–No Such Address" stamped in the lower-left corner. I hadn't understood the significance of the poster at first, but knew more by now about the severity of the Israel-Palestine conflict.

When I reached the first floor, I trotted down Student Street, past a spiral cement stairway, the childcare center, brushed silver chairs

Canceled Palestine envelope poster.

clustered around tables. Near the café I spotted Noam. He was surrounded by tributes to MIT "hacks": a plastic cow from the Hilltop Steakhouse and a reassembled campus police cruiser, both of which had been hoisted onto MIT's dome overnight. Nearby, a fire hydrant was hooked up to a drinking fountain. He shook his head as he walked to me and squeezed my hands. Sighing, he looked up at the glass ceiling panels and hanging brick half-walls overhead. "So, this is the new place."

"What do you think?" I asked, reminding myself to allow the silence, to let him process his own reaction. Despite years of practice, I could still speak impulsively, a habit cultivated from trying to be heard or make the funniest joke in my vocal family. I would later overhear Noam say, in an interview with *Real Simple*, "Silence is hard; there's a fear of awkwardness. We simply prefer speech, and we'll make huge compromises ... to keep it going." Had he understood my unease? Anyway, what did I have to prove? It wasn't as if I had designed the building.

From my vantage point, Noam lived a mostly internal life, with a cursory awareness of his physical surroundings, unless he found something amusing. "Pretty impressive, but I still miss the old building. It was kind of fun when loose windows fell out into the parking lot." When I joined him in Building 20, I was thirty-nine and fit enough to play racquetball with grad students Heidi Harley and Jonathan Bobaljik. As I approached the Dreyfoos Tower elevators, the new students seemed so much younger, the professors' faces more deeply carved by the inevitable passing of time. I'd stopped playing racquetball. The polished stainless steel of the elevators bore no resemblance to the dark wood stairways of Building 20, sticky with layers of dust and wax. There was no going back.

The elevator blinked 6–7–8. On the eighth floor a cluster of red upholstered seating spread its puffy arms to welcome discussion groups, exhausted students, and guests. Noam wore a poker face. We zigzagged left, right, right again to our suite, hidden in back, just as he would have preferred.

Glenn was at his desk. "You found it!"

"Unfortunately," Noam said, sounding like *Winnie the Pooh*'s Eeyore. He opened his briefcase, just as he would on any morning, handing Glenn the day's backup and a flyer with two book titles circled, for ordering. I pointed to the shelves filled with his books. "There they are, Noam—all in order."

A hint of mischief in his eyes belied the tone of his reply. "I guess they all fit." He now looked and sounded more like Henry Fonda's Norman Thayer character in *On Golden Pond* than Fonda himself. Squinting toward the rows of bookshelves, as if seeing for the first time just how many he'd written, I half-expected him to say, in Fonda-esque style, "Who the hell *wrote* all those books, anyway?"

"Yup, they fit. And there's room for more."

"Oo-kaaay ..." He let the word out in one long breath. "Let's see the office."

During construction he had waved his hands in the air when I suggested that he look at the plans, lamenting his usual, "I don't care.

Gondry's drawing of his meeting with Noam at Stata.

I won't be able to understand them anyway," followed by a sardonic "Surprise me." I hadn't pushed.

I tried to view his office through his eyes. Crooked walls pitched up from the floor at steep angles. Two leaning concrete towers allowed space for only two upright file cabinets and two bookcases. Family photos attempted to cozy up an inconveniently deep window-sill. He must have felt he was looking at the place through Alice's looking glass. He hadn't seemed to notice his new desk. What do you call a desk without drawers? A table. Its skinny, telescoping legs were nothing compared to the thick metal legs of his old gray desk. Unlike this high-tech Formica table posing as a desk, that desk had stories to tell. It knew the routines of the day—where the new mail sat, where the publications were piled, how many manuscripts could be stacked until they spilled over. This new desk had no idea of the act it had to follow. Since he was unimpressed by anything *state-of-the-art* (even mechanical pencils), I knew he would cringe when he took a good look, but the tilted walls had seized his attention. "Boy, Mr. Gehry might have realized that we need shelves for our books. Where are we supposed to put them, with all these slanted walls?" Noam had always surrounded himself with books.

His first interview was in an hour, so he settled in to sort through the piles of mail arranged on his desk. He emerged at lunchtime, a small white pharmacy bag holding his usual white Lender's bagel with fake cheese. "Uh, Bev, would you mind if I sat at your worktable out here to eat my lunch? The walls and the Leaning Towers of Pisa in there have given me a case of vertigo." He read through a library book as he ate (I'd never seen him eat by himself without reading). He had decided long ago not to dwell on insignificant nuisances. I had learned that a simple sigh signaled that the conversation was over, the deed done, the fight finished. From my witnessing chair, I saw his lack of tolerance for wasted time. I knew he would soon see beyond the configuration of his office and move on to the work at hand. He was in this building, this office, slanted walls, vertigo, and all. He would go with the flow and save his energy for bigger things. Following his lead, I had two bookcases made for a space beneath a far window and arranged three tall new plants strategically in his office to restore his sense of balance and to reassure his head that the reliable up-and-down physics of the universe still held sway.

Despite my efforts, some visitors experienced what I called *leaning sickness* in his office; I caught a Canadian journalist as she listed forward while photographing piles of books on Noam's desk. I would like to say that we adjusted over time to the building *Boston Globe* critic Robert Campbell called "a drunken barn dance," but like Oz's Scarecrow, I tripped each time I approached his windowsill, since the wall below the sill slanted two feet into the room. I never did come to terms with The Sail outside my window, which blocked my view, or *was* my view, of the rest of MIT. That said, Stata's design did offer the cooperative experience Frank Gehry had intended. Still, though I needed to bring more fun into my work life, I'm not sure I would have chosen to have it happen the way it did.

7

Roxy Joins Us at Stata

Bev pleads her case to have her dog come to work.

A year before our move to Stata in 2004, Laura and I took home a matted, wild-eyed, year-old chocolate cocker spaniel tethered to the end of a gray rope. She had a plaintive look in her eyes that begged you to buy what she was selling. We changed her name from "Rexy" to the more feminine Roxy and had her groomed and de-ticked. With a newly exposed soft white spot on her belly, she settled in and thrived. Weeks after our move to Stata, I came home to find her wagging her tail from the arm of a sofa, as if to say, "Hey, my person, it's raining inside!" Roofers hadn't tarped our exposed roof before a storm, and now rainwater was dripping down newly painted walls and a ceiling light fixture onto wood floors, carpets, and her curls. I pulled her to me and heard a crack on the floor above. We ran upstairs in time to watch the bedroom ceiling collapse. Noam and Morris agreed to let Roxy come to work with me during the two-month renovation.

They were not dog lovers, but when our house was livable again, I made a case for her to join me permanently at dog-friendly Stata. She had been great for those two months, but I was worried about Morris, who liked a quiet, professional atmosphere, even discouraging laughter within his earshot. I respected his views, but nevertheless could forget myself. More than once he had emerged from his office shouting, "What is this hilarity?" Putting an index finger in the air, he would remind us, "This is not a place of merriment!" Whether my laugh-mate was a professor, Glenn, or Noam's next appointment, his half-joking message was as clear as the Pantheon's recording: *Silencio!* I tried to laugh quietly, and in time Morris learned to live with, and even add to, the gaiety. Bringing Roxy to work every day would change the office atmosphere, but it would bring joy to me, dog-loving visitors—and maybe in time, Noam and Morris.

I made my case with apprehension, hoping our eleven-year relationships would sway them in my direction. "You won't even know she's here," I promised. When they agreed, I felt loved. Roxy would greet eighty people in a typical month. I remedied her barking with a sign: "Please don't knock. Come in!" Things went smoothly, not counting the tuna sandwich she stole from Morris's backpack.

After years of eating lunch at my desk while fielding email and snacking on sugary gifts from grateful Chomsky admirers, I was feeling it. Roxy became my fitness coach, extricating me from my work. We started with a run up the stairs to the outdoor amphitheater. Sometimes we made it across campus to the student center, and once in a great while we crossed Memorial Drive to the Charles River. When I picked up lunch from a food truck, an extra bit of protein was thrown in "for the pup." She carried sticks back to the office. We stumbled upon art installments I would never have seen, and walked in rain, sleet, and snow on days when I would rather have stayed inside. She became my touchstone, my work Prozac as discussions about the failures of our government and the approaching demise of our Earth accelerated. She added an atmosphere of fun. One morning Noam brought me an article he had cut out of a newspaper about the benefits of people bringing their dogs to work. When the dean's office sent a potential million-dollar donor to chat with Noam, they had spent most of their visit petting Roxy. Had she sealed that deal?

Stata's maintenance guy, Ron, greeted us daily with, "Hi, Bev! Hi, Fluffy!" (His brother was a leg-breaker for Whitey Bulger, but that's another story.) She drank spring water and napped on a big fleecy bed under my desk. During her MIT tenure, she was photographed and gifted with treats and toys (some meant to bribe me to extend appointments). People were shameless, but it worked. Some of them planned for years for a short meeting with Noam, yet Roxy meandered into his office looking for food scraps, unimpressed by his accomplishments or rock star status.

In winter, her hair longer, she would pop out of an elevator, startling someone who had mistaken her for a bear cub. "Can I say hi to your dog?" students asked, eyes glistening, remembering their family dogs. "Is she a student here?" some joked. I'd say, "Of course not. She's a professor." Like Morris and Noam, she was my teacher, reminding me to stop, sniff, and listen, especially during the summer months.

Some Some Summertime

My job was the best on the planet. Except when it wasn't.

"You have the best job on the planet." I heard these words enough to believe them, except for one glaringly persistent and undeniable problem. Summertime. Glenn's part-time schedule coupled with his stockpiled vacation days allowed him to go off on long bicycling and camping trips. In early June, before Noam deserted me as well, we rode the elevator to the first-floor farmer's market. He said a friend had just written a book about pleasure. I suggested he do the same, to lighten his mood. "What's pleasure?" he asked. He'd barely slept the night before, he said, to explain his dark humor. I asked what kept him awake more, fears about his own problems, or the world's. "It's not fear. It's more worry. About the world's problems. Mine feel small in comparison." He told me that not long ago, in Russia, someone pressed the button to send the command to launch a missile armed with a nuclear warhead, but the launch was canceled at the last moment. I held in reserve an image of him as the world's night watchman, for the times Morris had warned me about, when our days were far from warm and fuzzy. We both needed a summer break.

Each June we filled two big mail bins with envelopes, stamps, reams of typing paper, packs of sticky notes, sharpened pencils, Noam's favorite pens, a few books, and a stack of correspondence for transport to his Cape Cod cottage. Then we met to review his sparse summer schedule, honoring the one recurring variant on the theme of *No Summer Lectures*: Mike Albert's Z Media Institute (ZMI) in Woods Hole.

In the mid 1960s Mike Albert, an MIT grad student who opposed the Vietnam War and supported the Civil Rights Movement, joined MIT's chapter of Students for a Democratic Society (SDS), which campaigned against the US military's funding of MIT. MIT responded in 1970 by suspending Mike on trumped-up charges related to his activism. He later became a founder of South End Press and Z *Magazine,* both major players in Noam's political world. At the Z Media Institute, Noam, Mike, and the Harvard Trade Union Program's Elaine Bernard taught radical politics, media, and organizing skills to labor organizers and activists. Visualizing the folks at ZMI helped me sleep at night.

I handed Noam a library book, which he opened and leafed through with one hand, rolling a piece of scrap paper between the thumb and forefinger of his other, visually scanning a page, flipping ahead, scanning. When he handed it back to me I was confused and asked if it was the wrong book. "No, it's the right book. I got the information I needed. You can send it back." He hadn't written anything down.

My typical wrap-up routine included sending address changes to journals and newspapers—the *Boston Globe,* the *New York Times,* the *Financial Times,* the *Wall Street Journal,* the *Washington Post, Haaretz.* He also read nonmainstream news sources and online columns: *The*

Real News, FAIR, Salon.com, Dollars & Sense, Peace Action, American Prospect, Le Monde Diplomatique, In These Times, and *The Nation.*

Updating our summer form letter was the last order of business before I tucked his schedule into a mail bin. Loaded up, Noam, Glenn, and I took our end-of-term trek to his car. I would see Noam over the summer only on his half-days in. One such time, I made the mistake of wishing him a happy Fourth of July.

"Do you know the real story behind July Fourth? Maybe you can bring home the article I wrote, called 'A Few Words on Independence Day.' I fished a copy out of the file cabinet. That night, I barely got past the start: "Independence Day was designed by the first state propaganda agency, Woodrow Wilson's Committee on Public Information (CPI), created during World War I to whip a pacifist country into anti-German frenzy ..."

•••

Many of his writings would help shape my thinking, but this one almost ruined my summer. I had to put politics aside to relax. Noam must have tried to do that as well. He sent photos of grandchildren flying across the water in his boat, playing in the pond or on his deck. Imagining the lovely chaos, I wrote: "I THOUGHT IF I WROTE IN CAPS, YOU COULD HEAR ME ABOVE THE ROAR OF VISITING GRANDCHILDREN." Noam replied, "NOTHING CAN OVERCOME DIN."

As the days slowed, the pace of email would accelerate. With extra hours on their summer clocks, people had more time to mull over the world's problems. Noam pointed out that if people were as consistently active, concerned, and vocal as they were in the summer and during elections, we might see real change. Some wrote with light-hearted requests. A man sent a photo of a bodybuilder with Noam's head superimposed on the body, to be signed for his wife's birthday. A letter of gratitude and a plea for Noam to relax more arrived with a pair of plastic flip-flop sandals sporting fake grass inner soles.

Noam petting Roxy on the green recliner where he prepared his class notes.

Fortunately, Roxy's needs, and mine, pulled me away from the hypnotic glare of my computer screen. We took brisk walks, strolling MIT's silent halls and quadrangles. On a mild day, we dodged bicyclists along the Charles River, where I watched small craft sail by and Roxy sniffed out food crumbs (our inner lives differed). Scarce student activity meant fewer posters, virtual reality glasses, robots, Frisbees, or electric cars. My days dragged. With the enthusiasm of an automaton, back at my desk I sent form letters and forwarded email to Noam, often adding my own clarifying notes. Every August I vowed to never endure another summer of bored abandonment. One day a week during the summer my childhood friend Deb rescued me. We walked and chatted about my writing and her knitting, likening the tearing apart of a piece of writing to the unraveling of a sweater when the rows, or words, didn't add up, didn't match our mental pictures.

I had read stories of "recognizing" someone at first sight, as if we had met them before. That's how I felt when I first saw Deb, blond hair and braces glinting, as she skipped down her front steps. That January of 1966, I was as tanned as she was light; when she first saw me, rather than sensing we had met before, she thought the new white family had a Spanish daughter. We were similarly creative, a perfect match. We made troll houses, sewed clothing from patterns, swam, and played rummy on her front steps. She taught me to play her piano. Even fifty years before, she had lit up my summers.

As difficult as summer workdays were for me, they were harder on Noam. Not because he had a place on the Cape to relax and garden, nor because his desk looked out at the pond. Not because he explored the crevices between the stones and the trees with grandkids, grandnieces, and grandnephews on the path to the pond, where they searched for dragons and other creatures. Those were the spirit-rejuvenating joys of his summers.

The difficulties for Noam began in June, when his move to Cape Cod offered a little reflection time. I knew from chats with Carol and managing his emails that he felt he hadn't done enough. He corresponded till 3 am, perhaps wondering what amount of personal exhaustion was enough to join, initiate, or revive some momentum of change in our country, our world. Noam and Carol's friend, political science professor, author, and activist Norman Finkelstein, saw Noam's specific goal as a more humane world. Was it becoming more, or less, humane? I thought both. I asked Noam what he thought, but it was a question he replied to only vaguely. Did he still have hope?

Carol and Noam met when he was five and she, three; their parents were friends. Who knows when she began to protect him from constant work, too much time away from the sunny pond, the open ocean, or their garden. When family and friends left in early September, the furniture, sunfish, and kayaks were returned to the shed, and the motorboat put to sleep for the winter, and he piled his laptop, papers, and journals back into the mail bin and returned home to Lexington and to his MIT life.

I want to say he arrived with a smoking rifle and jingling spurs and hung up his cowboy hat ("his floppy canvas hat" doesn't have the same cachet), looking slightly more wizened, and always more wise, to bring the challenges of discourse, justice, and commotion back to the ranch. Because the activists, advocates, and atmosphere swirling around him like a windstorm were the things I'd been missing, I felt again like I had the world's best job. This attitude helped as I struggled through my fiftieth year, taking a few people, like Noam, prisoner.

Minimalism and Menopause

Bev gives Professor Chomsky a (small) piece of her (compromised) mind.

"Of course tomorrow isn't Wednesday. Tomorrow is Tuesday, so I'll see you tomorrow. You have to listen to what I'm *thinking*, not to what I say or write." These clarifications were more common as I began to plod through menopause, as were mood swings, hot flashes, and bursts of irritability. Confusion and impatience were neither strangers nor my friends during this time of my life.

The next day, a Tuesday in 2004, this scenario played out: "Uhm," I said, my voice trailing off. I looked at him. "Do you have any idea what I was about to say?" Now I was the one asking for clarification and reminders.

"No." He looked up from the book he'd been leafing through.

"You need someone younger working for you," I said. This was not my original thought, but once I had relieved my mind of the task of digging, it slipped back in. "Now I remember. It was about your Paris trip. We have to let Pierre Pica know whether to add the meeting with the union people to your schedule."

"Oh. Yeah. Right," he sighed. "It's just that there's already so much happening in Paris, all following a long trip to Ramallah and Beirut. Incidentally, did you send Avi her tickets for the Palestine trip?" I was juggling Ramallah, Beirut, Paris, Palestine, Pierre Pica, and union people. No wonder this peri-menopausal person was perplexed.

A while later, he pulled the extra chair up to my desk so we could look at requests, letters, and books to be signed. My small workspace was four feet from the coffee machine behind a partition, low enough for me to watch our entry area but high enough that I could duck my head and disappear if I chose not to be seen. "You met this guy last month and asked him to write with specifics. He wants to make a documentary about your activism," I said, handing him a letter, hoping to get through the pile in five minutes, before his next appointment. I was mid-sentence when someone spotted him.

"Hey, I saw the *Democracy Now* interview on Friday. I guess Amy kidnapped you again? Oh ... Hi, Bev!" Noam told the intruder the show had been taped a few weeks earlier, when he was in New York. After a brief exchange, the intruder left us.

"OK, where were we?" Noam asked. I handed him a book, and the door opened again. An old student, now visiting faculty, asked to make an appointment.

"I'm meeting with Noam now," I said, trying not to sound obviously ironic. "Can you give me fifteen minutes?" I cracked a smile and turned to Noam, who put down the book he was supposed to be signing to ask the visitor about a paper on the Minimalist Program. Normally, I found these impromptu chats fun; they broke up my day, informed me, stumped me, but I hadn't been myself for weeks, as menopause crept in and stole my humor and lighthearted spirit. In the mix was my growing frustration with the hierarchical system of the university. My friend Deb had recently been talking with a professor about a database she was developing at Harvard Business School when, mid-sentence, the professor squeezed her shoulders and physically moved her aside to talk with a passing colleague.

These things happened to female staff way too often. It wasn't just the staff being moved aside. MIT, like many universities, had since its inception discriminated against hiring female faculty and in admitting female students. Noam's friends and colleagues Louis

ZINN, Howard & Roz   1/88
Department of Political Science
Boston University
232 Bay State Rd.
Boston, MA 02215
(home)244-0779
(work)353-2540
         3683

(Auburndale)

Unpacking some of the tools of our trade.

Kampf, professor of literature and women's and gender studies, and Louis's life partner, anthropology professor Jean Jackson, each worked toward bringing that discrimination to the table, with the goal of leveling the male/female playing field at MIT.

We got through a few more items before another faculty member came in and yelled across the office to Noam, "Do you usually have a police presence at your talks?" I waited, heat rising in my chest and spreading to my neck.

When they finished, Noam asked, "Anything else?" I assumed he could see I still held papers and books. I couldn't hold myself back. Blame my hormones.

"You let three people interrupt us, Noam. Our conversation was just as important." *Was I doing this?* "I can't get back to people until I check things out with you." I *was* doing this, letting my emotions take over, as if I were standing outside myself, frustrated at feeling like chopped liver.

"Why don't you meet with Adam and we'll finish this later," I said, relieved to have spoken up, surprised to be backing down, and horrified that I was seeing Noam, one of the kindest people in my world, as inconsiderate. Plus, the room had become quite hot.

He looked down to open a paper clip to its full length, then looked at me as if I had just appeared in front of him. "Uh, I talked with a teacher you're taking a writing course with. He said your pieces are very funny." How he came to talk with my humor-writing instructor wasn't the point, so I didn't ask. I felt immediate regret at my reaction. His "I've gone too far and it's time to pay attention" technique seemed sincere. I supposed he'd learned this from his family, who had to share his attention, even during Cape Cod summers.

"My class does get a kick out of my titles." Now *I* was looking down. "You, you're good," I said in my best *My Cousin Vinny* voice, smiling, not expecting him to get the movie reference. "You can go. Adam's waiting. He brought vodka." He promised to finish our chat later, but I dropped it. He had gotten my point. Plus, my mood had swung back to normal-ish. Fortunately, the duration of this "change" was brief, less than a year, during which I kept myself focused on our office's ongoing challenges.

8

Convenient Blindness

They showered me with gifts, but once the filming began ...

Despite having set up systems to manage the needs of film crews, from submitting release forms, taking photos, and collecting contact information afterward, filmed interviews in our cramped suite remained a challenge in 2005, twelve years into my job. It helped to keep things moving when crews set up and broke down in the outer hallway. Most crews were manageable, but some took more effort to keep in line.

The documentary producer arrived with his crew to interview Noam about the anti-war movement, and handed me a box of chocolates. I was not shy about revealing my chocolate addiction to someone who wanted to thank me. Gift or bribe, dark chocolate, high in antioxidants, helped me sustain a sense of love during stressful times. We received all kinds of generous gifts from people who wanted to give thanks to the gatekeepers: flowers, candy, t-shirts, CDs, DVDs, and books. A painted Noam statue, small gnomes, a candle bearing his likeness. Baskets of cheeses, crackers, cookies, and oils. I had a cabinet full of wines from around the world. Someone had given me small totems carved from the branch of a particular tree that supposedly lulled the sculptor into an intoxicated state, with no need for sleep or food.

As if to prove them wrong, Roxy nibbled on a wooden mushroom and promptly fell asleep. People brought ethnic treats made by parents and grandmothers, and cans of maple syrup tapped from their own trees.

I grabbed my schedule and made my way around bulky equipment cases to give a last-minute warning, asking the crew to move the cases to a safer spot. Noam was reading in Morris's office. I hated to interrupt him, but this was exactly why I was there. Readying him for the next interview felt like bringing in a newly caught fish. I hooked it and reeled it in, watching it jump and fight before settling at my feet. Not that I fished.

I touched his arm to ground him into the present and asked if he was ready. His long sigh indicated to me not weariness, but a changing of gears. As I rolled strands of gray hair from his sweater where he couldn't reach, he asked, "Uh, Bev, what's this one about?" I held up the schedule. Although he could read at the speed of light, his squinted eyes followed my finger: Documentary on the anti-war movement and the courage of resistance, *30-min setup, 40-min interview.*

Noam was no stranger to resistance. He had helped found RESIST (A Call to Resist Illegitimate Authority), organized in 1967 by Louis Kampf. This was "the first academic group devoted to supporting draft resistance to the Vietnam War. In 1968, Louis and Noam were two of 130 MIT faculty members to sign an open letter to MIT's president, Howard Johnson, urging him to end MIT's relationship with the US Department of Defense" (MIT Press, August 2020). RESIST took on other forms of opposition over time. Noam continues to sign their yearly appeal letters.

People always asked me—and him—where his compassion came from. He never wanted anything to be about himself, so didn't reply. Early on, he was profoundly affected by his time in Laos, a story Fred Branfman told beautifully in a 2012 *Salon* article, "When Chomsky Wept." Following a flight cancellation in February 1970, Noam hopped onto the back of Fred's motorcycle and learned more about the secret US war there. Fred hoped having Chomsky join him might make the bombings known to the world and contribute to ending the war:

> [W]hat most struck me by far was what occurred when we traveled out to a camp that housed refugees from the Plain of Jars. I had taken dozens of journalists and other folks out to the camps at that point, and found that almost all were emotionally distanced from the refugees' suffering ... [T]he journalists listened politely, asked questions, took notes and then went back to their hotels to file their stories. They showed little emotion. ... Our talks in the car back to their hotels usually concerned either dinner that night or the next day's events. I was thus stunned when, as I was translating Noam's questions and the refugees' answers, I suddenly saw him break down and begin weeping. ... Noam himself had seemed so intellectual to me, to so live in a world of ideas, words and concepts, had so rarely expressed any feelings about anything. I realized at that moment that I was seeing into his soul. And the visual image of him weeping in that camp has stayed with me ever since. When I think of Noam this is what I see.

Fred and I had corresponded since he and his wife, Zsuzsa, stayed at Noam's after Carol died. I felt his loss when he died of ALS at age seventy-two, but was happy for him that his *Salon* article, which revealed Noam's more vulnerable, human side, had brought so much recognition to his work.

At his doorway, I leaned in to remind him that the day was only half over, and that his voice was already hoarse. "Don't make me have to tap dance to get you out of there," I whispered. "That would be embarrassing for both of us." His laugh meant that he had heard me, despite having left his hearing aids at home.

My instinct was to walk him through the wild tangle of wires, cameras, and cases that had transformed his office into a high-tech studio, but instead I stayed close as he shook hands with the enthusiastic young activists flooding the room with positive energy. When I called out to arrange for someone to make eye contact with me at the five-minute warning, two people called out a cheery "I will!" I reminded the crew they had a forty-minute time limit, and that they should ask their last question before my warning knock. Noam's replies could be lengthy. I heard an OK as their focus slipped away from me and toward Noam. Juan handed him the mic, which he slipped under the waistband and through the neck of his Irish knit pullover so I could clip it to his shirt. I stepped over wires toward the door and then stood back to watch them gobble him up like a swarm of ants to a crust of bread, satisfied that I could do my part. I loved this part of my job.

As a rule, once in Noam's office, crews morphed into squatters, pushing my boundaries by asking, even begging, for extra time. I don't think it was intentional, but Noam was usually seated facing away from the door, making it impossible for me to give him a two-minute warning, or to signal that time was way up. Even so, he was just as likely to be the perpetrator of our schedule going awry. When caught up in an interview, he ignored hand signals, verbal cues, even tap dancing. But I persisted, not only because it was my job, but because we both needed to walk, rest, eat, and breathe. The cooperation of this crew was its own brand of fresh air.

With Noam's time now spoken for, I used my forty-minute guarantee to run outside with Roxy while Glenn managed things. I was deep into my chocolate high when we reached the outer courtyard near the amphitheater. I dropped Roxy's leash and she shot ahead of me, looking for squirrels, sticks, crumbs. After our break, I greeted Noam's next appointment as I poured fresh water for Roxy and me and refreshed and checked Noam's email in-box. Another sixty messages. "Take a break, peeps," I said aloud. The alarm I had set prompted me to end the interview.

I gently opened the door and held up five fingers toward each of the target people. I got no eye contact, just a shifting of eyes and other incomprehensible signs from the crew, all begging, "But we're

Gnomes, Noams, and other gifts we received.

only on question two ... We've waited so long ... We were kidding when we said we would cooperate. And the big one: 'We don't see you, invisible lady at the door.'" The crew had become conveniently blind. I hated this part of my job.

I knocked loudly, which I'm sure displeased their sound engineer, and stood waiting to be acknowledged, with no apologies for the commotion of Glenn's copier. When Noam finished answering what should have been the last question, the interviewer turned to me. "One last question?" Are. You. Serious?

Noam looked at me and nodded. I walked away. We had talked too many times about the difficulty of ending a filmed interview, mostly because of what I called the "one last question" syndrome and his acquiescence to most "last questions." It didn't take a linguist to know that there could be only one last question. It was his show, but it left me frustrated. I was convinced that every film school offered a course called "How to Ask One Last Question, ad Infinitum." I could decorate his schedule with gold stars and graffiti, but how a day played out was ultimately up to him. I had seen his lunchbreak, a time he and I had both promised Carol would include a long walk and hydration, dwindle from sixty minutes to fifteen because he had extended a morning meeting far beyond its end-time. Fortunately, Carol was familiar with this ongoing struggle, so if she learned I had lost a battle, she (almost) never blamed me.

Taking Its Troll

Noam has an appointment with a duck.

Carol joked that a duck could get an appointment with Noam. It's true that we may have unknowingly entertained a few ducks—a duck could look a lot like a credible person until it began to quack. One such duck was Ali G, a controversial Sacha Baron Cohen character known for trolling celebrities. People often asked how Ali G, a gold-suited (in our scenario) sunglass-wearing rapper, sneaked by our radar in 2005. I have no idea. He had to have lied about who he was, and about the nature of his visit. Was the gold suit concealed under a long coat? A guy who set up an MIT talk by Cohen years later didn't even have a direct number for his agent.

Once inside, he introduced Noam as his main man, Norman Chomsky. His first question was innocuous enough. "Why is studying language important?" Noam said it was the core property that defines us. The interview slid downhill from there as Ali G asked the father of linguistics, "How many words does you know?" and "What is some of them?" When I watched the interview on YouTube (it took months to gather the courage), I thought Noam had played it straight; the outcome was not as ridiculous as Ali G might have intended. If Noam had excused himself and asked me to end the interview, it wouldn't have been the first time. One afternoon, Noam came out fifteen minutes into a meeting to beg me, wild-eyed, to end it. When I then knocked on his door moments later, the visitor was furious: "You said thirty! I wrote it down!" I diplomatically took the blame and apologized for overbooking the day.

I couldn't always tell what was going on behind his closed door. We assumed people sent honest inquiries, but over time the number of unscrupulous requests grew and we became more picky. Ali G's appearance was one catalyst for this decision. Another was a young man who showed up more than an hour early, hyped up way over the top. After half an hour, Noam came out and asked, "Did you see that guy? He tried out for some show called *American Idol* and was rude to the judges. Had to be escorted out. He was proud that he'd been all over the news for a few days. He had written us with a completely different agenda." I all but screamed, "How can we keep this from happening again? It's a waste of your time!"

As for Sacha Baron Cohen, I lost cool mom points for not knowing his Ali G character. I do clearly recall Noam standing at my desk afterward and making the firm proclamation: "No more men in gold suits." Well played, Ali G. Now tell me: How did you pull it off? (And where did you put it on?) Ali G seemed innocuous compared to what I came up against the next week.

Staple Gun Control

Today's schedule: No appointments or commitments,
followed by possible life-threatening drama.

A middle-aged man glowered at me near our doorway. His stature wasn't intimidating, but his eyes were dark and spiritless. His white-knuckled hands gripped opposite ends of a three-ring binder, colored tabs sticking out at angles from dog-eared pages. It was a Monday, so Noam would not be in. Glenn was off, and Morris was in Paris. The man told me he had used his disability check to travel 1,800 miles to talk with Professor Chomsky, and he had slept outside waiting for me.

I recalled a lesson I had learned on an African safari in the 1990s: *Never turn and run from a predator. It will smell your fear and chase you down.* Roxy stood beside me, brown and fluffy at all of twenty-six pounds. Her bark was shrill, not menacing, but she and the office key I had positioned between my thumb and index finger were my only lines of defense. "I'm sorry, but Professor Chomsky won't be in today," I automatically replied.

"Are you his secretary?" he asked in an eerily even tone.

"I'm his assistant. Our part-time assistant isn't in today." I was nervous, and I wasn't making any sense. It would have been wiser to tell this guy that my *muscular* assistant would be right back. It didn't matter that Glenn, though athletic and tall, was neither big nor visually muscular, because he wasn't coming in. That was my second mistake. My first mistake had been to ignore my instinct to back away. But my office wasn't the Serengeti, so when he gently asked to talk with me for a few minutes, I unlocked the door and let him in. So much for caution. I guess on some level I took my cues from Noam, who was kind first and asked questions later.

At my worktable he turned the pages of his notebook and pointed to highlighted bits. "This proves that a government agency is following me, using mind control to get me to join them. This group of criminals—those in the government *are* themselves criminals—are inflicting relentless pain and torture on me."

I said with sincerity, "I'm sorry you've had to endure this, but it's time to go," and I stood.

He didn't budge, but instead asked me if I thought he was a dangerous person: "I have never in my life committed a crime, yet you're afraid of me."

I'd seen many anguished people seeking out Noam in a frightening world. Most people deifying Noam were innocuous. I generally felt safe at work, but once in a while a visitor with dark energy slithered in and coiled around my feet.

"Bev, I asked a question. Do you or do you not think I am a dangerous person?"

"I don't ... I'm not afraid of you," I lied. "But I have a lot of work ..."

He pushed his chair back and stood, hoisting our heavy-duty stapler from the table and waving it at my head. "If I were a dangerous person, I would smash this stapler over your head. And *that* would be a crime."

I upgraded from concerned to scared somewhat shitless, holding my breath to keep him from smelling my fear. Feeling both disconnected and hyper-focused, I found the breath to ask, "And I trust you are not going to do that."

"Of course not," he said with more than a little sarcasm, as if I were some kind of idiot to suggest it. "In fact, I've wasted my time and money coming here."

Words rasped from my throat. "I'm sorry, it's better to call first ..." Had I expected him to apologize for not following protocol, then leave with our it-looks-like-a-weapon-to-me-now weighty stapler in hand for his trouble?

"Lady, don't talk down to me. Frightening things are going on in our world, and Professor Chomsky, *I thought* ..." His voice cracked, and his speech slowed. "I thought you could help, but this office is no different than anyplace else."

I sidled over to our water cooler and filled a plastic cup with water; I would under no circumstances place a hefty ceramic mug in this man's hands. I realized I was standing by the door, and I offered to walk him to the elevator. I was relieved when he disappeared behind the sliding doors. My concern for my own safety and compassion for him were in a dead heat, but mostly I felt helpless. He was clearly disturbed, yet there was a smidgen of truth in his words.

I pulled on my office door. It was still locked, so only someone with a key could have gotten in to help me. I slipped my key into the lock, and then called Noam to fill him in. "You can't take this lightly, Bev. I want you to arrange for an escort out of the building tonight, maybe get Campus Police to walk you to your car. Don't take any chances." I took his advice and got one of our strong male faculty to escort me to my car after work. Bertrand Russell had it right: the suffering of mankind is undeniably unbearable. I hope the man has since found some solace.

9

Noam Chomsky in Bev's Hometown

An evening event sparks childhood memories.

In early 2007, we learned that Carol Chomsky was terminally ill. She called to say it was time to put the financial portion of Noam's travel "into your capable hands." My doubts about matching the precision of her organized record-keeping were dwarfed by the thought of Noam losing her. We pared down his schedule for the next six months as a start and canceled all but a few local talks. Some cruel hand of fate had also recently diagnosed Howard Zinn's wife, Roz, with cancer.

Back Pages Books owner Alex Green wrote our office later that year to ask Noam to give a filmed reading from his latest book, *Interventions*, at Waltham's Embassy Cinema, the rebuilt version of the once impressive Embassy Theatre of my childhood. Howard Zinn had recently spoken there, and I encouraged Noam to accept, suggesting a discussion and Q&A, since he never did readings.

Noam and I had jumped a number of hurdles together in fourteen years, especially since Carol's diagnosis. Over the months, I had driven to Lexington to walk with Carol's exhausted caregiver, and I had filled out forms for a temporary disabled parking placard. When she lost interest in drinking anything but sarsaparilla, I ordered cases of it with colored labels declaring it "Carol's favorite soda." Noam seemed willing to grant me small wishes, so I was hopeful that he would say yes to this Embassy Cinema affair in Waltham. Most importantly, the young activists inviting him to speak, their independent bookstore, and the discussion topics were all people, places, and things close to his heart.

Noam replied to Alex that he would be pleased to try and work out a discussion and Q&A. To me, he wrote, "Your wish is my command." Once I stopped noiselessly cheering, Alex and I arranged a January 2008 event date.

The theater was at full capacity, but by start time he hadn't arrived. I stood outside scolding myself for not insisting that I pick him up, then saw his car and flagged him down. Relieved hugs followed. It was heady to bring Noam to Waltham under my watch, and I was grateful that he had made it despite the life changes he was enduring. I hoped the evening would be good for him, and I gave his arm a squeeze as we walked in together. My mother and sister, her husband, Paul, and our friend Al sat with Laura, Noam, and me in the front row until he took the stage. I felt at home in all ways.

My mother and Noam had never met in person. She had an uncanny ability to call me at work at exactly the wrong time. When I could chat, she half-jokingly accused me of killing time. Once I asked her to hang on, but left her on hold for ten minutes (I'd forgotten), during which she wrote a country-western song, with this reprise: *So I'm not hangin' on, I'm hangin' up.*

She called one day while Noam and I were meeting. I said I'd call back, but trying for funny, she said, "Nope, I'll only be a minute." I handed the phone to Noam, whispering that my mother, Charlotte, wouldn't hang up.

Noam: "Hi, Charlotte. How are you?"

Charlotte: "Hi … who am I speaking with?"

Noam: "It's Noam."

Charlotte, in her finest stage voice: "Oh. Hi, Noam!" Mumbling …

Noam: "Charlotte, do you mind if I borrow your daughter for a few minutes?"

Charlotte: "Oh, of course! Tell her I'll talk with her later. [Mumble …] Bye-bye."

She had gotten a kick out of it, she later said. Six years before, I had invited her to my Harvard Square stand-up show—realizing too late that my routine poked fun at her. For instance, about her and my father's smoking: "Ash Wednesday was my parents' favorite holiday." She said afterward, "I *am* like that!" Crisis averted.

Noam's dialogue with Alex touched on the media, politics, and a changing world. Though the new, less awesome Embassy lacked the personality of the original, we Waltham folks retained our unique, quirky character. A wave of sentiment hung in the air as family and friends joined the Q&A. A journalist from the Waltham *News Tribune* interviewed us as we filed out. My mother, a long-time Waltham resident in her late seventies at the time, told the journalist in her best news-anchor voice: "It was interesting to hear Chomsky mention experiences that were linked to the time period I grew up in. I am just thrilled." The *Trib* had interviewed her before. Asked about my brother Ron's *Sammy Sumner* book, she had replied, caught off guard during a nap, "Well, it's no *Gone with the Wind*."

That night I learned more about Noam and saw how far our team of two had come. The structure of the event set the stage for a new format better suited to Noam's conversational style: a twenty-minute talk and a forty-minute Q&A. That night I felt a braiding together of my childhood and my work, as Noam, a humble, accidental rock star, illuminated people, one city at a time. In this case, my city.

At the end of 2007, my mother was diagnosed with cervical cancer. My sister and I took turns bringing her for radiation and chemo treatments. I was grateful that, unlike Carol and Roz, this cancer would most likely not take her life.

Saying Goodbye

Noam pisses off William F. Buckley; difficult losses.

The death of author and intellectual William F. Buckley Jr. in early 2008 pulled a YouTube video of a contentious 1969 interview to the forefront of a surge of emails to Noam. I knew of Noam's appearance on Buckley's acclaimed show, *Firing Line*, but only now, nearly forty years later, did I learn that Noam had pissed off Buckley by swerving from his host's script, and by repeating truths contradicting Buckley's assertions and making him explain himself. When Buckley claimed that communist insurgencies existed prior to the Nazis, Noam countered that there were communist resistance bands fighting against the Nazis, but no insurgencies. The video shows Noam's insistent, cool demeanor, as his frustrated host throws out snarky remarks like a heckled comedian, demonstrating to Buckley and his audience that Noam was a force to be reckoned with.

Sadly, Roz Zinn passed away that spring. As Carol's illness progressed, Noam gave phone interviews from home on the stock market plunge, bank bailouts, and the treatment of the US public as irrelevant onlookers. Visits from family and other good, caring people, like teacher-activists Chris and Gene Fogler, helped lift Noam's spirits. They even brought Roxy a knitted sweater.

In late November, I drove to his house. Carol was in the dining room, in a hospital bed. I could see from the front door that Noam was reading to her, so I walked quietly in. The *Winnie the Pooh* books they had read to their children brought them both comfort these days. As she lay listening in a half-dream, I touched his shoulder. When he looked up and saw me, coincidentally holding a Winnie the Pooh balloon, he cried in my presence for the first time. My heart broke, as it had for my father when I first saw him cry, at my grandmother's grave. My father's tears had me running for the car, but our extra degree of separation made it easier for me to stay by Noam's side until he was able to continue reading.

When Carol died in December, I met with the family to find a venue for her private memorial gathering. Noam asked me to frame several photos, which Deb cropped and printed for me. With Carol's photos bearing witness over the months, Noam recalled stories of their early years together. His sadness was palpable.

Soon after, I saw him with a big sticky cinnamon roll and asked what it was. He replied, "Breakfast." From then on I brought him lunch from home. I never thought twice about it until I handed him a dish of chicken and vegetables in front of a friend. He had put his arm around me and said, "I have a few guardian angels keeping me going." I felt a seismic shift in my heart whenever he revealed a fondness and gratitude toward me. I felt the same toward him.

His daughter Avi was another guardian angel, converging with friends to cook for him. Close friends had him over for dinner and made him meals and desserts to take home. I remember Bob Berwick arriving with a wonky apple pie in one hand and a large old-fashioned rotary phone in the other. He had rigged up the cordless rotary so that it rang when someone called his cell phone number. This somewhat typical MIT sight had us, even Noam, laughing. He healed slowly.

PART II

Life After Carol

10

Figuring Out a New Normal

Walking this way.

In the spring of 2009, Noam attempted to slide back into work mode. Avi, Judith, or granddaughter Ema traveled with him on sporadic trips. I joined him for local talks, and life at the office began to pick up. My mother believed, like many, a Fox News report that President Obama's healthcare proposals meant government-sponsored panels would decide which patients would be treated and which left to die. I shared her fears with Noam, who brought up the issue in an afternoon interview on the Affordable Care Act.

One morning he arrived sporting a much-needed haircut, courtesy of his granddaughter Sandi, just as I read an email from Avi about his high blood pressure. I suggested we schedule a checkup, but he had a better plan. "My brother has two dogs, and he said if I pet a dog, my blood pressure will go down."

"Let's test that out." When I held Roxy up, she licked his face, and he recoiled so severely that you would have thought I had pointed a gun at his new haircut.

David, a young man from New York, had volunteered to train Noam monthly in Lexington and soon had him planking on a yoga mat. When I asked Noam if he planked on his own, he said his exercise consisted of leaning over to pick up the yoga mat to vacuum, then throwing it back down in the same spot. David and Noam had a less healthy pizza dinner with Laura, Jay, my nephew Bobby, and me at our house after a meet-up plan snafu. Ultimately, their workouts turned to political discussions, and despite David's valiant efforts, the sessions petered out over time.

Carol had taken care of life at home, circumventing questionable situations. When strangers called with a "quick question," as if their promised brevity made crossing the home boundary intrusion OK, Carol had redirected them to Noam's email. But now he was on his own. When he told me a woman was ringing his home at all hours, I was livid. When she called our office, I told her that his home was off limits. (She did not take it well.) He needed a private number. Not because I wanted to show her who was in charge, but because he needed privacy, and sleep. Plus, I wanted to show her who was in charge.

"If I make my phone number private, can I still use the same number?" he asked. I put my hands on the back of a chair and leaned forward, my head tilted. "If your number—the same number—became unlisted, those who already have it, or those with an old phone book, could still call ... right?" There had to be some logic to his question, but I was too tired to see it.

Noam had hired a guy via a newspaper ad to make a minor repair, and I had concerns as the repairs grew. Jacki, Noam's bookkeeper, saw his house repair expenses growing exponentially. When we spoke, it wasn't about whether, but *how*, to step in; we wanted to be respectful. Early on, Noam had told me a story about Carol calling a plumber to fix a bathroom leak. She had explained the problem by phone, in plumber's language. The plumber arrived and insisted Carol "call her husband" into the room so that *he* could describe his fix. Carol insisted that she was more knowledgeable, but the plumber insisted on talking to the bespectacled man typing madly in his nearby office. She roused Noam to come stand next to her and nod when appropriate (while writing a lecture in his head). Once the plumber had settled his repair plan and costs, Noam returned to his typing.

Jacki and I double-teamed Noam. The bottom line: he had paid the same amount for *repairs* over nine months as he'd paid for his *house* decades before. He let us change the locks. When Jacki told the handyman to stop repairs until checking with Avi or Harry, he was, she said, "pissed," but he packed up.

With Noam's handyman gone, I grabbed a small rectangle of drywall, screws, seam tape, and joint compound and repaired the area above his kitchen window, where moisture from a leak had cracked the wall over time. As payment, I accepted Noam's offer of treats from tins of holiday gifts sent by friends and followers.

I tried to reinfuse our week with playfulness, perhaps to offset the handyman saga. When Noam asked where an old book was shelved, I hunched my body forward and faked a limp. "Walk this way," I said in a throaty voice. He of course didn't get the reference, so I told him it was from the movie *Young Frankenstein*. "There's a hunchback—his hunch moves from one side to another on a given day—who says to his guests, 'Walk this way,' and they lean over and walk behind him like hunchbacks."

"David and Judy [his brother and sister-in-law] have seen the movie a million times. Carol and I didn't find it funny."

I became animated. "The main character, Gene Wilder, is sitting with a scalpel in his hand, lecturing a class of medical students. He smacks his fist down to emphasize a point, accidentally plunging the scalpel into his leg, then slowly crosses his leg to hide the scalpel. His eyes glaze over as he utters, a syllable at a time, 'Class-is-dis-missed.'"

Noam laughed, head bobbing. "If you had acted out the movie for us, we would have loved it." I promised to act it out when we had free time. (As if.)

It was still cold in the late spring, but Noam had neglected to wear his coat into work. During a break I looked up when I heard him say, "Uh, Bev ... (he always began our conversations with "Uh, Bev"), I'm going to the pharmacy to pick up a prescription. I need the exercise." I asked him how he planned to do that without a coat. It was forty degrees outside. "Don't worry, I know the secret underground route to the medical department!" He flashed his boyish smile and left. Noam seemed to straddle several worlds. The serious academic world, the political world, our small MIT world, and his world of family and friends. I had watched in awe as he segued from talk of a devastating national disaster to a memory of boating with grandchildren the previous summer. When he returned from the pharmacy, I showed him what I saw as a funny email:

Hello Noam—Sorry to be impolite with the last email asking if you were alive or not. I am doing a Cognitive Science degree and was doing research for a presentation on you and could not find any dates of death because being stupid I thought all famous psychologist were dead. Again, so sorry if I offended you by asking you were alive or not ... I was being inconvenient.

After wondering aloud why the guy hadn't done a web search, I suggested that he may have misremembered Laura Ann Petitto's announcement made years before:

Dear Colleagues,
Nim Chimpsky died on Friday, March 10, 2000, at the age of 26, from a heart attack at the Black Beauty Reserve in Tyler, Texas. Many of you will recall that he was the subject of the Columbia University Language experiment in the mid-1970's ... [I]t is the passing of a life, albeit a chimpanzee's life, and one that—whether or not he ever intended it—contributed greatly to our knowledge of how human children learn. Good bye, Nimbo.

The chimp had been named for Noam as a nod to his role in ongoing debates on which aspects of language were unique to humans. We later received an email telling us a fossil spider in amber had been named for him in Burma. The write-up noted, "The first Left-Wing Spider in Burmese amber, *Retrooecobius Chomskyi*, named after Noam Chomsky."

Noam asked if I could imagine going down in history as a spider. I could not. A bee species was also named after him in 2013—the leaf-cutter bee *Megachile chomskyi*. A creative follower sent us a 3D model of the bee, supposedly named for its long tongue. Noam's response to this news was that he hoped to be able to thank the bees personally one day, so was practicing his waggling.

The Situation: Late 2009

And now for a little comic relief.

Roxy had a much less discrete way of helping herself to Noam's treats.

Scene 1: It was midday. I was working at my desk, surrounded by scattered film equipment. Noam's office door was slightly ajar. The only light in the darkened room was trained on his upper body as he answered questions about the Israel-Palestine conflict, his voice low and even. "The balance of terror and violence is overwhelmingly against the Palestinians." Glenn's desk was neat and orderly, mine was piled with folders, papers, books. Glenn had paper clips, staples, and other items separated into containers on his desk. Aside from the murmur of voices coming from Noam's office and the clicking of keyboards, our suite was quiet. Then I heard "the sound." I had *never* heard it during a filmed interview. I snapped a look under my desk, knowing what I would see, or what I would *not* see: Roxy.

"This is not happening," I thought, taking long, tiptoed strides toward Noam's office, fists clenched, elbows pumping like a slow-motion runner. I peeked into Noam's darkened office. "Take, for instance, the idea of a two-state system ..." CLANG!

I dropped to my hands and knees in the doorway, crawling to keep out of view. Had the crew heard the commotion? Noam was focused on his reply, lights on his upper body. "The press responded, too, by refusing to publish ..." I spotted Roxy under Noam's desk and slithered slowly forward, eyes straining to grab light in the dim room. I got to within two feet of the dog. My cherished furry best friend had become, simply, "the dog." Her expression said, "YAY. My person is here to get me that piece of sandwich from the trash. GOOD person!" She lifted her paw. The voice in my head screamed, "Nooo!" Another CLANG rang out as my hand grabbed her collar and I crawled with her to the door, her jingling tags loud as a dinner bell to my ears. She resisted, no doubt thinking, "Hey, my person, you forgot the most important thing, back there, in the trash ..."

My face burned as I closed the door behind us and got to my feet, then turned to her, arms madly waving, a harsh guttural sound working to escape, and not escape, my lungs. She wagged, happy at our new game, despite her lost spoils.

Scene 2: I sat at my computer feeling like a remorseful child, Roxy tethered to my desk leg. Had we ruined the interview? He should fire me. Noam appeared around the corner and stood at the coffee machine. "Uh, Bev," he began. If I wasn't fired, at the very least I couldn't bring her in anymore. I wouldn't blame him. He lifted the coffee carafe and twisted the top and sighed. I held my breath, waiting. "Is there more coffee? Oh wait, there's another cup in here."

"Was he not going to say anything?" Aloud, in a robotic voice, I said, "Oh, good. Drink that. I'll make another pot."

"No, don't bother. I've had enough today." Did he mean *I've had enough*, as in—and I heard my mother's voice shouting at four rough-housing kids—*I've had just about enough*? I was happy for the commotion of the camera crew packing up.

"I'm sorry about the dog. That shouldn't have happened."

"What happened?" he asked.

"Didn't you hear Roxy clawing at your trash can during the interview? I was *mortified!*" I dragged out the word, rubbing my elbow. Was my residual Catholicism making me confess to something I had apparently gotten away with?

Noam faced me, beaming. "Well, I heard something, but I couldn't tell what it was. Anyway, we need more comic relief around here."

My laugh "Haha!" was a nervous release. Who would have guessed that this little brown cocker spaniel, a matted mess when we found her at a year old, would be Noam Chomsky's comic relief. Hearing me laugh, she got up from her bed and sat at Noam's feet, staring at his mug, hoping he would share. We admired her audacity.

Roxy and Bev.

Noam's last meeting of the day was with linguistics professor Michel DeGraff, one of my favorite faculty members. Michel, who had been instrumental in bringing Haiti's native Creole language to Haitian schools, kindly gave me a chocolate treat. I did not share it with Roxy.

That night I finished reading Tracy Kidder's *Mountains Beyond Mountains,* a book about Paul Farmer, a Boston-area doctor focusing on HIV/AIDS and tuberculosis. I had met him early on, when he had shared a panel with Noam, putting issues of global health on my radar. It was no wonder Noam wasn't concerned about Roxy infiltrating an interview. He didn't sweat the small stuff—in her case, twenty-seven pounds of it.

Noam was my perfect father figure, forgiving and endearing, generously offering impromptu teaching moments. He didn't carry a big stick anywhere near me, but he did ask me to bend the truth a little, and then wrote me things like: "There was a front-page article in the *Globe* today about how people aren't going to confession as often as they should. Take note. Signed, Noam, head bowed."

At home, Laura and I were sweating other things, including some sad news about Jay's best childhood friend, Nathan, who had lived with Jay and my husband and me for two months as a teen. He had died on his motorcycle. I hugged Roxy close. My personal constant.

11

Howard Zinn

Howard Zinn takes his leave in the middle of everything.

Laura had the task of sharing more bad news in January of 2010, as she handed me the *Boston Globe*. "Bevy, I'm so sorry ... Howard Zinn died last night." I looked at the headline, then at Howard's photo. He and I were in the middle of an email conversation, and it was my turn to write. He had been worried about Noam's health. I'd told him that Noam had sent me a note to remind him to go to the infirmary for another bloodbath, suggesting they "must be hiding a vampire there." Anthony Arnove, Noam and Howard's agent, had promised Laura and me tickets to a New York performance of *The People Speak*, a show that grew out of Zinn's *A People's History of the United States*. Howard would be there, and we looked forward to it.

I ran to the living room and turned on *Democracy Now!* Amy Goodman was soberly announcing, "Howard Zinn died suddenly on Wednesday of a heart attack at the age of eighty-seven." Our Howard, historian, revolutionary, playwright, and activist in the civil rights and anti-war movements, had died. Amy now had Alice Walker on the phone, Howard's Spelman College student in Atlanta during their 1960s desegregation campaigns. I needed to get to work to manage the email that would no doubt be pouring in, but I stayed put when Amy announced that we would hear next "from MIT professor and linguist Noam Chomsky, contemporary and friend of Howard's."

"We wanted to end the Vietnam War," Howard had told me as we had chatted near the coffee maker a few years before. He recalled the 1967 March on the Pentagon he and Noam participated in when I was a naïve teen. Folk singer Joan Baez, another national treasure, had joined a half-million American protestors on those marches. Recalling the extraordinary strength and commitment of the Baez, Chomsky, and Zinn triad underscored the depth of our loss.

I closed my eyes and leaned my head back. Noam, Carol, Howard, and Roz had been friends and political allies since the 1960s, and Noam was now the sole survivor of their foursome. In an interview, Howard said he'd met Noam on a plane. Noam told me they had met at a rally. It didn't matter *how* this dynamic duo had met, only that they *had*. I had believed what I'd learned in school about our country's history. I hadn't considered problems of democracy, freedom, or our government's actions for the first half of my life. I hadn't questioned my news sources. Daniel Ellsberg's MIT lecture had started my slow journey, and the work of Noam, Howard, Amy and others like them had kept me somewhat informed.

Though I hadn't recognized it, my unplanned education in labor and social issues had been simmering in me since I was eighteen, when I first heard Baez sing about an outlaw sliding money under his plate when a poor family offered him a meal. I usually pushed the fast-forward button to skip "We Shall Overcome" and her celebrated Woodstock rendition of "Joe Hill," preferring her love songs. Her rich vibrato evoked for me a world of long ago. If her music had any connection to my working-class family, I was oblivious. The discussions taking place in the Chomsky home in the 1960s and 1970s about unfair labor practices and threats to democratic freedoms were not taking place in mine, but there was at least one similarity. Noam's daughters, he had told me, listened to Baez as teens. I wonder if he had listened closely to her lyrics?

Noam's TV voice pulled me back as he recalled Howard's involvement in acts of civil disobedience, publicly and persuasively insisting

Howard Zinn and Noam sharing a laugh with photographer and videographer Roger Leisner.

that we get out of Vietnam, period, with no conditions. Near the end of Noam's interview, I rushed through my morning routine, leashed Roxy, and got into my car for my Cambridge commute.

Noam worked from home on Thursdays, and I was sitting at my desk preparing to call him, studying a photo on the wall nearby. He and Howard were flashing electric smiles, having found great humor in something, or someone—probably Roger Leisner, an animated and eccentric peace activist and vocal supporter of marijuana legalization who videotaped and photographed most of their talks. Despite struggles born of their life choices, the photo reflects their infectious delight, perhaps at living the lives they were meant to live.

Later that day I re-read the days-old message from Howard in my in-box. He had been getting over a bad flu and asked me to make sure Noam, who had also been sick, was taking care of himself. I regretted not getting back to him in time and shook off the image of Noam, six years Howard's junior at eighty-one, as a subject of Amy's future tribute. Two days later Irene Gendzier, Noam and Howard's friend and colleague, called to invite Noam, Laura, and me to a memorial gathering honoring Howard at Boston University. We had a lot to get through before the late March event.

Walking Their Talk

Helping hands for Haiti and East Timor.

Noam and Amy Goodman met for a Q&A on Obama and US foreign policy, hosted on March 6 by Harvard Extension's International Relations Club. Noam's beige winter jacket sat next to me in the church pew. (Note to self: Take Noam's jacket to wash when you look for his extra car key.)

Amy talked about her trip to Haiti following the January earthquake, and about Noam's dedication to the people of East Timor. He had inspired Amy to visit the country during her early years as an activist. While she was there, a member of the Indonesian military, whose weapons and training had been funded by the US, fractured her friend's skull. By the time the East Timorese won their independence, the Indonesian military had massacred close to one-third of the population. At East Timor's independence celebration, Amy got Noam on the phone and they broadcast the whole thing back to the US. Noam's commitment to help the East Timorese was one of the first things I had learned about him. "Noam's voice cracked during that broadcast," she said.

I thought of Noam's message that night. "Fighting for democracy is something you have to fully embrace. You can't just stick one toe in. You have no choice but to fully immerse yourself." I was grateful he hadn't drowned in the process.

At the end of the Q&A, Noam and Amy rose to an emotional standing ovation. Afterward Laura and I helped with the book signing, and Noam invited us to join them for a walk to the nearby Au Bon Pain. The idea of joining two great minds in conversation wasn't as intimidating as it used to be for me, but to be honest, it still brought out my insecurities. A small grudge I held toward Amy made me bolder, and we accepted.

As we walked and chatted, I felt more at ease. When she pulled out her wallet and ran to put in an order for our table, she proved she was no prima donna. It took some doing, but I convinced her, by reminding her that I chat with Noam almost daily, to sit with him and let Laura and me get the food and coffee. He and I would square up the bill later. We made Noam eat, as he tended to ignore his hunger. (Ongoing note to self: Don't believe Noam when he says he's not hungry.)

I felt like a member of the in-crowd as people did a double take outside the café window. A man and his ten-year-old daughter came inside to thank Noam and Amy for taking time to speak at the church. He explained to his daughter as she shook their hands how hard they both worked to protect our democracy. Overwhelmed, he left in tears, which of course brought tears for Laura and me.

Amy explained that her parents and Noam had attended the same summer camp, where the campers spoke only Hebrew, and where Amy's mother was voted the funniest camper one summer, the most serious the next. I saw in Amy both attributes. When the conversation moved to language concepts, Noam's face brightened. "Amy, do you know Bev talks backward?" Admitting to this is a crapshoot. People are either skeptical or fascinated. She looked surprised, but before she could ask me to perform, I turned the focus away, sharing my thoughts about developing a universal sign language. Amy held her wrist in the air, jerking it up and down. "Can you imagine Noam, repeating the things he's said over the years? He would end up with repetitive stress injury!"

I liked her, a lot, and forgave her on the spot for the times she had kidnapped Noam to tape a segment or two of *Democracy Now!* while in New York, even when he was exhausted and tried to beg off. It was always his choice in the end.

Amy cringed at the idea of being driven by town car to Logan

Airport, but I urged her to accept the students' gift: town car drivers had to make a living. They picked up where an earlier chat had left off. "So Avi and Diane each have two children, and Harry has one ..." Laura and I took in the truth of where we were, and with whom, pondering how we got so lucky as to bear witness to two people who had, like Howard Zinn, soberly walked their talks, and still managed to find humor. ·

Howard's Memorial: March 27

The puzzle pieces of Noam's and Howard's lives snap together.

Laura and I sat in a front pew at Marsh Chapel. Noam sat on the opposite side with other invited speakers. Center stage was Roz's larger-than-life portrait of Howard. The atmosphere was ethereal, Howard's presence palpable, as family, friends, and colleagues told stories of his legacy as activist, humanitarian, playwright, and teacher. Noam spoke about demonstrating with Howard, particularly against the Vietnam War, while underscoring Howard's infectious humor. A young Iraq War veteran turned anti-war activist told the audience stories Howard had shared with him about his time as a World War II bombardier. Afterward, deep soul searching had convinced Howard to become a critic and protestor against acts of aggression.

Noam had told me he had no choice as a human being but to be an activist, and Carol protested for the same reasons. Howard held these same beliefs, but it also seemed to Noam that Howard *liked* the activist's life.

Many assumed I had absorbed all of Noam's teachings, everything he'd written and lectured on. They would ask what Noam would say or think, how he would react. I had been with him over ten years, and still had my head down most of the time, looking up to glance at the spinning plates, pull down the most urgent, throw a new one up, pass something on to Glenn, give the plates another spin, and repeat.

Howard Zinn often mentioned the "Wobbly spirit." The daughter of a Wobbly (Industrial Workers of the World, or IWW)—I can't remember her name, nor her father's—had come to interview Noam in the early 2000s, after learning he was the only living second-generation member. She talked excitedly with me beforehand, leading me to blurt, in a moment of self-conscious honesty, "Who are the Wobblies?" The look on her face begged, "How can you work for Chomsky and not know?" Had she asked me, I might have explained. I didn't tell her that one of the reasons I had gotten this job was precisely because I wasn't a groupie. Not yet.

A young Irishman now stood nearby, at the front of the chapel, his strong a cappella ringing out the story of "Joe Hill," permeating every floorboard and pew, piercing every wall and ceiling beam in that sacred space, possibly summoning the presence of Joe Hill himself.

And standing there as big as life
And smiling with his eyes.
Says Joe, "What they can never kill
Went on to organize,
Went on to organize."

From San Diego up to Maine,
In every mine and mill,
Where working men defend their rights,
It's there you'll find Joe Hill,
It's there you'll find Joe Hill!

I dreamed I saw Joe Hill last night,
Alive as you and me.
Says I, "But Joe, you're ten years dead."
"I never died," said he,
"I never died," said he.

Laura, Noam, and Bev backstage after a talk at Harvard.

By the last note, tears flowed all over. I'd had moments of awakening in my life, but for me this was like Helen Keller connecting language to her world, the letters to her doll. In a perfect storm, I felt a convergence of Joan Baez's lyrics and Noam's and Howard's words. This trio had offered strength and visibility to those whose voices were shut out. The story of Joe Hill, a migrant laborer and activist wrongly executed in the early 1900s for murder, became my mental background track as puzzle pieces snapped together. The people I had come to know and care about over sixteen years, whose unswerving focus on human struggle and resistance I'd witnessed, stood with us in the chapel. Migrant workers, filmmakers, activists, ex-prisoners, teachers, Wobblies. I had been too busy keeping all the plates spinning in the air to be able to see clearly what had been in front of me: my father's short, dark crew-cut, a carryover from his Marine years, his thick workingman's hands, circles under his eyes from moonlighting as a shoe salesman. He had worked for the Federal Tea Company since I was a toddler, watching over us four kids and checking in on his aging parents. When the company changed hands, he took a job as union representative and arbitrator with the National Association of Government Employees (NAGE). Long before *Requiem for the American Dream* was a reality for most, my father, with his eleventh-grade education and a doctorate in life experience, went on to work with lawyers and politicians to help working men and women negotiate salaries and benefits, because he had been in their shoes. He may even have sold them their shoes. Joan Baez had been singing about the people in my world. Noam and Howard Zinn had been fighting for the rights of *my* family. After a decade as a waitress, my mother put to use her unique kind of intelligence and life experience to help at-risk students graduate from high school. I wrote Noam that night.

Hi Noam,
Your memorial tribute to Howard yesterday was very moving. I know how tough it is for you, being the last of your foursome … the difficulty of your day wasn't lost on me. I looked up Joe Hill this morning to read more about him, the Wobblies, etc. It occurred to me that the artwork of the bronzed miners in your office is probably related to the story of Joe Hill. (Did you know Joan Baez performed "Joe Hill" at Woodstock?)
    Joe Hill's ashes were found at a post office in the '80's. One small packet of ashes was scattered in a 1989 ceremony, which unveiled a monument to IWW coal miners buried in Lafayette, Colorado. Six unarmed strikers had been machine-gunned by Colorado state police in 1927 in the Columbine Mine Massacre. A famous Wobbly, Carlos Cortez, scattered Joe Hill's ashes on the graves at the commemoration. Did you ever write about that? Many things connected and came together for me when the Irishman sang in Joe Hill's voice.

Noam replied:

Awful to watch how humans find ways to torture one another. Like the miners in Iquique, the strikers in Lawrence, and much too much more. The bronze miners is an even more horrendous massacre, maybe the worst in labor history. It was in northern Chile, the very valuable nitrate mines, British-owned then (American later). I visited there in October 2006. It's up in the Andes. Almost unlivable. Not a green shoot in the ground for many miles. Howling winds and dust storms. The miners and their families lived in shocking conditions. The owners lived in the comfortable seaside town of Iquique.

In 1907, workers and families marched down some 25 miles to Iquique to plead for a very slight improvement in living standards. The owners were quite accommodating, put them up in the Santa Maria school, and invited them to a public meeting in the schoolyard. They gathered there, and were massacred by the state security forces. No one knows how many, maybe thousands, men, women and children. Chile has a very brutal history, for which the British share a lot of responsibility (then the US, when it took over). Pinochet was not as much of an exception as is often thought. It's all been kept under wraps. There's virtually no literature on it until very recently. Now activist groups and some historians are unearthing the whole story. The first conference on it was about a year ago. The photo [in my office] is of a small monument outside the school, put up by local activists not long before I got there.

I don't recall when Hill's ashes were found. It's probably covered in recent labor history, maybe in later editions of Howard's *People's History* ... I was also moved by the Irishman's song at Howard's memorial. Always am when those days are brought up. One of my evenings in Paris was at the metalworkers union building, a panel of union activists, some with an anarchist background. Hardly a main current, but much more alive than here.

The US has the most violent labor history of the industrial countries. Workers were being murdered into the late 1930s. Nothing like that had happened in the rest of the world. The right-wing British press in the '20s was shocked by the violence against working people here, and bitterly mocked the great philanthropist Andrew Carnegie when he was traipsing around Scotland while his goons were murdering working people in Homestead PA. I wrote about it a little, in *Year 501*, last chapter.

—Noam

I couldn't get the young anti-war veteran-turned-activist out of my head. I wrote later to ask about Carol returning to school. I asked him to say more about his father joining the Wobblies, and went to bed wondering how Noam responded to questions like this eighteen hours a day. By the time I fell asleep, I knew the answer. His work was his passion—it was who he was. Our conversation continued the next morning:

It's odd how little Carol and I talked about the fact that I was very close to a long prison sentence when she went back to get her degree after seventeen years away. As to what that young fellow went through, and how [he] dealt with it, hard to find words.

My father was a Wobbly. He told me when I was a kid. Parents and children didn't talk much in those days, at least in our circles, but we did talk about that. He explained how he joined. He was barely off the boat, steerage, penniless. He didn't know any English, working in a sweatshop in Baltimore. Some man came around through the shop trying to sign up the workers there. My father couldn't understand what he was saying, but he seemed to be for the workers, so he signed up. The story of the Wobblies is remarkable. I suppose I'm the only living second-generation member, but now it's mostly symbolic. They were largely crushed by Woodrow Wilson—one episode of what's called Wilsonian Idealism.—Noam

I answered, "Noam, Thanks for this. Not bedtime reading, but an important part of history. I'm learning—The miners, Pinochet, Wobblies, Marxism, juntas, coups ..."

Everything Noam—always the teacher—taught me was part of a web, one fact leading to three more, and on and on. Carrying our correspondence inside me for a few days, another puzzle piece clicked into place. I had been seeing the Chomsky family as cooler than my own. It was a judgment I had made based on economic status and my parents' limited education. Though I can't pinpoint why, I felt a bubbling up of the truth of my family. Their strengths and accomplishments were different, but not less important. While the Chomskys' academic training led them to do outstanding work in education and for social justice, my family had its own victories to celebrate. Our family was perfect in its imperfection, as are most, whether professors, secretaries, waitresses, union arbitrators, or shoe salesmen. We're all Joe Hill.

In His Shoes

Noam walks a burro up a muddy mountain.

On the subject of shoes, it's only right to give a shout-out to Noam's ever-present black "shoes." The word *shoes* is in quotes due to our ongoing disagreement about whether his black leather sneakers were shoes, as he insisted, or sneakers, as I had.

Shoes or sneakers, they represented something completely different when they were, more or less, resurrected. Noam never traveled in summer, but a trip to China at the invitation of his friend and colleague Jim Huang, to lecture, lead discussions, and receive an honorary degree, was a welcome distraction. He approved my catalogue order of shirts, socks, and pants for the trip. Purchasing his shirts brought me back to my father. He had recently reminded me that he had always been a sharp dresser. When he died weeks later, I buried him in his own off-white shirt, rather than the impersonal one offered by the funeral director, a decision I regretted when I saw him in his casket. Buying new shirts for Noam felt like a betrayal of my father, but my guilt soon gave way to self-forgiveness. I picked up a new tie for Noam, and asked if he wanted to bring a second. He said, straight faced, "If I bring two ties, I'll have to bring a second suitcase. They take up too much room." With clothing bought, he assured me he had good shoes.

After his China trip, we received a box containing plaques, a ceremonial gown, and event photos and videos. In a photo of Noam kneeling to receive his honorary degree, his Velcro sneakers stuck out below his gown. I pointed this out to him.

"They're not sneakers. They're formal shoes. They're black!" he insisted, smiling. When I tried to take a look at his shoe size to replace them with a newer pair, he told me he planned to walk into his grave in those shoes. I got the gist of his message. No new shoes. Or sneakers.

Our debate over the sneaker/shoes was put on hold. The Colombia Support Network (CSN) directed and co-founded by his friend Cecilia Zarate-Laun, was dedicating a forest in Carol's memory, and they wanted Noam at the dedication. The mountain area provided most of the region's water for drinking and irrigation, and the program dedicating "La Carolina" would raise awareness for the protection of the eco-system of La Vega from the threat of mining operations. The ceremony helped Noam to heal and gave him hope, just as learning about programs like this gave me faith. After the trip, he wrote to the CSN folks: "I cannot imagine a more lovely place for Carol's spirit to rest, under your gentle care. And I hope, fervently, that her spirit will help you protect the water and the forest and the natural beauty of La Vega."

This was the one and only time I heard Noam talk about a spiritual world. Back in the office, he dropped a grocery bag on my desk, saying nothing. We wordlessly locked eyes before I peered inside the bag to see if he had brought me a gift. What I saw instead were two sneaker-shaped mud cakes. Not that he hadn't thought about bring-

ing me a gift—Cecilia later told me
he had wanted to buy me jewelry
but couldn't remember ever seeing
me wearing much of it. (He was
right.)

"I think they're finally ruined.
I guess just throw them away."
He'd had a problem managing his
burro on the trek up to the ceremony and had to walk up sections
of the muddy mountain by foot.
He was eighty-two, but I think his
burro issues had more to do with
his inexperience as a "horseman."
A follow-up email to me from
Cecilia read: "Can you imagine

Noam's IWW membership card.

giving a step, and your foot comes along but your shoe doesn't? The
horse-riding he said it was the first time in his life … He reminded
me of Don Quixote that romantic beloved hero fighting for justice."

This was a perfect opportunity to lose the shoes, but I figured
since he had chosen to carry them back, somehow through customs,
caked in mud, he wasn't ready to part with them. That night I scraped
mud from them as if on an archaeological dig. I wiped them down
inside and out, let them dry, and sponged them off again. Then I polished them—twice. The resuscitation effort took two hours. The next
day I dropped them on his desk in a clean paper bag.

He opened the bag. "You bought me a new pair of shoes," he
sighed, looking somber. I told him they were his old sneakers/shoes.

"How?" he asked, staring. "This is a miracle …" His words weren't
far from the truth. Maybe I'd had a little help from La Carolina.

My father knew a sneaker from a shoe. His reputation as a great
dresser extended to his feet. He sold and wore the best: suede oxfords,
wingtips, penny loafers, even tasseled leather slippers. When my
brother Ron worked as an orderly at the Metropolitan State Hospital,

he asked my father to donate his old shoes to the residents. My father agreed, separating the new from the still good-looking older shoes and slippers. Ron took the wrong box, giving the residents our father's best shoes. My father had a fit, but those who didn't prefer to be barefoot loved their fine leather footwear.

12

The Man Who Couldn't
Say No: 2010

Disabling Noam's "yes" key was a real challenge.

"I don't know why people don't hear *no* when I write to them," was Noam's frequent lament, with slight variations, like: "Look at this email, and tell me how they interpreted my *maybe* as a *yes*," and, "How much more clear can I be?"

Oh, Noam. Let me count the ways. People do hear what they want to hear, but Noam was his own worst enemy when it came to saying *no* in a clear, concise way to a friend, colleague, or stranger. He had debated William F. Buckley, Jean Piaget, Michel Foucault, and B. F. Skinner without breaking a discernable sweat, but preferred that I be the naysayer, the killjoy to the inquiring public, I think because of his ambivalence. He hated saying no. Responding to a lecture request for a small college's speaker series, which he was sure conveyed a *maybe*, and most definitely not a *yes*, he wrote: "Would like to work something out if we can manage. What possibilities do you have in mind? Schedule is very intense, and we have few options." He always held out hope. In fact, I thought his response looked much more like a *yes* than a *maybe*, for three reasons.

1. It began, "Would like to work something out." Most people won't read any further. They will never hear what follows: "if we can manage."

2. He asked, "What possibilities do you have in mind?" Sounds like a *yes*, right? And a real kiss of death if you're trying to say *Maybe*.

3. They will also read "we have few options" as "we have *a* few options." The two phrases have an almost imperceptible grammatical difference, but their meaning differs greatly. Hopefuls won't want to see, so won't catch, the caveat.

When documentary interviews began to take up more of our schedule, Noam decided to shut them down for a while. I would help discourage documentary requests, since it was difficult for him to say no. My baby finger was still curled in from our pinkie promise when I saw that Noam had sent a new email agreeing to a documentary interview. Had he skimmed it, overlooking the obvious? "Noam, this is a *documentary* request. I can send regrets," I wrote.

"Well, this is one I *should* do. They've been after me forever." I reminded him that most film or documentary producers would settle for a short video or written statement like the one we had recently sent advocating the reduction of ocean plastics. The string of exceptions following his proclamation to take a hiatus from documentary films left me head scratching.

But wait, there's more. Noam noticed his photo on a flyer announcing him as keynote speaker at a European summer conference. He asked me to take a look. I did, and took it down, annoyed with the organizers for fabricating his participation at a conference alien to both of us. A thorough email search turned up a vague reply, definitely *not* a yes, and *barely* a maybe. Noam had a long-standing rule to keep summers free for family and writing, a rule that was broken twice, fifteen years apart, for sound personal reasons.

Still, he insisted he couldn't get out of it. Maybe the conference hit a nerve or fit into some internal, private plan, or he had talked with someone about it way back, uttering a *maybe* that sounded a lot like a *yes*. He told me he has what he calls "buffers," or little drawers in his brain that he opens to retrieve conversations and memories, even from fifty or more years ago, an ability he thought for a long time everyone had. So he would remember this *maybe/yes*. He ended up attending with a family member.

Office appointments were not exempt. Trying to make time to prepare lectures for an upcoming trip, Noam asked me to "keep the 22nd clear." I marked an X across the calendar page. The ink was still wet when he wrote in an email, "I added someone on the 22nd." After triple-checking, I wrote, "Noam, you asked me earlier today to keep the 22nd clear. Is the date a typo?" Why, oh why, hadn't I learned to cross things out in pencil?

"I should do it, these are really good people," he said, and the day filled up. As a kid, Noam must have loved the much-recited mnemonic rule-of-thumb that every English-speaking child learns by the second grade:

i before e,
except after c,
or when sounded as "a,"
as in *neighbor* and *weigh*.

Just as some authorities deprecated the rule as having too many exceptions to be worth learning, I made my own compromise and conceded to *his* many exceptions. I should have disabled the "yes" key on his keyboard years before.

Only after exhaustion had him again fighting consecutive colds and flus did he admit his need to slow down. When he asked me why I hadn't been tougher on him, I explained emphatically that he had ignored my pleas to say no to projects far afield from what he saw as crucial. To prove he was ready to heed my advice and change his wicked ways, he drew up a contract on a piece of legal-sized lined paper and wrote in green marker: "Formal Agreement. BE TOUGH on Noam Chomsky." We signed it, and Glenn signed where Noam had scrawled "Notarized." I taped it above my desk, and I pointed to it now and then. But alas, nothing changed.

This contract, drafted by Noam, was taped to my desk. It asks me to "be tough on Noam Chomsky." It should have been taped to his watch.

One day I was working quickly and thought I had forwarded a message to him by mistake, so I sent a second note asking him to ignore what I'd just sent. Then I realized that the message he was supposed to ignore had never been sent.

Noam: "Here's a question of logic that you can ask Sylvain [Bromberger] about next time he comes in: Is it possible to ignore a note if you haven't received it?"

Me: "I don't need to ask Sylvain. I know the answer. If you don't receive a note, but I tell you to ignore it, then you can't ignore it. You must then write a note like this, which I cannot ignore, because I now have to admit that I sent the original note (which you were supposed to have ignored) to the wrong Chomsky address. But I didn't know this until I opened *my* incoming Chomsky mail and saw that the note you were supposed to have ignored had been sent to me by mistake. So, where was I? After realizing you hadn't been sent the original note, I should have written to tell you to ignore the note to ignore the note. But that might have been confusing. Unlike this message. OK, once more, this time with feeling ..."

Noam: "These are the kinds of things that brighten up a gloomy day."

To a woman in Asia who'd asked for an interview, Noam wrote, "Sorry. I'm scheduled to the hilt, and beyond." The woman replied, "[That] sounds bad though I do not know what 'hilt' means. I'll try another time." Maybe the trick to saying no was to cause confusion.

My efforts to say no to interlopers flip-flopped when I encouraged some outside his close circle to visit Noam after Carol died. Daniel Ellsberg had recently called asking to meet. I told him Noam was working from home for a few days and suggested he call him there and ask to drop by.

"I couldn't do that," Dan answered. I loved him for not wanting to invade Noam's personal space, for not assuming his own reputation entitled him to ask too much. I offered to suggest a meeting to Noam, and Dan agreed, saying he would email later. He told me not to worry if we heard he was arrested in DC the next day, as that was his plan. When he was released from jail, he and Noam spent the evening together, talking about what they always said yes to—exposing the truth.

13

Oy to the World

Sometimes guardian angels switch places with those they guard.

January 2011

Between work and my mother's cancer treatments, I was exhausted. In my car on Memorial Drive on the way home after a long week, I became aware too late of the glaze of black ice invisible beneath a thin layer of falling snow.

The resulting multicar collision was so sudden and forceful that it felt like I was watching with my eyes suspended in front of me— my body pushing toward the windshield, my hand reflexively snatching Roxy in midflight, front and back fenders cracking and snapping as the speeding car hit me from behind and I hit the car in front of me. In a final crescendo, my eyes sprung back into my skull and my body snapped back against my seat faster than Ashkenazy playing Rachmaninoff. My car finally settled six feet from the banks of the Charles.

When an ER doctor confirmed a concussion the next day, I felt what it must be like to suffer from dementia, when you know early on that something is wrong but hide it from yourself and others. It wasn't as if I could not remember details as much as I had to retrieve them from somewhere else when they should have been easily accessible. Most disturbing, yet refreshing, my emotional and social filters had been ripped away. Nice or naughty, I said what I felt. Noam wrote praising my finesse in putting off one annoying request in a "gentle yet persuasive manner." I replied, "You make me sound like a laxative." I hoped that I wouldn't have written that under normal circumstances.

I vaguely sensed as I pulled out of the rental car lot on Monday that I shouldn't be driving. I wasn't spinning my usual plates at work, and some were smashing to the floor. Noam and Morris had what they thought was a covert meeting in Noam's office. I could see them talking through Noam's doorway, my two guardian angels huddled, glancing back at me, shaking their heads, Noam's hands flipping up and out as if lecturing. Morris retreated into his office and Noam approached me. "Uh, Bev, Morris and I are concerned that you're not giving yourself time to heal." They didn't even know I had just sent Noam's flight plans for a Europe trip to an organizer of an upcoming Boston talk. *Smash ...*

"How can they confirm a concussion without a CT scan? Morris will walk you to medical for another neurological exam. Roxy can stay here with Glenn and me," Noam insisted. Morris and I donned winter coats for the walk to MIT Urgent Care. They confirmed my concussion, but declined a CT scan, citing unnecessary radiation exposure. Over Noam's protests ("Stay home and recover") and Morris's refrain ("You are not taking this injury seriously enough") I worked from home for a week, but still, Noam admonished me for working on a Saturday. "Bad enough that you show up weekdays instead of getting rid of those ills."

Me: "Ills, schmills. This work doesn't get caught up on its own. Does it count that I'm still in my pajamas? I'll bet you haven't had a drink of water since my accident."

Noam: "Oops. Just took a drink of water. Pajamas? You get a half-credit. Your work will wait. Never mind the mish-mosh. I goof off all the time. Impressed that your Yiddish innovative capacities are picking up."

Bev and Morris.

Me: "I didn't know mish-mosh was a Yiddish phrase. Good about drinking water, IF you're telling me the truth."

Noam: "How could you see the black cross on my tongue from that distance? I'll go right now and have a drink. Hope it washes off."

I had shared with Noam that as a kid, if my mother suspected I was lying (I never was) she would ask me to stick out my tongue to see if it had a black cross or a black spot on it (her observations varied). It had become an ongoing joke between Noam and me.

Me: "The black cross only disappears after you recite the Act of Contrition a thousand times. It could take weeks."

Noam: "Learn something every day. In my ignorance, I forgot about the Act of Contrition. I'll memorize it."

Me: "It begins like this: 'O my God, I am heartily sorry for having offended Thee, and I detest all my sins, because I dread the loss of heaven and the pains of hell.' As a kid, I misheard the words and recited, 'I am hardly sorry for having offended Thee ...' See? Catholic guilt, right there on the page."

Noam: "That's pretty heavy. I mentioned it to a long-lapsed Catholic friend, who spouted if off from memory. Scary business, Western religions."

Months before, he had told me that he was drinking plenty of water at home. I knew he wasn't, and I told him he'd never go to Catholic heaven. His reply: "You don't know about how I bribed the Pope." I should have asked him to elucidate, because while I was at it, I could have thrown it back at him and blamed it on my concussion.

"Huzzah!" Noam wrote when I said I was ready to return to work. I replied, "One more thing. We have the gold letters J-O-Y hanging on our living room wall. I nailed them up two years ago at Christmas and never took them down; I figured the world needs more joy. So this morning, Laura hit the J with her head and knocked it off while opening a window, leaving O-Y. OY to the world. Probably more appropriate."

Noam wrote, "Oy. I hope Laura doesn't have a head injury. Maybe she was just jealous and wanted to match yours."

Back at work, Morris mentioned the passing of a close friend as we made tea at the hot water dispenser. "You know what I always tell you. There's only one way out of this life. There *is* no alternative!" he said, laughing and shaking his index finger toward the sky. His words struck with an unexpected sharpness, and I choked up.

"Morris, I adore you guys. I want you both to stay around for a long time."

"Well, let's not think about *that* right now," he roared.

"I wish I could *not* think about it. How do *you* cope with the certainty of death?" I asked, remembering my friend Shelley telling our Totem Mamas group that she learned in Bhutan to think about her death for five minutes each day.

"Beverly, I thought about death once, and it depressed me so much I decided not to think about it again!" Oddly, this lightened my mood. I had imagined myself to be spiritual about death, but when I put faces of those I loved on the concept, I was not so Zen. I took his advice and stopped thinking about death for a while, may the Bhutanese forgive me.

Soon after, Morris quietly revealed to Noam, Glenn, and me that his memory loss was progressing. *Smash ...* Then he asked me to drill another hole in his adjustable cane, so he could stand up straighter. This didn't surprise me. Two years earlier, after witnessing a fatal car accident on his way to work, he had come in and announced, "I'm not driving any more." Later that week he arrived at MIT by the T. "I hung up my keys." He and Noam shared that practicality: *Here is a difficult problem, here are the ways it can be solved, I choose to go forward this way and get on with things.* I know little about how they approached linguistics issues, but I have to guess that practicality figured into those, as well. Their way of looking at things energized me. I was soon spinning plates again.

Staying Grounded: Still BFFs After All These Years

In March, a series of catastrophes in Japan shifted our focus toward our mortality. The idea of a nuclear meltdown had scared the hell out of me ever since I read about Hiroshima and had an anxiety attack. Reading the article, I learned again what Noam always came back to: that so many world events go largely unreported.

I found comfort chatting with Morris. He claimed to be the luckiest man on earth, even while recalling devastating stories of his youth. His father, a businessman, fled to the US from Riga, Latvia, with Morris and his family just before the Nazis arrived and decimated Latvia's Jewish population, killing many of his relatives. Sylvain had told stories of his family fleeing France shortly before Germany's attack on Belgium. Both recalled Miss Buchner, who "taught English to foreigners" in 1940 at George Washington High, a school at the edge of Harlem filled with refugees. Morris, Sylvain, Jay, Noam, and Louis, another GWH attendee, all shared their childhood experiences of anti-Semitism, in interviews, and with me personally. They told their stories with humor, gently sharing the difficulties they'd endured.

I had met Jay Keyser, Noam's friend and colleague, and L&P's original department head, in the late 1980s, through a Grad Program Administrators Group I had helped found. As MIT's associate provost, he was the first speaker I remember at our monthly round-table lunches, where we addressed MIT student issues. He was delightful. During our serious and informative discussion about harassment at MIT, a topic then picking up steam on campuses, he inserted humor at suitable times, softening the subject, making it more palatable, so, more approachable.

I had known Noam's MIT pals, now in their eighties, for eighteen years, and I dreaded losing any of them. The dominoes fell too closely when in April 2011 they lost a dear friend, Professor Jerome (Jerry) Lettvin, a cognitive scientist most known for his paper "What the Frog's Eye Tells the Frog's Brain." My son Jay and I had met Jerry and his wife, Maggie, in 1974, when they were Paul's housemasters at the Bexley Hall undergrad dorm. Maggie had gotten into prime shape after suffering a back injury in a car accident, and introduced a still-overweight Jerry as "my husband*s*." I had exercised to her TV workout program, "Maggie and the Beautiful Machine" and was already smitten.

"Send your son to private school when he's old enough for it to make a difference," she said, two-and-a-half-year-old Jay on her lap. I took her advice and enrolled Jay in a private middle school, and then at Matignon High in Cambridge, where he maintained a solid A average. When he was a senior, his basketball team won the state championship. When I look back, I see how many of the older MIT folks, and even some students, inadvertently shaped and guided my life, and consequently Jay's.

That same spring of 2011, Morris was slowly losing his dear wife, Rosamond, a talented artist and mother of their three sons, to Parkinson's disease. One afternoon I felt a strong pull to visit Roz, to see what Morris was dealing with. Sitting alone with her, comatose in a nursing facility, I told her of Morris's devotion, and I promised I would keep an eye on him. I told him of my visit the next day, hours before she passed away, and then framed a trio of Morris's favorites of her artwork and hung it inside his office door.

14

Our Danny Boy: May 2011

A reality TV episode and a father.

It wasn't just the older people leaving us. Jay's father, Danny, called Jay and me to say his health was failing and asked us to visit. When I called him the next day to say flights were scarce during spring break, he said he'd rebounded, and not to come. Having inherited my mother's denial, I delayed our trip, with mixed feelings.

Danny had reminded me often that Jay and I were his home, and I had felt the same for a long time, despite everything. Seven years before, in 2004, Jay was planning to marry the lead singer in his cover band. They were one of ten couples to be videotaped for a month preceding their wedding for the Oprah Winfrey reality TV show *The Knot*. On the day Danny was due to fly in, Dean, the videographer assigned to film us, drove with us to Boston's Logan Airport. The question "Will Danny show up?" hung almost tangibly in the air. The last time we'd seen him, he was thirty-two, Jay's age now. I was rooting for him to fight his fears.

At baggage claim, Jay and I circled the crowd of people from his flight now gathering at the conveyor belt. "He's not here," Jay mumbled. "He's not coming." I spotted him first, the older but still handsome boy I had met thirty years before, his shoulder-length hair pulled back in a ponytail. His skin was tanned brown-red, as Jay's did in summer. A slight paunch pushed at a crisp shirt the same white as his perfectly capped teeth. My next memory is hugging him, then feeling Jay's arms around both of us. Our original world of three. When we broke loose, we were all crying. Even Dean, who was estranged from his own father, videotaped through tears. At dinner that night, Jay's father reminded us both of something he'd told me many times, "Even when I wasn't there, I was always there."

In the end, our episode was not aired, because we had said no too often. Danny told me later that the wedding had changed his life. We had all found some closure, and definitely forgiveness.

Weeks after Danny called Jay and me separately for long talks, we heard from his friend Jenn that he was hospitalized and unconscious. Jay and I made the decision, a foregone conclusion, to remove him from life support. He died that night. In June, we flew to Florida to clear out his things. We carefully wrapped a golden box holding his ashes and tucked it inside his truck with other treasures, and drove him home.

Some people I knew through our office heard that my son's father had passed away, but as in a game of phone tag, while in Florida I answered a few panicked emails from people checking to make sure Noam was still alive.

Weathering the Storm

I was often tempted to press the Delete button.

The day I returned to work, still emotionally immersed in Danny's loss and our glimpse into his world, I read a nasty email rant addressed to Noam. He expected and even welcomed disagreement, but the over-the-top rage of some had more to do with their own pre-existing agendas or personal issues, and Noam, having strong and specific political views, seemed a convenient vehicle for their anger.

Putting aside his significant linguistics work, Noam defended those whose voices, loud as they might be, went unheard. He wasn't alone

Danny and Jay: my guys.

in his distress over senseless, unjustifiable wars, or havoc wrecked by tsunamis, earthquakes, or radiation leaks, all pointing to the questionable survival of our planet and species. He worked beyond exhaustion, often refused compensation outside of his flight and hotel, and he paid his own way if necessary. He worked late into the night, having soundproofed his home office wall so that his typing and the towering piles of books occasionally falling wouldn't wake anyone.

The more I witnessed his dedication, the more I lost patience with ranting lunatics spewing thoughtless vulgarity, some of whom sent offensive, time- and spirit-robbing viruses. With each vile email, I was tempted to hit "Reply" and give the writer hell. I would say that Noam doesn't fabricate statistics or data. I would suggest they find the facts he quotes in journals, newspaper articles, books. I'd point out that he was a guardian of peace, even for those with opposing views. If a person suggested he leave the US, I would send a related quote, like this one from Howard Zinn: "If patriotism were defined, not as blind obedience to government, not as submissive worship to flags and anthems, but rather as love of one's country, one's fellow citizens (all over the world), as loyalty to the principles of justice and democracy, then patriotism would require us to disobey our government, when it violated those principles."

I would suggest that they seek out and read, with an open mind, credible news sources. If the reasonable ones were still up for a heated discussion after they had done their due diligence, they could have at it.

But it was my job to pass all of Noam's messages on to him, whether from a colleague or a ranter. I forwarded even those I would rather trash with one keystroke. So when I opened this especially ugly email, I jumped out of my chair, gathered up items for an impromptu meeting, and stormed into his office—well, I didn't actually storm. Noam doesn't respond to drama.

I excused myself for interrupting his reading and asked him if we could talk. He looked up with a touch of concern and nodded, and I launched right in.

"Noam, don't nasty, antagonistic emails from enraged people bother you? Considering how you live your life, how do you keep from blowing up?"

"Do you get angry with a hurricane?" he asked.

"No, I don't get angry with a hurricane, but I am upset when people are *hurt* by a hurricane ..." I was pacing.

Noam interrupted me, "But do you get angry with the *hurricane?*"

"No," I said, because I knew it was the right answer. Is this what his students felt—momentary cluelessness, with a moment of enlightenment lurking?

"Well, people are hurricanes."

"I'll think about that," I said, returning to my desk unenlightened. Was he suggesting anger was a big waste of time unless harnessed into action, or that hurricanes, like people, are unpredictable, and might erupt without warning? Or was he saying you can't control a hurricane any more than you can a person?

I went home and talked this over with Laura. As a therapist, she has witnessed anger and frustration in all sizes and shapes. "I think there's a way in which people carry their own weather systems," she said, going in a whole other direction. "They're affected by what's going on around them, what they've learned, what they've eaten, and their assumptions. Some people walk in my door and I can feel the storminess around them."

A few days later I wrote to ask how he kept from reacting to a writer's fury. Yes, it was the same question, but I worded it in a way that wouldn't hint that he might be answering a question I was supposed to have figured out for myself. He wrote: "People usually have reasons for being angry, however distorted and unpleasant. There's always some hope that they can be dealt with. Sometimes it even works, after a lot of effort. But what's the point in being angry about it? A three-year-old doubtless has a reason for an annoying tantrum, but do we get angry at the kid?"

•••

Most things I heard in our suite circled around again, in a colleague's email, an overheard conversation, a Skype interview I sat in on as an extra set of ears. These teachings wore a groove in my brain's neurological pathway until they stuck. I had learned that even hostile discourse can be a step toward understanding, and that many lack the ability to control reactions like anger, rage, or frustration. I would follow Noam's lead and don raincoat and boots to wait out the storm. Finding compassion in anger was no doubt one of my life lessons coming full circle.

It's only right to balance this out with one of the most awesomely well-timed phone calls I ever received at work. Noam had written a reply to a young man with a few questions. The guy was so moved when he got the reply that he called me. "Holy sh*t, this dude took time from his f***ing day to write to me. How f***ing cool is that?" Cool, for sure. I had f***ing needed his flat-out enthusiasm.

15

Spell Cast (All Keyed Up): 2011

My inner thoughts weren't always deep.

Noam's voice over my right shoulder startled me. "Hey! Look at that!" he said, his eyes intent on my keyboard. I jerked my fingers from the home row keys as if a twenty-six-legged creature with hairy, probing antennae were crawling toward my wrist, and looked down at my hands. "What?! I know, I never wear nail polish!" With that I coiled my fingers in toward my palm the way the wicked witch's feet curled in when Glinda removed her ruby slippers. My parents, both snazzy dressers, bore four children, only one of whom, my sister Denise, had more than an obligatory interest in dressing up. The one time I wore a skirt and heels to work, Noam had frowned and asked, "Are you going on a job interview?"

When I looked up again Noam was shaking his head. "No, all of your keys are *labeled*!" He spun his index finger in an oval circle to indicate my entire keyboard. "*My* keys have all rubbed off!" he said, cocking his head and grinning.

My mind's eye lit up with images of Noam's body hunching, hands hammering out thesis drafts, editorial letters, articles, statements of solidarity, petitions, lectures, professional correspondence, recommendation letters, arguments, and email. For decades. On countless keyboards. On manual and electric typewriters, then word processors, then progressively streamlined and ergonomically correct wireless keyboards, all the way to the smaller keys of his compact laptop, none of which cramped his fingers or hurt his wrists. His body, unlike mine, seemed to be built for endless typing.

"Really? You have no letters on your keyboard? None at all?" I looked down at mine. Small bits of my "e" and "t" were missing, but it was otherwise intact. "I'll get you a new one, but I'm curious. How long has it been blank? I'm assuming it has *no* letters, *no* numbers or symbols?"

"Right. I suppose it was gradual, which gave me time to get used to it. No need to get me a new keyboard. I know by now where all of the keys are. In fact, there are tiny white dots here and there to give me little hints." He squinted toward his thumb and index finger, held a sixteenth of an inch apart to illustrate, smiling at the concept.

My head spun. Pulled into another realm, I imagined infinitesimal specks of paint and plastic flying off his keyboard and embedding themselves beneath his fingernails, landing in his eyebrows and the waves of his graying hair until only the upper crescent of the "q," and the right most tip of the "t," remained. I saw him striking the "s" with spectacular speed while writing his earliest drafts of *Syntactic Structures.* I envisioned each subsequent keyboard heaving and wailing as the refractory "r" succumbed to his repetitive rage against the machine, leaving this last keyboard black and bleak.

Had he lost entire words all at once: language, morphophonemics, terrorism, thought, mind, and media? Just as he claimed there were an infinite number of sentences one could string together, so were the ways his keys may have rubbed off. Did neighbors "o" and "i" hold hands to jump the keyboard together, wearing only a diphthong? Did the "i" go before the "e," or did it make an exception? Was it possible that his most-quoted phrases, in a show of solidarity, leapt together, questioning even the simplest things? I could see colorless green ideas tumbling to his office floor, clinging statically to his slippers as he shuffled through the perpetually diminishing pathway to the printer.

Noam rolled a chair next to mine to review his new schedules. Was it real or did I imagine the word *censored* floating upward from behind his eyeglass lenses, toward his creased brow as he hiccupped a partly formed paragraph, which jettisoned under my desk, settling along Roxy's spine. No harm done. I reached down and pinched an entire sentence between my index finger and thumb. It struggled erratically, biting at my nails before relaxing into its gravitational pull. I stretched it between my hands and apologized before reading his mind aloud:

The general population doesn't know what's happening, and it doesn't even know that it doesn't know.

I shook myself free from my reverie. "I'll order a new keyboard tomorrow." Noam was losing his letters. I was losing my mind. And soon, the nail polish.

Kindled Spirits (A Day in the Lives)

If you assume that there is no hope, you guarantee that there will be no hope. If you assume there is an instinct for freedom, that there are opportunities to change things, then there is a possibility that you can contribute to making a better world. — Noam Chomsky

It took Noam months to admit to having a blank keyboard, but some things he would never admit to. Like jet lag. "There's no such thing as jet lag," he said to me a day after returning from Australia, where he gave a lecture titled "Revolutionary Pacifism: Choices and Prospects" and received the Sydney Peace Prize. (I'd been offered a first-class ticket to join him, but he wasn't ready for me to go along and "manage" him.) Peeking at me through slitted eyes, he poked an index finger into his temple and added, "It's all in the mind," then weaved toward his office like a half-asleep drunken sailor.

Nor would he ever admit to being sick. When I heard the conges-

tion in his lungs by phone the night before, I had asked if he was sick
from breathing contaminated airplane air again. He coughed back
one word at a time: "Can't-you-tell-by-my-voice-I'm-not-sick?" He
thought this was funny, but I wouldn't hang up until he agreed to call
Dr. Kettyle at MIT Medical if he wasn't feeling better by morning.

A slight detour. I kept him in full supply of throat lozenges
because he lost his voice a few days each month from nonstop talking
and exhaustion when traveling unguarded. Organizers promised him
quiet during car rides between events, but alas, they asked questions
for the full length of the drive, no matter that his voice might be
wrecked before the next lecture. No matter that he needed to prepare. This drove us crazy. It drove me crazier that he had broken
his vow of silence in the car. "Well ... they're good people," he
would say in self-defense, denial, and whatever else was going on
in his head.

The next morning, he threw his coat onto the rack, called out
a barely audible hello, and—I want to say *tiptoed*—into his office,
which convinced me that he was still sick. I brought him a mug of
hot herbal tea with honey. He was sitting at his table next to a pile of
mail, immersed in a journal article. I hovered long enough to watch
him circle a word in ink and draw a long line out to the margin,
where he scribbled a note in tiny, barely legible handwriting. His eyebrows were tightly knit as he thanked me and sipped the tea, never
losing focus. I pulled the door closed and took the few steps into
Morris's office. We agreed to give Noam a few hours to call his doctor
before we intervened. As if on cue, next door Noam let out a string
of hacking coughs that he had surely been holding in.

By late morning, after intercepting hundreds of emails, I hadn't
encountered any of the usual horrors. No video of a child in a war-
torn country crawling on her handless forearms, no imploring message from a desperate soul unjustly accused of a criminal act, and
no repulsive string of expletives denouncing Noam for speaking
truths someone didn't want to consider. A silent phone added to my
momentary bliss.

Talk of imminent disasters and catastrophic events scared, angered, and frustrated me. I had been trying for years to balance the serious and disturbing information I absorbed in that office each day about human suffering, environmental devastation, and the atrocities of unnecessary wars, in a way that allowed me to, sometimes, feel joy. On the positive side, the benefits of my job included discussions with Noam, Morris, and other professors and students who stretched my intellect. Many of our visitors were richly complex and extraordinary people—social reformers and other progressive thinkers trying to bring positive change to our screwed-up world. So while parts of my job were fascinating, even uplifting, it was becoming increasingly difficult for me to find my way through the dark and dreadful truths laid out in the steady stream of correspondence about terrorism, tipping points, and corruption that flew at me during my work day.

On those days I imagined squeezing my phone, my computer monitor, and its accomplice, my ergonomically modified keyboard, through the narrow opening of my eighth-floor window. Then I would grab my dog, my backpack, and my own ass, and make a neater exit through the front door of 32 Vassar Street, leaving no forwarding address. Midday walks with Roxy helped my outlook. Our drive home included a stop at St. Patrick's Cemetery near our house. After throwing balls and sticks, we were more centered by dinner. (Roxy needed to shake off my day as well.)

In light of Noam's cough, I was grateful for the sparse schedule I had made for his first day in after the Australia trip. Aside from a late-afternoon meeting with me, he had a two-part interview with David Barsamian for a book on the recent Occupy Movement. Founder of Alternative Radio, David had compiled other interview books with Noam, including *Keeping the Rabble in Line* and *Class Warfare*.

A half-hour into the interview, David burst out of Noam's office to run and buy a new audio card. This gave Noam time to look through mail and eat the hot soup I picked up from the café. Not that he could tell a café soup from Julia Child's boeuf bourguignon. Food was secondary to him.

When I returned to my desk I noticed some movement to my left. Maybe a visitor walking in to snag an autograph. I turned toward the intruder, making no effort to hide my frustration. Noam was staring at me from just beyond the file cabinets that provided me with a puny shield of privacy. I was unsure what to make of his expression, so I took a broad shot. "Do you need something?"

After staring at me, poker faced, he asked, "What do you do when the cat looks at you with those sad eyes?" He was not an animal person, but he had grown accustomed to seeing Roxy's face, even welcoming her into his home. Her first year with us, he had affectionately dubbed her "the cat." I believe it was affection, though it's possible he never took a good look.

"I know that face. She looks like that when she's begging ..." A quick check under my desk confirmed she was gone. "Is she in your office? Did she *eat your soup?*" He said nothing, but he looked amused as I ran to his office, where I found her, paws on his worktable, looking sadly, or guiltily?, at his nearly empty bowl six inches from her snout. "Roxy—get—away—from—there—now!" I said, thinking "Not again!" She didn't budge. I grabbed Roxy's halter, wide eyes focused on the bowl, body straining toward it, stumpy tail wagging wildly, and dragged her out of the office, lootless, and banished her to her bed.

I told Noam that David was ready to go, but he remained nearby. A quick check assured me that Roxy was snuggled in. "Can you show me how to use this new coffee maker, Bev? I can't wake up, and I need to make it through the rest of this interview."

"That's because you're jet-lagged, Noam."

"Never! I just haven't gotten enough sleep lately between trips."

"Right, they call that jet lag," I muttered, taking his mug from him and placing it under the spout where a fresh pod was about to deliver his coffee. I asked, trying to seem casual, "Would you like me to get you in with Dr. Kettyle today?" Mug in hand, he walked away, coughing and shaking his free hand in the air, a clear "No!" in Noam language. Coffee sloshed up alternate sides of his mug's lip with each

Morris and Glenn.

unsteady step. As I tried to settle back into my work, Morris's voice rang out nearby.

"Someone gave me this. It's called a Kindle, and all I know about it," he said, pointing to it, "is that this is the *on* and *off* switch." Glenn didn't own a Kindle, but Jay had bought me one, so I offered to show him how to use it. "What do I *need* this for?" he asked, turning the Kindle around in his hands and laughing, so characteristic Morris.

"Let's say you're going on a trip. Instead of packing six heavy books, you load them onto your Kindle and read them there." He asked how this was better than holding a real paper book, with its bulk and texture, and words printed on a page. Noam had written something similar: "With all of modern technology, electronic access cannot compare with having a book in hand, nor can the internet compare with the enriching and exciting experience of wandering through a bookstore or a public library to explore the cultural wealth that they offer in ways that are a unique and unmatched delight and source of enlightenment."

A few books had been loaded on Morris's Kindle, mostly Tolstoy. I clicked on *War and Peace* to show him how to open it. "I haven't read that in quite a while," he said. I began reading it aloud, trying to prove the Kindle's value, as if it were my own personal invention.

A few sentences in, Morris seemed amused, even settled in, so I continued, ignoring Noam's seismic sneezes from down the hall. On the third page, I read two sentences that asked the question I hadn't been able to figure out for myself; the one that touched me at my core and made it difficult to say "fine" when someone asked how I was doing. "Morris, would you mind it if I read that passage again?" I asked.

He nodded his head. "Yes, I know, this is something." Tolstoy:

"Can one be well while suffering morally? Can one be calm in times like these if one has any feeling?"

We sat looking at one another. He nodded and said that it's no easy task to be human. Morris's take on the book's theme was that one cannot control events. I thought about Noam saying that people, like hurricanes, can't be controlled. Morris and I had both uncovered gems worth pondering, and today's lesson was over. A while later, Noam resurfaced from his office and pulled up a chair to talk about his schedule. His smile was wide as he made a joke, despite his bad cold, about Roxy looking hungry. I reached down and stroked her head, scratching behind her curly ears. "She always looks hungry—that's just her face. But—did she eat your soup?"

"I'll never tell," he said, laughing his noiseless laugh. I laughed too, wondering how he held onto his sanity, knowing what he knew about the disorder of the world, never idly wading through the pain of it, but looking it in the eye and reasoning with it, wrestling with the beast that it is. If he could laugh, certainly I could. Was this his secret—knowing that we have to create the space for joy in order to have hope?

When I finally asked him months later how he remained centered, he shared a story that was, oddly, about his observation of someone else's coping skills, not his own. He was stuck in traffic in a busy city center in India with an activist friend, Aruna Roy, co-founder of the MKSS (Workers and Peasants Strength Union). People mobbed them, asking for money. A woman pressed her baby's face to the car's window. Noam, disturbed, asked Roy how she coped. She said she looked away, because if she let herself take in each person's suffering, she would be unable to continue her work. Not focusing solely on the pain of individuals seemed true also for Noam. When I talked with Laura about coping, she thought Noam had an exploded view of the world map, with countries needing to be stitched back together. My map is a more personal one, showing the frayed individuals. This may have been one reason we worked so well together.

I came to recognize Noam's practice of sidestepping whatever slowed him down, like fear, illness, or jet lag. When I asked again years later how he stayed centered, he said, "Through action." It seemed an obvious answer by then, since a steady pace had always helped keep me a step ahead of my own worries.

16

Activism and the Vietnam War

Which living person do I most admire? Noam Chomsky, Barack Obama.
— James Taylor, in a 2015 interview for vanityfair.com

I cleared my head, and sometimes found joy, by reading biographies and autobiographies of musicians, authors, and entertainers. I then read related articles and watched documentaries to learn the stories of people like Janis Joplin, Maya Angelou, James Taylor, Joan Baez, and Vladimir Ashkenazy. After a while I read about Howard Zinn, Edward Said, and others of Noam's contemporaries. Their journeys fascinated me.

People write autobiographies for many reasons; some to be understood when they've been *misunderstood*, or to demonstrate the price of fame. Jane Fonda vehemently protested the Vietnam War. Her political style and snafus at a time when rising anti-war sentiment left veterans feeling unappreciated alienated many. In her autobiography, she expressed regret for the hurt caused by her being photographed at an anti-aircraft gun, something she regretted doing when she realized her error.

The Vietnam War touched my family. Uncle Mike returned home from two tours in Vietnam with PTSD in his twenties. At thirty a stroke left him with aphasia and partial paralysis. When Mike was denied Agent Orange benefits, my mother asked me to step in and argue for an appeal, even knowing that my politics differed from

Mike's. For three months he came to my house with cane in hand, his military cap pinned with American flags, Vietnam signets, and helicopters. I took notes as he detailed his memories through crude and disturbing pencil drawings. He spoke single words, the deeper meanings of which I skittered above, unwilling to take in more than I needed in order to piece together his story. The details that leached in despite my safeguards fueled me to write a stronger appeal letter, which we sent with drawings and documents to the Board of Veterans' Appeals. This time they granted Mike his benefits. The victory provided him with much-needed compensation until he died, too soon, at seventy-one.

On the Tuesday after I finished Fonda's autobiography, I asked Noam, "Was Jane Fonda well-intended, if not misguided? Was her disapproval media-driven?" When he agreed to tell me about his experience with Fonda, I imagined pushing a magical "Pause" button, to stop time and pull out a microphone and a bag of lightly salted popcorn (blood pressure), prop up my legs, press "Record," and give him the go-ahead wave. Instead, I perked up my ears, hoping to remember key details. He was a good sport when I asked him later to fill in some blanks, this time about Fonda's New York City event:

> It was supposed to be a fundraiser for the anti-war movement. She insisted I fly out first-class (I flew back on my own, economy— I was more spry in those days). It was held in some extremely elegant ballroom, filled with people I was told were very famous. I actually recognized one face: an actor in a children's show that we watched with the kids, maybe *I Dream of Jeannie*. Comical to see his face in the crowd. There was a panel, and each of us talked for about ten minutes while the audience got bored waiting for the main show. Then the affair started. People standing up and announcing: "I'm Phil Ochs," huge applause, a ... statement, and so on. And yes, I ... left in the middle without telling anyone.

I still needed an answer, but waited two decades to ask again. Wasn't Jane Fonda well meaning in exposing the crimes of the Vietnam War? He said she was hated for her activism, for resisting the Vietnam War. "We all were, anyone was who would dare speak out against the war. It took years before anti-war sentiment caught on." He said Jane did a lot of good things. His answer seemed obvious to me by now.

It was the norm for celebrities like Danny Glover, Wallace Shawn, Peter Coyote, and many others with high public profiles to meet with Noam about human rights, peace strategies, the environment, and other crucial issues, and never their acting careers.

Some devoted activists who had Noam's attention and support still suffered marginalization, job loss, and worse. Dr. Ken Hildebrandt, author of the book *INFORMolution*, and his wife Elaine, a couple dedicated to exposing hard truths, were each arrested and stigmatized, after leaving their careers in pursuit of fair elections, leaving them struggling, all for speaking out against the misinformation we're fed.

Noam and Norman

We have to start meeting like this.

In early 2012, after reading Dwayne Raymond's book *Mornings with Mailer* (Harper, 2010), in which he describes his days as Mailer's devoted research assistant, right-hand man, and confidant, I wrote to him about my Chomsky book project. Life got in the way of our meeting, but we kept in touch, comparing and contrasting our bosses and our work. Both men had shown a great appreciation for our uncanny intuition. We each managed interviews, talks, travel, and inquiries. Most prominent was that we both underestimated our bosses' grasp of pop culture.

One morning Dwayne met with Mailer to consider an invitation from Martha Stewart's TV show. Mailer's questions, "Who is she? Doesn't she cook? Will a group of women try to get me to make a pie?" were so Noam-like. Dwayne's response, "Yes, but she also interviews artists, writers, and actors. Younger people could be introduced to your work," felt like many of my own. Like Noam, Mailer enjoyed a good scotch. He interviewed with Charlie Rose eleven times, to Noam's two or three. Conversely, Mailer had done a two-part *Democracy Now!* series with Amy Goodman in Provincetown, while Noam had been on her show countless times.

A later discovery surprised me. Past interviews with both Noam and Norman were highlighted (fully clothed) in a Japanese issue of *Playboy* magazine (June 2002). I couldn't put my finger on why the show *The Gilmore Girls*, on which Norman played himself, felt familiar until I remembered a 1999 call from one of the show's permissions-seekers asking to pin up a poster with Noam's likeness in a character's dorm room. Noam shrugged, so I said yes. Seeing it, a snarky roommate asks if she has any friends, aside from her poster of Noam Chomsky. Another scene:

EMILY: The government says you should have nine servings of fruit and vegetables per day.

LORELAI: Imperialist propaganda.

RORY: I think Noam Chomsky would agree.

LORELAI: I bet Noam doesn't dip fruit.

RORY: Or laugh. Ever see that *punim* on him?

LORELAI: Easter Island. [I looked up *punim*, Yiddish for *face*. I beg to differ. Noam laughs, and he enjoys dessert.]

Delving deeper, I asked Noam about his jail time. He said he had been jailed *seven* times in all, six times for Vietnam War protests, and the other for a protest against US intervention in Nicaragua. I asked if he saw similarities between himself and Mailer:

I met Mailer a few times, the first time in jail. We spent a night in adjacent cots in a huge detention center after the Pentagon demos.

He wrote a book about the whole affair, *Armies of the Night*, his best book I think. Pretty accurate, except that—interestingly—he downplayed his own quite significant contribution, though he was famous for the image of extreme arrogance and egotism that he constantly cultivated, with a passion. Will tell you about it some time. It's not in the bio, I'm sure.

Met him again on the Cape, where he was a Provincetown celebrity. Someone brought him over to our cottage—tiny, five kids running around. It was part of a long-time effort to get me to appear with him at some Provincetown affair where celebrities show off before one another. You can guess how successful the effort was. When he stopped the constant act he was trying to carry off, he seemed to be a decent guy—and there's no doubt that he had a lot of talent ... There are plenty of other differences. In many ways we were at opposite ends of the spectrum.

Noam elaborated on the significant contribution Norman Mailer had played at the detention center after the Pentagon demonstrations. "Maybe [the agitator was] a police infiltrator, trying to inflame the mostly young kids to engage in violent acts. Mailer walked over to where he was standing on a table haranguing, and quietly started ridiculing him. Soon the act collapsed. That headed off what could have been a dangerous outcome."

Dwayne and I continued our personal correspondence. He said, "Here's a key for when you write about Noam ... The song that the reader must hear is quite simple; they want to embrace the familiar. They want to be a part of something that they are already a part of, but need to be reminded of ... Not that I know anything, really. I'm just a poor guy, muddling on, hoping to not cause a big stain on the world in the end."

Sadly, Dwayne died too soon, in his sleep in April 2018. I had lost a friend, a confidant, one of "my people" who shared the exciting, outrageous, and mundane experience of working for and with a well-known person. I was grateful that I had reached out, that we'd

connected. His last note to me included this: "[Y]ou are one of the
few on the planet, like me, who understands what the day-to-day life
with these men is like, with their faults and fears and greatness and
gentle childlike nature ..."

17

Cape Crusaders

Noam's Scramble
From *Recipes for Peace*: A cookbook from members and friends of Arlington/Lexington United for Justice with Peace (UJP):

> Break 1 egg (per person) into a bowl. Beat the egg.
> Heat a pan on the stove and melt a tablespoon (or slightly less) of butter in pan. When butter is melted and pan is hot, pour egg mixture into pan.
> Stir as eggs thicken to desired consistency.
> Serve hot with wheat toast.

Noam continued to travel inexhaustibly, cramming in talks and Q&A's. Starting in January 2012, his lectures focused on the ever-present peace themes, on the issues of Israel-Palestine, revolutionary pacifism, and the Occupy movement. In June, the end of the MIT semester and summer's arrival begged his forgiveness and nudged him toward Cape Cod, where he worked in his lower-level office and, sometimes, had fun. And who knows, maybe he considered working to be fun.

The extended Chomsky family and their close circle of friends were a bright and extraordinary group of humanitarians steeped in global concerns: immigration, human rights, fracking, political science, mass media. Their time together on the Cape was, I imagined, filled with political discourse, eating, swimming, and boating. Noam had regaled me with stories of magical walks down the path to the pond, where he taught the younger kids to search for dragons' hiding places. Of the games he played, I loved most that he helped the kids plant branches in the sand during the day. While they slept, he swapped the branches for larger ones, convincing them at breakfast that they had grown overnight into tiny trees.

In the spring of 2012 he invited Laura and me to help open the house with him in June, and we agreed. I began to worry right away about exposing myself as a political lightweight. And boats made me sick. I packed Dramamine and *The New Joys of Yiddish* (Three Rivers Press, 2001). I had read *Chomsky for Beginners* years before, trying to memorize simple facts about him. I gave it another quick scan before we left. It couldn't hurt.

He was expecting more family to arrive in a few days, so he arranged for us to stay ten minutes away, in the guest cottage of his friend Norma Simon, a children's book author. Norma and I had met by phone four years before, when Noam asked me to call and check on her following surgery. Norma had lost her daughter, a young social activist, to cancer in 1978. Something pulled taut in me when I realized her daughter and I were born the same year.

Norma mailed me two of her books: *Hanukah in My House* (1960) and *Passover* (1965). I devoured them. Another delicacy I consumed were three-sided cookies from a tin she had sent to Noam. I declined at first, having had a cookie with breakfast. "Hamantaschen are *special* treats that *have* to be shared during Purim," he said, pushing the tin my way. My sugar-addicted inner voice pushed for clarity—it wanted, *needed* to be sure it heard right. "So, I *must eat* the haman ... taschen?"

He said yes, so I took two, out of respect. "I love a tradition that mandates the sharing of cookies. Show me *that* in the Catholic religion," I challenged him.

"What about the Holy Eucharist?" He was referring to the host.

I explained that biting the host was forbidden, but using your tongue to peel the tasteless plastic-y disk off the roof of your mouth for eternity was expected. Noam suggested Catholics find some Eastern European chefs to make a tastier one. He promised to tell me the real story of Purim another time. His expression promised it would be a doozy. What didn't kill me would make me stronger.

The hamantaschen cemented my eagerness to meet Norma in person. I hoped to try out some Yiddish phrases with her, Noam, and anyone who wanted to be entertained by a *goyish froy*, even if they thought, "That's *fakakta*." Besides, my Russian-Jewish maternal great-grandparents had spoken Yiddish.

Laura and I arrived before Noam, whose handyman had unlocked the door and turned on the utilities. The pond at the edge of Noam's property and Norma's favorite kettle pond would provide relief from Wellfleet's heat wave. He was hesitant to ask anything of me outside of work, but we had stopped to pick up Noam's usual foods: plain yogurt, nonfat milk, bananas, blueberries, tomatoes, celery, hummus, and low-sodium cottage cheese, as a thank you. "I eat mostly white things, the more bland and tasteless, the better," he'd tell me every time, as if I didn't know. He preferred the simplicity of dipping carrots and celery into hummus or cottage cheese to cooking. His one scrambled egg recipe appeared in a UJP fundraising cookbook. I couldn't wait to refrigerate the food and run down the path to check out the pond. We weren't due at Norma's for three hours, so we might have time for a swim.

A Chilly Reception

Or was it a warm reception?

I put cold water down for Roxy and opened the refrigerator. It was warm. I played with the dial inside the door, but no luck. The plug was in the socket. I would try and catch Noam before he left home to ask where the fuse box was hidden.

With Roxy at my heels, I started down the wide wood-planked stairway of the homey two-story gray clapboard cottage to get my cellphone from my car as a sand-colored sedan pulled in. It was Noam. His hair had been cut short for his three-day Scotland trip, and he wore wide black sunglasses. I imagined that his outfit, brown sandals, beige shorts, and t-shirt, was typical of his Cape summer wear, just as his blue Oxford button-down shirt, Irish knit sweater, jeans, and black Velcro sneakers had become his customary MIT uniform.

"I was about to call you," I said, my body straining toward the pond.

"And I was wondering where my cell phone was so I could let *you* know I was early! I see you've brought the cat. She looks hot, poor thing." Roxy was panting again.

"Is there a trick to turning on the refrigerator?" I asked, anticipating the fun of puzzling through the problem with him. Most things I had fixed for Noam were never broken. Like when he asked me to fix his garage door. Within two minutes I noticed that the "Lock" button on the control pad was depressed. My repair consisted of pressing "Unlock" on the pad, but Noam liked to tell people how Bev, the genius, miraculously fixed his garage door that winter, after he spent weeks pulling it closed with a rope. When he told the story in my presence, I countered with the words Noam used to describe the laws of language: "Any five-year-old understands this." He seemed to enjoy bragging about me, and I got a kick out of it, so I let him. Who wouldn't feel a swell of pride when one of the world's smartest people bragged about them? It was intoxicating.

"Oh, it's off?" he asked. "I hope it's not broken." It was typical of him to assume the worst. He slid open the heavy glass door to the main level of the cottage, and we followed him to the galley kitchen, where, humoring him, I stepped aside and poured Roxy a fresh dish of ice water, to let him try to figure out the problem.

He squinted at the inside of the refrigerator, looked up, down, left and right. Exposing his teeth in a Norman Thayer–style grimace, he touched the dial inside the door. I said that I had checked the plug and tried all the settings, to assure him I had thought this through. His head disappeared farther inside the fridge, near the left hinge.

"What's this *On* switch?" he asked, pushing it, making the refrigerator hum and whir in response. He emerged again, his mouth open and head lifted in joy and disbelief at the sound of the surging electricity, and pumped his fist in the air in victory. "I did something you couldn't do! I fixed something you couldn't fix!" He practically sang the words.

"What?! The *On* switch was where? But wait, I looked there!" I was beginning to sound like Dr. Seuss—*Not fair! It was where? I did not find a switch in there!*

Noam was gloating. "Are you going to write about how I showed *you* for once how to do something?!" He smiled so hard the space between his teeth widened. Still grinning at his victory, he helped us pull deck furniture from storage. When I lifted a fluffy white rug off the porch railing, gray tufts flew, and a horrible smell emerged. Why oh why had I never bought into the concept of rubber gloves? Something bad had happened on this rug. While Laura snapped together vacuum parts, I loaded a sponge with soapy hot water and scrubbed. Norma told me later that a squirrel had been trapped inside the rug over the winter, and the cleaning person had cleaned it before hanging it to dry.

Sweating in the heat, or *schvitzing*, as I had learned from my friend Kate, I had the brilliant/desperate idea to take the unwieldy two-person kayak down to the pond with Laura, where it would spend its summer adjacent to the shore. Finally at the pond, I waded in and splashed my face with cool water, tempted to jump in, clothing and all—not unusual for me—but Norma was waiting. Roxy plopped down and took a long drink from the clean water. She was, I swear, smiling, as was Laura as she walked barefoot along the short length of sand. We made a plan to drive to Norma's, say hi, and shower. Noam would meet us there.

Meeting Norma

Confessions of a matzo/matza/matzoh thief.

It's funny how you draw a picture of someone in your mind before meeting in person, and when you do meet, you feel a strange disconnect between imagination and reality. In-person Norma, in her eighties and still publishing, was fit and pretty, with a perpetual smile. Despite profound losses, her robust humor and zest for life shone.

Her guest cottage, like Noam's Lexington home, exuded the warm intimacy of family and an unaffected hominess. We unpacked and showered before dinner.

Eating appetizers, we learned that Norma and her late husband, Ed, had met Carol and Noam through a friend who taught Carol to fish. In a photo gracing Noam's work desk, Carol squats, tan and fit, behind three big bluefish (just "fish" till Noam filled me in) laid out on the dock. I told Norma that actor Catherine Keener had invited Noam, Laura, and me on a road trip to the home of children's book author and illustrator Maurice Sendak to videotape a piece honoring three eighty-three-year-olds: Keener's father, Noam, and Sendak. I had met Keener when she joined a friend for a shoot at our office. She won my trust that day by diagnosing Roxy's intestinal issue. It didn't surprise me that Norma knew "Maurie." Sendak's sudden death canceled our trip, but Keener kept in touch, encouraging me to deepen my writing.

Noam cleared his throat. "Uh, I thought I would take you both down to see the boat tomorrow, before Judy and her gang show up." I wasn't worried—after all, he had said to *see* the boat, not *ride* in the boat. "Norma can join us." This wording implied that we might *go out on the boat*. Petting Roxy, I saw a possible way out.

"Why don't I stay back with Roxy while you three motor around," I said.

"Why? We can bring her with us." I considered running west,

away from the Atlantic Ocean. If I had to ride in a godforsaken boat, at least she would be with me.

Over pie, Norma asked Noam about his recent trip to St. Andrews in Scotland.

"It was the usual—I gave a lecture and they gave me an honorary degree," he said, without a hint of irony or self-importance, never mentioning the last-minute venue change due to the overflow crowd. "The usual," Laura repeated, and the three of us chortled. Never dwelling on personal honors, Noam changed the subject. "Norma, did you know Bev has made me into a *schnorrer*?" (Yiddish for moocher.)

"Oohh, how so?" Norma asked, her voice spanning the musical scale.

"She brings me free lunch from home. Now I have to lose weight."

"Don't blame me! I've seen you spread butter on matza—matzo, crackers—which is it?" I wasn't sure about the "crackers" part, but that wasn't my point.

"Matza ..."

"With an 'h' or without?"

"Both. It really doesn't matter."

My friends call me the spelling police, so the fact that Yiddish words have multiple spellings never sat right with me. Speaking of police, I told the story of a gift of matzohs (*matzohs* was on the box), which may have been a criminal offense.

A few years before, at Passover, a package came for Noam. I unwrapped it. Inside was a cardboard box with the caption "6 matzohs" printed above a photo of a big round cracker so dry my lips chapped looking at it, but Noam was away and I was hungry. I opened the box and ate one, covering the "6" with a sticky note marked with a "5." The matzoh was at least better than the communion host. Catholic guilt percolated. Had I crossed a religious boundary by opening a sacred box? Still, I munched until 2½ remained, and wrote that number on the box in ink. Viewing the evidence of my offenses the next day, he looked at me, then at the box, reading aloud the phrase "Watched from time of planting." As a finale, he stared with rapt attention at the box, eyes wide, hand in a frozen, open claw to demonstrate the unceasing labor of the designated Watcher. For once Roxy hadn't been the guilty party. Nor was she afraid of boating.

Boat Slip, 2012

> I worry about stupid things. Like, will my
> twenty-two-year-old cat get old and die?
> —from Bev's Harvard Square stand-up routine

Months before, Noam had asked me, "I have a big boat cover, and I can't get the zippers to work. Do you know anyone who can replace zippers?" Usually when he asked, 'Do you know anyone ... ?' he meant me, if only subconsciously. I said I would try to get them to work. He told me fixing them was hopeless. I said nothing.

The next week I left his house with a big plastic bin stuffed with the blue boat cover, wondering if I consistently led Noam to believe I was capable of *anything*. At the same time I wanted to prove to him that I *was* capable of anything. After "fixing" his garage door months earlier, he told me there were two kinds of people in the world—those who believed things could be fixed, like me, and those who believed they could not, like him. I enjoyed the challenge of living up to his great expectations, even when he might be pulling my leg. Using a spray lubricant and a bar of glycerin soap, I managed to get the zippers to glide, then jammed the cover back into the bin and returned it to him. I had put it out of my mind until he emerged from his cottage the next morning, the cover overflowing in his arms like a rogue papier-mâché wave. New fears ran through me. What if the zippers didn't work? What if I got seasick on the boat, or stuck my hand in the churning wake and lost my finger, but kept it to myself to save our outing? I think these things.

"When we get there, we can put the cover on the boat every

wrong way until we figure out the right way," Noam warned. I was too busy worrying to speak.

I have only negative memories of boating. Years before, I had boarded a friend's cabin cruiser with five-year-old Jay and my then-husband, Alan. An athlete, he had warmed up tennis pros, flown a hang glider off Mt. Washington, and skied the Swiss Alps, and he loved fast boats. Jay and I spent the afternoon lying very still on the lower deck with motion sickness. I vowed to never, ever, set foot on a boat again. But as one forgets the pain of childbirth, my faded vow had me joining friends for a fortieth birthday celebration, a three-hour gambling excursion at sea. A three-hour tour. I should have been very afraid. Gripping my roll of quarters, I pulled the slot machine lever just as the boat swayed, then I stopped, dropped, and crawled to a chaise, eyes squeezed shut. Every half-hour, my friend Cindy whispered, "Can I have another $5 in quarters? It doesn't look like you'll be spending them." As she fished the coins out of my pocket, I tried in vain to form two words: *ginger ale*. This sealed it. No More Boats. To add my mother's empty threat, "*Don't* make me say it again."

Is it me, or do most people over the age of seventy-five begin their days at the post office? We waited in the air-conditioned car as he made his way in, his torso leaning slightly forward, his elbow pushing through the last strands of the shirt's faded blue fabric. He looked like someone's thrifty grandfather. Noam hated fussing and shows of ostentation, like five-star hotels and limousines. He had barely worn the new shirts we had ordered, and I puzzled at his hesitancy to take a taxi, as if it meant foregoing a contribution to a nonprofit. When I asked if I was out of the loop on Wellfleet summer chic, he said his granddaughter paid for torn jeans, so his shirt must be in style. Our next stop was the pharmacy. When he got back into the car holding up a jar of Vaseline, an early childhood scene shot through my mind of my mother taking our temperatures—not orally. Noam's voice jolted me back to the present. I tried to separate my memory from the image of my boss holding up the jar of ointment between index finger and thumb, as if promoting it in a TV ad.

"I buy this every year, then I lose it," he said. "I have to put it" … the scene took on a dreamlike, slow-motion quality "… *on*" … boundaries dissipated … "*my*" … please God … Then he finished the longest sentence in our personal history "… *boat*." His boat! I would gladly help put Vaseline on his boat! Whatever that meant.

Norma, standing on the dock next to an older fifteen-foot-long white motorboat, hugged us and handed me a hat. I don't look good in hats. Ask anyone. But this ample hat could conceal my fears, so I put it on. It was hot even at the ocean, and I was thankful for Laura's habit of bringing water everywhere. (Note to self: never give Laura flack for taking time to fill water bottles.) She had brought the only water bottle, and we all sipped from it with the ease of pre-Covid life.

Noam positioned one foot firmly on the dock, threw the cover in, and placed his other foot inside the boat. In a moment of eye-popping fright, the boat drifted slowly away from the dock, spreading his legs far apart. He gripped my arm and the boat's windshield, and pulled his other foot in at the last minute. Apparently this does *not* happen only in movies. The rest of us, even life-jacketed Roxy, got in without incident. I felt OK, despite the boat's rocking. Noam took the Vaseline from the pocket of his khaki shorts, and got to work rubbing it on the snaps of a big metal frame at the back of the boat. Now it made sense. What Noam had been calling a *boat cover* was actually an overhead *canopy*. We followed Noam's lead, rubbing until each snap oozed Vaseline.

We spread the cover over the frame, the wrong way, as predicted. Flipped, the snaps, flaps, and zippers matched perfectly. I silently cheered. This fine blue canopy would protect the landlubbers in back from sunstroke. Noam untied the boat and pulled the starter in back, where Roxy, Laura, and I spread out on a long bench. I sprinkled water on Roxy's head, and when Noam hit the gas I spilled the rest.

Noam, our Cape Crusader, sat on his well-worn white leather seat and flew across the waters he had navigated every summer since the 1970s. Laura leaned toward me. "This is great, Bevy." I managed a smile and exhaled a long sigh, thankful to not be nauseated.

"Around Jeremy Island is Provincetown at the tip of the Cape Cod arm," Noam yelled out, pointing as he slowed the boat to show us where he and his family had pulled up to a sand bar to swim, picnic, and watch the moon rise. Spending the day in the company of Noam, an endearing, enduring peacekeeper, Norma, and Roxy, was perfection. Hands tucked inside the boat, I took in the glistening panoramic view, but those two up front were the real attraction. Like a scene from *On Golden Pond*, Norma hit Noam on the knee, and yelled, "Isn't this fun, Noam?" In my mind I heard, "Isn't this fun, *Norman?*" How was it for them, reliving boating trips with family, some now gone? I hoped our expressions proved to those two energetic octogenarians that they hadn't schlepped us along for nothing.

Back at the cottage, I looked up the Yiddish word for nauseated: *Ibbledick*. What's not to love? Laura said later that she would love to retire on the Cape. If we settle there in our dotage, there will be no motorboat. Don't make me say it again.

18

Zoned Out

Walking a mile in Noam's raincoat.

In September 2012 we packed our schedule to make up for impending time away in Italy. While Noam walked to stretch his legs, a film crewmember of Celik Kayalar's documentary 99% sat in his chair and slipped on Noam's glasses so the cameraperson could correct for glare. Wearing his glasses for other crews at other times, I felt more insightful, even argumentative, but it had made my head ache, as if his last thoughts clung to the lenses, anxious to get back to the business of thinking.

Noam returned and sat next to me while the crew finished setting up. He had another cold, no doubt from germ-ridden airplane air, and coughed between sips of tea. "How's your mother doing?" She had finished radiation and chemo for cervical cancer, but recently cancer cells had resurfaced in her lungs. This new cancer meant more chemo.

"She's having a rough day. The few days after chemo are always hard," I said, wincing at his hacking cough as much as the thought of my mother's struggle. He looked pensive, nodded, then sighed. We talked until the crew collected him.

During his interview, I borrowed his familiar hooded raincoat to walk Roxy. I had hung it up when he was late, walked beside it down

MIT's hallways and to the farmers' market across campus, ridden with it in the elevator. The stories of his life encircled me as it sheltered me from a light rain. Roxy bounded up Stata's triple staircase in her water-repellent dog jacket. Trailing her, my shoulders felt the weight of Noam's life and losses. The occasional scents of mothballs, coffee, and fertile earth wafting from it evoked visions of him planting daylilies in the loose Wellfleet soil, trimming rose bushes, taking early morning walks down the pond's steep, tree-rooted paths with his grandchildren. I imagined him building up and reinforcing the slope at the edge of the unpaved road to prevent its sandy dirt from sliding toward his gray, bedecked clapboard house. I felt our connection as I walked, more or less, a mile in his shoes.

After our walk I felt the recurrent urge to drive to my mother's house to steep her a pot of tea and play a game of Scrabble. She played strictly by the rules. I once whispered something non-Scrabble-related to Laura, and we snickered when she accused us of using a secret code to cheat. She had trained her kids to be competitive. Why would I help anyone else win, even Laura?

"Hey, I heard that!" she had called out, though it was clear she couldn't have.

"Hey, I said that!" I'd called back. I remember her head silently bobbing in laughter the way Noam's often did. Was that a generational thing?

Two days before, my mother had sat back in her recliner and said the darndest things. The woman receiving another specially mixed chemo cocktail in a nearby chair laughed with us until the room quieted with a collective holding of breath while she struggled to swallow a piece of dry bread from her complimentary sandwich, sobering us with a stark reminder of where we were. Tensions eased when she sipped from her water bottle, and soon my mother's humor had us laughing again. I thought we were in trouble for carrying on when a nurse entered with purpose: sliding curtains open to their end points to expose our room to the hallway.

"It's true, you know, laughter really is healing. Just … thank you," she said, wiping tears as she returned to her desk down the hall.

My mother had survived cervical cancer, but this lung cancer was not curable. Her doctors said that chemo treatments would provide a longer, better quality of life, but that didn't prove true for her. Sitting in her dining room drinking tea with her one afternoon, she had sighed, "I've stayed too long at the fair." Her words had broken my heart.

"Is that it for me today?" Noam asked as the last crew packed up and he tucked the next week's schedule into his briefcase.

"Yes. Go home and get into bed, please."

Noam laughed and gathered up his other briefcase. When he picked up his raincoat, I had the sensation of his carrying me with him. "I'll be sure to follow your sage advice," he said as we hugged goodbye. We both knew he would be up late, answering emails as new thoughts and ideas circled his eyeglasses searching for a place to land.

PART III

Traveling Chomsky-Style

19

Italy: September 2012

Laura and Bev's Italian Holiday.

Rome and Siena

Laura and I would spend three days in Rome, with a quick detour to her cousin's Siena villa before my business in Italy would begin in the northern town of Pavia. There I would oversee two full days of talks, meetings, meals, interviews, Q&A's—even an opera written in Noam's honor. His colleague and friend, Professor Andrea Moro, director of Pavia's Center for Neurolinguistics and Theoretical Syntax at IUSS, made it possible for Laura and me to take our first overseas trip with Noam, to help navigate noisy, hectic airports and train stations and to manage events.

My impression of Rome, after the taxi ride from Rome's Termini Station to the Hotel Portoghesi, differed from Elizabeth Gilbert's in her book, *Eat, Pray, Love*. My book would be tiled *Run, Pray, Live*. Each time a cluster of people crossed our path, I expected our taxi driver to clip them and fling their bodies cartoon-style across the piazzas. I watched vehicles squeeze through openings narrower than a Boston sidewalk and asked myself why no pedestrians lay dead in the streets. I was willing to bet that Italians were served moving violations only when a body was pried from their car's front grille.

Before that unforgettable, unfathomable, cab ride to our hotel, in an Alitalia bus from Rome's Fiumicino Airport to Termini Station, we passed ancient ruins. One looked like the Colosseum. Just as I thought it was too close to be a world wonder, a fellow passenger yelled, "Look, the Colosseum!" I, or more accurately my son, could have thrown a stone at it from the bus. On a tour the next day, we learned that throwing stones was the least of what took place in that glorified hellhole.

"Laura, it's 9:30 in the morning here, but it's 3:30 a.m. at home. If we nap now, what will happen to us?"

"I know what will happen if you don't nap, Bevy, and please don't count backwards anymore." On the Roman streets two hours later, we were out of step, eyes hyperfocused, palms clinging to buildings for safety. In sharp contrast, Italian pedestrians crossed traffic-filled streets at a normal pace, seemingly unaware of the cars at their hips. What was their secret?

The next morning after breakfast (a 2 a.m. snack in Boston) we set out to explore. After barely a day in Rome, Italians had instructed us to "go this way to the taxi, the Trevi Fountain, the bus stop," mostly unsuccessfully. Looking for the Pantheon for an hour, a beautiful Italian man pointed and said, "Go that way, then take a left." There we spied the promised brown sign with beige lettering no larger than our street sign at home, spelling "Pantheon." Had we walked past it, expecting a grander declaration? We funneled in through a narrow alleyway opening up to the Piazza della Rotonda. *Bellisimo!* Our frustration dissipated inside this awe-inspiring building of dome, portico, and oculus. Laura stood transfixed by the architecture, while I knelt at the altar praying for my mother's health, with a shout-out for the safety of the world and its pedestrians. It couldn't hurt.

Leaving the Pantheon, I dipped lapsed-Catholic fingers into the holy water font, relieved when they emerged unscathed. I may burn in hell, as my mother used to say, for breaking one or two of the Ten Commandments, but in Rome I felt the benevolent presence of the Jesus of my youth. That afternoon we visited Cristina, our Pavia host Andrea's childhood friend, an architectural historian who directed a yearly research program for thirty American Fellows. We walked with her up a rise to a stone cottage where Galileo had stayed, by invitation of a group of scientists wishing to develop his innovative work on the telescope. "His work changed our relationship with the universe; now we were no longer at the center of it, as we had thought," Cristina said. It was mind boggling to imagine Galileo observing celestial objects through those same windows four hundred years before. The concepts of time and space overwhelmed me more than once in Pavia.

As we sipped prosecco at sunset on the rooftop, Cristina explained the Italian driver-pedestrian conundrum. "The drivers see you. They have a plan. The trick on both sides is hesitation. Just don't. And never look afraid. That confuses them. The thing is the timing itself. The driver judges where the walker will be in a few seconds. The walker understands this, and keeps going, without hesitation. Also, Italian cars are smaller, more maneuverable." We lifted our glasses to Cristina, who had solved one of Rome's greatest mysteries for us.

Layered over that enigma was the pervasiveness of Catholicism in Rome—strolling priests holding thin, black briefcases and nuns of varied ages grouped together on street corners in flowing off-white gowns and oversized rosary beads. These scenes threw me back to a childhood of church bells, catechism class, and prayer. Despite leaving the Catholic Church, I felt an odd presence of my seven-year-old self dressed in white—miniature wedding dress, veil, and patent leather shoes. Hands pressed in prayer, I climbed the wide church stairway with the other children toward my First Communion.

My brothers and I walked to Waltham's Saint Mary's parish church on cold Sunday mornings, snug in our matching hooded bench-warmer coats. My mother stayed home to prepare a hot Sunday meal while my father read the paper and watched football. After mass we endured forty minutes of Catechism class, memorizing the Ten Commandments and the Act of Contrition, reciting the Lord's Prayer, the Hail Mary. A gospel lesson focusing on acts of forgiveness, kindness, and full-scale miracles followed. The saving grace to our long morning came later, when we each spent a nickel on a small circular loaf of bread smelling of yeast and sourdough, baked by a local Italian family working small ovens in their garage near the church. The bread, crusty on the outside, steamy and pliable on the inside, warmed us for the mile-long walk home, obliterating the lingering aftertaste of the papery host, fragments of which still clung to the crevices in the roof of my mouth.

Rome exudes the smells of pizza crusts, breads, and yeast, and when a similar scent wafted out from a bakery, I automatically turned in, but the exact smell and taste of *that* crusty Sunday treat remained elusive. Walking the streets, I expected to look down and see my yellow Easter-morning t-strap shoes and matching clutch purse. But looking down might have been interpreted as hesitation, so I walked ahead, chin up, imagining the symbiotic dance of the driver and pedestrian, each swaying and weaving together the way sidewalk and street intertwine at the seams in variations of gray cobblestones and pavers.

Noam had warned us that everything in Italy takes *dieci minuti*— ten minutes literally, but two hours in reality. Sated and sleepy after a three-hour culinary affair called supper (rather than dinner), we returned to our hotel for one last night, unaware that we would return with Noam in less than a year.

After a scenic train ride into Tuscany, we drank red wine at the Piazza del Campo in Siena with Laura's cousin Julie. Inside the Cattedrale di Santa Maria, or the Duomo, as it's also known, I knelt at the confessional to take a rest. "Bless me father, for I have sinned. It has been forty-five years since my last confession. These are my sins," I whispered, looking up to see Laura and Julie staring at me. "I was a docile kid, so I had to make up sins at Saturday confession," I admitted.

"Well, at least you had a lie to confess to the next week," Julie pointed out.

"That never occurred to me. Does that mean my whole Catholic childhood was a lie?" It was time to go to Julie's to rest.

Denise had taken our mother to chemo two days before, and I called to check in. Her voice broke, and soothed, my aching heart. After a meal of homemade pasta hours later, Julie's daughter Katy sang in English about homesickness. We cried, of course.

The next morning emails about permissions, interviews, video-taping, and dinner invitations had us packing up for Pavia. On the afternoon train we caught glimpses of picturesque Cinque Terre's pastel colors through gaps in the rail tunnel, and vowed to return someday. But for now, a full Pavia schedule beckoned.

Pavia

Sign language Noam-style.

We shared an Italian feast with Andrea, his friends Franco, Giovanni, and others at a restaurant in Piazza Vittoria, where Andrea works and lives, shortly after arriving. Giovanni asked what was up with Noam's hand gestures, touching fingers to forehead and waving his arms to demonstrate. I thought that American behavior might indeed be curious—but should Italians be mocking hand gestures?

I hadn't realized that I held a view on Noam's personal sign language until I shared it. "I think he is physically moving and organizing his thoughts with his hands. He pushes both hands to the left or the right, palms splayed slightly down, as if to say, 'Let's put this thought over here,' or 'That refers to this group.' He may come to center, fingertips of both hands pointing inward toward his chest, then fanning all fingertips forward and out to the sides." I illustrated each movement as I spoke. "It has always looked to me like his thoughts are in the space in front of him, and he's illustrating them as he speaks."

As a sidebar, I shared something Noam had told me. When his daughters were little, he might be writing something in his head while they told him stories. When they noticed his hands moving, they would ask, "Are you listening, or working?" I would say he was doing both. After dinner Andrea and I reviewed the packed two-day schedule in his apartment before Franco walked us to our hotel.

Halfway there, he knocked on a board over a hole in a wall. We were stymied until a small door at eye level slid open to expose a gelato bar. We devoured our delicious magic trick before settling into our room at Collegio Borromeo with full bellies.

I wrote to Noam to check in and told him that his room was the one reserved for visiting Popes. I also confirmed that, as he had surmised, holy water flowed from our faucets. Laura and I anticipated the high energy, curiosity, and play his arrival would bring. We would sit with him at an opera exemplifying the six passions of the soul: wonder, love, hatred, desire, joy, and sadness, written in celebration of his life's work.

Noam, Laura, Andrea, and I lunched with Father Paolo at the hotel the next day. Curly pasta with a delicate tomato sauce, tiny sliced peppers, and onions, then a plate of lightly fried white fish with artichoke hearts and risotto. A bowl of fruit ended the meal.

"How many emails do you answer each day, Professor Chomsky?" Father Paolo asked, moving the fruit to the center of the table for all to reach.

Noam turned his head in my direction. "Bev can tell you that."

"I opened more than a thousand emails on a Tuesday morning at the end of a three-day weekend," I said, hoping to impress him.

"But Bev deals with two hundred of them before sending them on to me," Noam said. I thought he was exaggerating, but when I thought about it later, I realized that between redirecting, replying, and trashing some, I probably filtered a couple hundred each morning. How had he guessed?

"That includes the occasional crazy person. Those we usually delete," I added.

"If someone needs psychological help, we refer them to Laura," he said, looking at her and laughing. "An anarchist asked me to solve an argument between his girlfriend and him." I pondered what Father Paolo was thinking by the time Noam finished with, "If a request is really nutty, I make the cat answer it! Roxy will do anything for food." It was useless to explain to Father Paolo that Laura was a psycho-

Noam ... thinking.

therapist, that the cat was a dog, or that Noam considered *himself* an
anarchist.

In a 2003 interview, "The Double Life of Noam Chomsky,"
Liesbeth Koenen had asked Noam whether he still called himself an
anarchist. He said people should be able to take their lives into their
own hands, and should be skeptical about hierarchies and domina-
tion. This defined anarchism for me beyond the stereotypes I'd held.

Father Paolo apologized that the fruit was not ripe, which led to
the question of what the fruit *was*, if not ripe. I said unripe. Noam
said it would be raw, recalling a book sent to him years ago called
something like *Cooked vs. Raw*, which I insisted had nothing to do

with this argument. It blew my mind that he could recall most of the hundreds of unsolicited books mailed to him yearly.

During our stroll to the evening concert venue, we picked up some of Andrea's students and Noam's friends, Luigi Rizzi and Adrianna Belletti. The surprise ending to that stroll through the Piazza de Leonardo da Vinci was ducking into a concealed entrance at the rear of the venue. We were the Secret Service, an entourage traveling an underground passage to the stage with our rock star.

After the concert, Laura whispered, "Bevy, look where we are. I feel so lucky." I looked around, taking in the love and appreciation for Noam, overwhelmingly grateful for my front row seat. As we left the building through the side door, a bicyclist yelled, "Hello, Professor Chomsky! Welcome to Pavia!" Noam waved back, beaming.

Observing Noam in a Q&A with Andrea's students and colleagues at IUSS was a mentally stimulating highlight of our visit, as he addressed questions like, "What is thought?" "What is the mind?" "What is the difference between the mind and the brain?"

After the Q&A, the crowd mobbed Noam, shoving books and papers and microphones at him, requesting statements and autographs. The chaos I managed back in Cambridge seemed trivial by comparison. "What should I do, Bev?" Andrea asked, panicked. Finally, I could do something to earn my keep.

"Can you announce that there will be no interviews, and ask those seeking autographs to line up?" I asked. He nodded, eager to regain control. "Ask them to print their names on one of these and stick it onto whatever they want autographed." I pulled a packet of sticky notes from my bag and handed it to Andrea, then tapped Noam on the shoulder to let him know I was there to help. He looked relieved. For forty-five minutes, while Laura chatted with the lingering crowd, I moved people along, thinking that this was what probably happened elsewhere when I wasn't around to prevent bedlam.

On our last night in Pavia, we attended a dinner with Andrea's neuroscientist colleagues. I don't know who Noam was chatting with, but my conversation was a mindblower. Neurolinguists were studying the brain–language connection by hooking up electrodes to the exposed brains of people before surgery, noting which parts of the brain lit up when answering questions. The patients were conscious, with exposed brains. It's good that I was drinking when they described this to my queasy self. Incidentally, the number of drinks I consumed in Italy was cumulatively equal to the number I had by then drunk in my entire life. When in Pavia, or when imagining lying on a table with an exposed brain … it's best to do as the Italians do.

That Pavia Q&A inspired me to begin my blog, "Through Progressive Lenses," with Deb's technical guidance. "From Here to Pavia" was my launch pad, the rough, first-born post of what would eventually develop into this book, about my relationship with Noam Chomsky, the person, and our adventures.

20

Don't Mind Me

Noam asks a profound question, sparking Bev's deep ponderings.

Soon after our Pavia trip, Noam and I met to outline his upcoming talks during MIT's Apartheid Week organized by groups like Palestine@MIT and the Harvard Solidarity Committee. He had given an Edward Said Lecture, and the Boston Women's Fund would honor him with the "Men Take a Stand—Social Justice in Action Award," after his talk "Language and the Limits of Understanding." Our spring trip to Ireland, with its own complicated schedule, would follow these events.

Mid-meeting, he looked up from a letter and asked, "Bev, can we count our thoughts?" It wasn't unusual for him to run something by me while considering a lecture topic or thinking about an article he had read, but this was a real mind-teaser. I dug for an impressive retort, because jousting with Noam Chomsky in a game of wit gave me a little high. I admit that underneath the play, my straight-A child self felt an internal need to get the answer right—*if* there was a right answer.

"Can we count our thoughts?" I repeated, stalling for time, hoping that, if not a great rejoinder, at least a brilliant repartee might be set in motion. Seconds passed. One, *one thousand*; two, *one thousand*; three, *one thousand*. Nothing insightful, remarkable, or even witty was coming to me, but I was determined to throw out a guess. I was in awe of his thoughts, words, and deeds, but I was having fun thinking about thinking, rather than over-thinking, my thinking. Years spent chatting with brilliant MIT minds had reassured me to some extent of my own strengths. When did this shift happen?

"No," I said. "Counting your thoughts is thinking. You would have to count the thought about how counting your thoughts is thinking, then … it's an endless loop."

He smiled and nodded his head, and while a nod from someone else might have been a positive sign, a *mere* nod from Noam was underwhelming. What could I say? I know what I could have *asked*— had he ever tried to count *his* thoughts? He had once told me he thought about a problem before going to sleep, and usually had an answer by morning. In fact, he was once so deep in thought before a Boston lecture that he hadn't taken note of where he had parked his car, so he took the T home afterward. In his sleep that night, he saw an intersection with two street signs—and that's where he found his car the next day. If his brain worked all night, did he keep a running tally of his thoughts? My brain does something at night, but I'm not sure it's problem-solving, unless I've laid a specific tarot card by my bed, asking for clarity. I suppose our methods are similar.

Before another interview, Noam looked down at his schedule, then cocked his head and looked at me. "Bev, what is the definition of *courage*?" My mind shot to Oz's cowardly lion, but I chose to be serious. He shook his fist at my guess. "Perfect! I'm going to use that in the interview!" More ironic would have been the question, "What is memory?" because neither of us could recall what I had said. For months I suggested, "Courage is essential in the face of fear," and variations using key words and phrases like *strength, bravery, evil necessity*. Each time, Noam shook his head. "Nope. It was better than that." Why hadn't I written it down? Shades of Ali G—I couldn't even pinpoint who had asked the question.

These are the games we played. Some were amusing, while others threatened my sanity. This was the price I paid for working in a department where almost *everyone* was thinking about language, thinking about the brain, thinking about thinking. Maybe they weren't counting their thoughts, but this *was* MIT.

My complex relationship with the art of thinking may have begun twenty years before when a grad student named Knut stood in my office doorway in a beautiful red sweater (sure, I can remember that detail) and said, "I haven't been the same since I thought too much about the concept of Time. I can't get the idea of the constant passing of time out of my mind. There is never a *now*," he said, "because even when you try to think of *now*, it's not here anymore. Even this conversation becomes something of the past as soon as our words are out." Maybe Knut thought time was the coolest concept ever, but from that day on, I had to work to not overthink being in the moment, which defeated the purpose of being in the moment. My reward for my angst was his red sweater, his gift to me on his graduation day.

When I was ten, my eight-year-old brother Paul, the one who studied at MIT to become a physicist (I saw that coming), introduced the idea of eternity to me. "Time never, ever, ever, ends," he said. I was pumping hard on a silver playground swing, minding my own business before his words blew my head apart, as if I had fallen ten feet onto the asphalt. I looked down at my new white sneakers to distract myself, thinking about the night before, when our two neighbors and Paul and I put on our whitest sneakers and rushed back outside just before the sun set, taking turns running in a big circle in front of the others until all we could make out in the growing darkness was a pair of disembodied sneakers racing around the edges of the playground. Trick of the eye, trick of the mind.

What is the mind anyway? I was reminded (*re*-minded?) twice in December that nobody knows. First when I read the transcript of Noam's Q&A session in Pavia, where questions of mind and thought had blown Laura and me away months before. And again when my brother Ron described a Deepak Chopra lecture he had attended with his wife, Lynne. "Dr. Chopra asked us to recall our childhood homes in our minds. He said, 'Nobody knows how we can form an image in our heads, nor how thought, or our minds, work.'" Until recently, I thought *they*—the world's great thinkers—knew the answers. I emailed Ron this paraphrase from the Pavia class:

"What is thought?" Noam asked the audience of graduate students. "You can say a couple of things about those aspects of thought that are expressed in language, but then we are talking about language. What about those aspects of thought that aren't expressed in language?" he asked, going on to say that nobody knows what thought actually is, and concluding that "there are a lot of things going on beyond the level of consciousness that we try to move to consciousness and even to the external world, often failing, which means that there is a lot of thought going on, and we have no grasp of it ... In other words, I know what I'm trying to say, but I can't find the words."

For weeks after returning to our relatively concrete and tangible routines, the concepts of mind and thought lingered, loitered, persisted, like the awareness of your tongue in your mouth. Best to pay no mind to that tongue if you want to remain on this side of sanity. Reading the transcript of the Q&A, the fuzzy beginnings of an answer took shape in my ... mind. I cornered Noam the next day at the coffee maker.

"Noam, remember when you asked me, 'Can you count your thoughts?'" He did. "Well, it took ninety minutes in your Pavia class, the reading of the transcript of that class, and weeks of processing to figure it out. Here's what I think: We can't count our thoughts because nobody knows what thought, or the mind, is." I waited.

"That's good," he said, smiling and pumping his fist in triumph. I would have liked, "That's *right*," but I still felt a personal victory, considering many of my observations hovered and dissipated like a cloud's fuzzy image, as new information vied for space.

Who needed mind-altering drugs with these questions in the air?

Martin Luther King, peace sign, and Howard Zinn buttons.

I heard soon after that the cells of the human body regenerate every few months. So the skin, lungs, and heart I have in August are not the same organs I had in May? That couldn't be right. Or is it every few years? In either case, we wouldn't grow old. I would look that up as soon as I stopped thinking about my tongue.

Here is another of my favorites of Noam's quotes, also from the Pavia Q&A:

> It is important to learn to be surprised by simple things—for example, by the fact that bodies fall down, not up, and that they fall at a certain rate; that if pushed, they move on a flat surface in a straight line, not a circle; and so on. The beginning of science is the recognition that the simplest phenomena of life raise quite serious problems: Why are they as they are, instead of some different way?

My earliest lesson had come in my first months of work, in 1993. I don't recall the specifics, but I had read and thought I'd understood an article on whole language, which I mentioned to Noam. "Read the first four lines again," he said after taking a glance. "Now what do you hear?" I couldn't grasp what I was missing. He questioned me until I understood the article's underlying message, the one I hadn't seen at first, having filled in spaces with my own assumptions. I later shared an article about people cheating "the rest of us" with false disability claims. I'd re-read it only once before recognizing who the victims were. Noam agreed, saying that the vast majority of people who receive disability insurance have legitimate needs. The article, like many, had people mistrusting one another, instead of focusing on the actual culprits—unscrupulous lawmakers, media, and corporations. I wish I could go back and tape every conversation.

At the mini-revelation that these types of conversations made me Noam's student, a voice in my head shouted, "How cool is that?" People had suggested I was both his student *and* his teacher. I would have to give that some thought.

The Peace Sign

Noam shares inside dope on the peace sign's design.

A string of lectures, most recently on prospects of freedom in Gaza and the upcoming elections, triggered the usual case of laryngitis for Noam. We managed a brief appearance in the MIT Korean Gangnam-Style video in October of 2012. In his short clip, he was instructed to say, "Oppan Chomsky style." If he had been able to speak, I would have urged him to make a brief statement for peace, like, "Give peace a chance." Had he done that, five million people would have heard his words when the video went viral less than two weeks before the US Obama–Romney election. At my desk, I hummed the Beatles' song lyrics, popular during the peace movement of the sixties and seventies, at the height of the Vietnam War, when a country of peace activists wanted all US troops out of Vietnam: *All we are saying, is give peace a chance.* I was about to tack those words onto my email to Noam when Glenn handed me a box.

Over the years, Roger Leisner had sent DVDs of Noam's lectures, and photos of Noam with peace, hunger, climate, and human and civil rights activists he had shared a stage with, like Edward Said, Mel King, and Michael Moore. I have a framed photo of him with Moore, both looking amused. When it was mailed to me following FAIR's

25th Anniversary celebration, Noam told me that just before it was snapped, he said to Moore, "Finally, a photo that will impress Bev."

"I wonder what Roger sent," Glenn said, rattling the box.

"More buttons, I'll bet," I said, remembering the Occupy movement buttons he had made. I spilled the contents onto my desk. Buttons. A Black fist caught my eye, the symbol of Black Power in the sixties, and more recently a symbol of solidarity, resistance, defiance, and strength. Another read: *"I was never aware of any other option but to question everything—Noam Chomsky."* A kid in a candy shop, I read the next: *"Dissent is the highest form of Patriotism—Howard Zinn."* I pinned the Zinn button to a Colombian artisan's wall hanging and fastened another to a poster of Noam flexing a muscle above the caption *"Got Peace?"*

Noam and Carol were friends with Howard and his wife, Roz. Both dedicated, vibrant couples made hefty personal sacrifices in the name of peace and human rights. All were committed to opposing the war in Vietnam, and subsequent wars. When they talked family and politics, a second dialogue was going on between Carol, a Harvard professor and musician, and Roz, an artist, musician, and actor, about their fears that their husbands might serve significant jail time for their activism.

Sweeping the remaining buttons into the box, I flashed on primary colors inside a black peace sign and took my glasses off to get a closer look. The top read "All We Are Saying Is" and the bottom, "Give Peace a Chance." Really? This sort of thing happens to me a lot. Call it coincidence. Sufi calls it "The Truth." Noam appeared at my desk as I pinned it on. "What's all this?" he asked, admiring my peace sign button. "Roger sent us more buttons." I held up one of Noam's face, and he winced, never wanting to be revered, while I reminded him once again that people's admiration showed they were paying attention.

"Have you heard of Peggy Duff?" he asked. "She was responsible for the peace sign's design." I looked her up. She'd been general secretary of the Campaign for Nuclear Disarmament, and while the flag positions for C, N, and D created the peace symbol, nothing indicated that she had designed it. I wrote Noam that evening to double-check. He said it was common lore among activists in the early days of the peace movement that Duff was behind the design. It was to be a symbol of the International Peace Movement, with the circle around the CND flag positions indicating the world. Noam told me he had lectured on peace in London more than once by Duff's invitation when none of the British intellectuals would step up to do it. Those involved in the peace movement were aware of her impressive accomplishments, which would merit the Nobel Peace Prize. In the foreword to Duff's memoir, *Left, Left, Left*, Noam cited Duff as "one of the unsung heroes of the struggles for peace and justice post–World War II ... founder and leading figure in the CND, which was instrumental in bringing the dire threat of nuclear war to general attention."

Peggy died in 1981, a dozen years before I met Noam. I had hung out in Harvard Square in Cambridge in the late 1960s and early 1970s, where hippies and the homeless begged for spare change and folk singers begged for an end to war. I crossed the bridge over the Charles River to Boston Common in my crop top and frayed bellbottom jeans to hear Baez, Dylan, and others sing for peace.

The business of finding peace was not, I was learning, for the faint of heart. I showed Noam a box of books I'd collected from overstuffed bookcases, mostly gifts from authors, to decide which to donate to the MIT libraries.

"You should read this. Alex Carey was a friend," he said, handing me an inscribed copy of Gabrielle Carey's *In My Father's House* while telling me the background story. In the late 1970s Noam had invited Carey to MIT as a visiting faculty member, and they spent a year in collaboration. Noam and Ed Herman had dedicated *Manufacturing Consent* to Carey, citing his work as a major inspiration for their own. Carey broke open the field of corporate propaganda: his collection of essays, published posthumously in 1995 as *Taking the Risk out of Democracy: Corporate Propaganda versus Freedom and Liberty*, is a classic. Carey's life of activism was largely to blame for his depression and eventual suicide, just as depression, stress, and heart attacks plagued many activists. Once I began posting stories about Noam's time spent with family and friends, activists began writing to thank me for "giving them permission" to bring more balance and joy into their own lives. As one person wrote, "Noam Chomsky has a boat?" The image of him motoring on the ocean seemed incongruent with the driven life of a dedicated man answering email until 3 a.m. The satirical journal *The Onion* had once posted a photoshopped image of Noam relaxing on a porch glider. The fact that he had no reading material in his hands proved it was a fake.

Multimedia ads bombarded us mercilessly for months, as I wondered again why candidates and their speech writers couldn't simply speak this one, positive truth: The most important thing is peace. One of Noam's quotes, to me the most salient, was printed on a small black and red poster sent to us by a student that read: "We can be fairly confident that either there will be a world without war, or there won't be a world." On Election Day, peace button pinned on, I voted for the one I thought cared most that there would be a world to which we could bring peace.

21

His Mug Runneth Over:
December 2012

What do you get when you cross a Caféphile with a Technophobe?

Once he tired of declining my offers, Noam graciously accepted help with simple tasks. Aside from legitimate fixes like changing his hearing aid parts, I picked up a few groceries for him when I shopped. My brother Paul and I dropped by more than once to check Noam's printer and reglue a strip of laminate to the rim of the kitchen table Noam had built years before. Rehanging a door between his kitchen and dining room, I had spied faded pencil marks on the doorframe documenting the heights of his three children, and at the very bottom, their cat. Laura joined Noam in toasting my efforts with a single malt scotch.

Noam felt familiar; I had shared the same good-humored teasing with my family, especially my father, who had also loved imaginative wordplay and storytelling. Also familiar was his occasional impatience. He tried not to let it show, but I saw it in his body language, and on his face. With a ton on his mind, I had to call him back to my desk more than once when he stood during our meeting before signing a book, or okaying an interview. It could have been, as I think about it, more dedication than impatience pulling him back to his office. From my vantage point, most things outside of his thinking, writing, and lecturing were distractions.

I handed him a fresh mug of coffee. "Thanks. It looks a lot better than the coffee I make at home."

"What do you mean?"

"Around the third or fourth time I run the water through the filter, I end up drinking beige hot water with coffee grounds floating on top." He was laughing, but I could tell he was serious by the way he illustrated the floating grounds, wiggling his bent fingers the way a child does when he pretends to be a monster.

That weekend, I picked up a Keurig coffee maker with his work charge card, since his home office qualified for the purchase. One pod per cup. Simple. We called to ask if we could drop by later with a surprise.

"Only if you share a healthy drink with me," he said.

"Irish whiskey?" I asked.

"Of course," he said. "Doctor's orders. I have to drink more fluids."

"He's talking about water."

"I add ice," he said. It was no use arguing. We'd had this conversation before.

At his house, we set up the coffee machine and gave him a lesson, writing down each step: insert disposable pod into receptacle, fill top with mug of water, close the top, position mug under spout, press button.

A couple of weeks later we showed up to drop off holiday gifts mailed to the office and replenish his coffee pod supply. He said he was just eating dinner.

"You're eating buttered matza crackers and calling it dinner, again?"

"What's wrong with that?" he asked.

"Protein is what's wrong. There's no protein in butter. It's healthier to have cheese or smoked fish with your carbohydrates."

"Really? I thought butter was a protein. I'll add cheese next time." He'd be spreading butter on his matza for eternity. (I liked to imagine he would live forever.)

Laura grabbed two highball glasses from a cabinet near the sink;

ironically the only cabinet not already opened wide, and poured two single malt scotches while I checked out his coffee stash. The one open box still held a few of the original eighteen pods. He drank a few mugs every day, so the math was way off.

"Noam, why do you still have so much coffee in here?" In this case, "in here" referred to the inside of his outdated Sears microwave affixed permanently above a harvest gold electric cooktop and oven, surely a fancy, modern appliance back in the early 1970s. Noam seemed pleased with his reassignment of the now-dead microwave as a coffee pod storage area.

He put down the *New York Times*, which he read daily, and turned to me from his seat at the kitchen table. "What did you say?" he asked.

"I was asking why there's so much coffee left over. You've used barely a dozen pods."

"I've been reusing them," he confessed, turning back to his newspaper.

"How many times?"

"What?" he said, turning toward me again, squinting like Norman Thayer.

He wasn't wearing his hearing aids, so I moved around the table to face him. I spoke more loudly. "How many times do you use each pod?"

When he laughed and refused to offer a number, I made a sour face and lifted my fist in the air, shaking it. He returned the gesture. This was not our first dispute over his extreme frugality. Or maybe he enjoyed drinking loose coffee grounds floating in beige water.

"Another problem you might be able to fix," he said, possibly admitting to his thrift as the first, "is how to keep the coffee from spilling onto the counter."

"Are you filling it twice? It's easy to do if you're distracted," I said. Laura handed him a glass, lifting hers in a toast, each of them taking a slug. I reached for her glass and took a token sip—just enough to clear my sinuses.

"I followed your directions to the letter. There must be something wrong with the machine. Maybe we should set up the old Mr. Coffee again." He shook his head at the consistent failure of technology. I ignored his fatalistic position.

"Show me how you do it," I said. Laura looked on, sipping her scotch.

Noam Chomsky was voted the world's top public intellectual in 2005 in Great Britain and has been compared to our greatest thinkers—Plato, Aristotle, Freud, Einstein. I tried to keep this in mind as I watched what he did next.

He lifted the large mug next to the coffee maker, filled it to the top with water, and poured it into the Keurig. "I'm not sure whether I already filled this," he said. Then he popped the pod into its slot, waited for the water to disappear, and closed the lid. So far, so good. Next, he pulled a smaller mug from the cabinet and set it under the spout. Laura put her glass down. "Noam, stop! I know what's happening here," she said.

Noam looked puzzled. "What did I do wrong? I did it exactly as you said." He loved to watch other people problem-solve, particularly because of his conviction that technical problems have no logical solutions.

"You've been adding water from a larger mug, so that amount of water is pouring through the pod into the smaller mug, and the excess coffee will overflow into the lower receptacle. If you continue to put in more water than the receiving mug can hold, the extra coffee will overflow from the receptacle onto your counter.

"And eventually flood your house," I deadpanned.

"So the mug I pour the water from and the mug I drink from should be the same?"

"Or at least the same size. Filling the reservoir once and making your coffee right away will also help," Laura said, closing her argument with a pull of scotch.

Looking at Laura, he raised his own glass to his lips and drank. "Surely there's protein in scotch!" His eidetic memory didn't extend to protein or a coffee mug's size, but only because they were the least of his worries.

Cross Words

Malignant: bad, invade, destroy.

My mother loved crossword puzzles, so we bought a newspaper at Dana Farber the day of her last chemo infusion of the year, eight days before Christmas. I had never warmed to these puzzles, but on treatment days I found myself leaning toward her, away from the surrounding scenes. We worked the puzzle as the chemo cocktail was prepped.

"Twelve down is 'aria,'" I said. She nodded, penciling it in. I was on her sacred ground; her nods were consecrated. As she filled in the squares, I saw her sitting in our living room with the evening *Trib*, pen to folded paper, or at the kitchen table with the *Boston Sunday Globe* after breakfast.

"Cancer is big business," I said to my mother as I looked around. "Years ago people died with cancer cells in their bodies and never knew it. Now people have to go through *all of this*." I swept the room with my hand. I knew *all of this*, radiation and chemotherapy, also saved lives, but I was dubious. When such a high percentage of the world's population develops cancer, you have to wonder what's going on with our environment, food, water, stress levels. I had read a few books on the subject that authors had sent to Noam.

A nurse called out "Charlotte B.!" She raised her hand and called out, "Present!" in her obedient Catholic-school voice, chuckling at me. The nurse wheeled my scared and courageous mother away for chemo-port insertion, and I snatched the paper from the tabletop to work on the long, puzzle-length clue. "Something you do before going to bed." I filled in letters until I got it. *Shutthelightsoff.*

My mother was returned to me, and I threw the paper onto the table like a caught thief. "I found the long phrase for you, here,"

I said, picking the paper up again, pointing, hoping I hadn't ruined her fun. Nodding, she checked the words I had filled in as I wheeled her to our meeting with her oncologist. "Do you remember when we were little, what we did when you and Dad left the upstairs light on after putting us to bed?"

"Yes, you would all sing from your beds, *Shut ... the light off*, and you would repeat it over and over again until we shut the light off."

"Why do you suppose we sang it that way, with a pause after *shut*?" I asked.

She said she didn't know and turned away, as she did when straying into emotional territory. There would be a time when I couldn't ask her a simple question, but I didn't want to think about that any more than I wanted to remember a flat gray rock at the shore of Penobscot Bay near our Maine cottage. I had named it the "Roxy Rock," because its shape resembled our dog Roxy, the ears and nose identical, with thick paws sticking out from beneath a blanket. One day I would stand on that rock and release her ashes into the bay where we had played year-round. Now, sitting with my mother pre-chemo, I was thankful that both she and Roxy were still here. *"Just this,"* as my Sufi, and my Laura, would say. I often needed the reminder.

My mother yelled a lot when we were growing up, despite our being well behaved. When one of us asked her at a family gathering years later why she had yelled, she yelled, "When I die, I want you kids to put this on my gravestone: '*I was never yelling. That was just my voice.*'" We had laughed then, but sitting with her now I felt compassion, and sadness.

Noam and my mother were different in this way. He was a soft speaker—in twenty years I had heard him yell only once, during a phone interview after a sleepless night during Carol's illness. His voice rose from his open office door.

"If you're going to ask me a question, then you need to let me answer!" A pause, then he repeated, "I said, if you're going to ask ... You asked me a question, and I would like to answer ... ARE YOU

GOING TO LET ME ANSWER? ... YOU ARE? ... THEN STOP TALKING AND LET ME ... I'M GOING TO HANG UP IF ..." And for the first and only time in my memory, he slammed the receiver down. I sat at my desk in the ensuing quiet before getting up to make tea.

"Charlotte B!" the next nurse called, and I wheeled her into the chemo twilight zone, where we talked and joked and pretended we were anywhere but in a hospital watching chemo enter her veins to make her sick so she could live longer with a terminal illness. She would have the next three weeks to enjoy a different kind of normalcy before another round of chemo and crosswords. This would likely be her last Christmas, her favorite time of year. I would talk with Noam about the business of cancer after the holidays, and his return from Turkey, where he would give the Hrant Dink Lecture. Upon his return, the January 18, 2013, *World News* headline on reuters.com read: "Chomsky Urges Turkey to Pursue Kurdish Peace." In Turkey he had, as usual, offered up the truth, doing his part to bring peace to the world, one word at a time.

22

The Tie Project: February 2013

Ties to water.

In early 2013, Noam was sick with a bad cold, so I drove to his house to collect backup and drop off his mail. "Incidentally, sometime yesterday I lost my hearing aid. I've looked everywhere for it, and it's nowhere. Can I order another—just one?"

"You don't need to order a new one," I said, after suggesting he check the pockets of the bathrobe he was wearing over his jeans.

"Why not?" he asked, hands in pockets. He was squinting to hear me.

"Because I can find lost things," I said, raising my voice.

He sighed. "It's hopeless, it's probably in the trash somewhere."

"So it looks like you lost the right hearing aid?"

"Yes, but you really shouldn't bother. You're wasting your time."

I questioned him to ensure that he hadn't left the house since he last wore it, then I asked him to leave me to my detective work. He waved his arms in protest, mumbling something about Sherlock Holmes. I waved mine back and began sleuthing. Roxy sniffed close behind as I searched obvious spots in his 1960s bathroom. Then his bedroom: bureau, bed, carpet, bedside table, pockets of jeans thrown over a chair. No luck.

It was sweater season. This took me to the wide closet between his bath and bedroom. On the left side, a couple dozen ties hung on a rotating rack like the one my grandmother Florence had given my brothers one Christmas (along with a glow-in-the-dark Jesus on a wooden cross—imagine their glee). I felt mildly invasive jostling them, but let go of any fears of intrusion when I recognized a gray tie I had bought for his China trip and then considered the changes to our relationship since Carol died. Two identical coral-colored ties hung from the rack. One was the tie he wore on the cover photo of Robert Barsky's biography, *Noam Chomsky: A Life of Dissent*. Barsky had interviewed Noam for the book on topics like RESIST's formation and the role of the university as an institution.

Finding nothing among the ties, I searched the closet floor and inside Noam's shoes. Then my "I find lost things" phenomenon kicked in. I stood before his closet and mimed him removing one of his ubiquitous Irish knit sweaters, pushing my arms into the air and following the trajectory of an imaginary airborne hearing aid to a space behind a perpetually opened door. There, sitting in a perfect hide-and-seek corner that nobody would ever search, was his hearing aid.

I called Noam in and held it up. "Where did you find it? How?" he asked, shaking his head in disbelief. The closet caught his attention.

"Look, there are a lot of clothes here that I haven't worn for years." He knitted his eyebrows and scanned the closet. "Where can I take what I don't need?"

I recognized this as a fund-raising opportunity. When I told him what I was thinking, he looked puzzled. "Why would anyone want to buy my old clothing?" I promised to call an agency to pick up most of the clothing, but I would be keeping a few items, and all of the ties. Again, he asked why.

"Because most of these ties have stories to tell." I wondered if he still had the tie he wore to Japan in 1988 when he received the Kyoto Prize. He had traveled there again two decades later wearing, he and Carol saw from photos, the same tie.

Ten years before that, when a UN hearing went on too long and

Noam had to catch a flight, he and his friend and colleague Arnold Kohen planned a scheme. They would switch ties, and Arnold would pretend to be Noam. "We're so far away, they'll never notice," Noam had said. I checked out an office photo of Arnold taken at the hearings but found no matching tie in Noam's closet. I wrote Arnold, who of course had kept the tie. He said he could never relinquish such a conversation piece.

"I can sell your ties," I repeated. He looked at me like I had lost my mind. He had fifteen ties I could sell to raise money for the Carol Chomsky Memorial Fund (CCMF), which his friend and colleague Jennifer Loewenstein had set up in 2010, primarily to benefit Palestinian refugee camps in Lebanon and the Gaza Strip. Noam didn't usually accept talk honoraria, but he was willing to accept charity donations. He agreed to my plan. Not that I had one.

My decision to donate to this particular fund goes back to 2010. Laura and I had joined Noam for a fundraiser in Portland, Maine. We sat across from him at a table in a church auditorium while a speaker told the filled room that the children in Gaza, when asked what they wanted most, said they would like to have clean water. Noam nodded when he saw tears streaming down our faces.

To prove my project was legitimate, I bought iron-on material to bond to the backs of the ties, and videotaped Noam signing them. When I told my siblings about my idea, my brother Paul offered me $300 for two ties—one for himself, and one for Ron. I bought one for Jay. The math was easy—if I sold a dozen more ties for a donation of $75 to $150 each, I could raise about $1,500 for the CCMF. Friends bought three, and I sold six to long-time activists, donating one to a fundraising group. I bought one for the teen son of Diane Gee, a bright and intense woman who had interviewed Noam in 2012 on her radio show, *The Wild Wild Left* ("Gaza: How to Create a Revolution"). Noam was dumbfounded when he learned I'd raised about $2,000. His ties would have new adventures.

The CCMF received other donations beyond Noam's honoraria. A standout for me was from Beth Goldring, whom I met in the

1990s in Building 20 just before she shaved off her thick red hair. In 2000 she developed the Brahmavihara Cambodia AIDS Projects, a Buddhist chaplaincy project based in Phnom Penh. She once asked via her newsletter for contributions to a human rights fund in lieu of birthday gifts. Despite operating on a shoestring herself, she donated several times to the CCMF.

After the last tie was sold, I found an old pair of his jeans and his original Irish knit sweater in my closet. I had taken the pants home to measure for a new pair, the sweater for repair (it was too far gone). I would donate them, but not yet. After going through Noam's old clothing, I flashed on my mother's wardrobe. With a sense of sadness, I knew that someday I would go through her closet. These two elders were my constants. I felt protected by and protective of both. Each was, in my life, an eccentric powerhouse, with his or her own endearing and complex humanness. Both were my cheerleaders, encouraging my capabilities and strengths. Each had their own pessimistic optimism. Though I had lost my father fifteen years before, with Noam in my life I felt I still had two parents, though my mother's unconditional love surpassed all.

Going Home: March 2013

Charlotte expresses zero interest in visiting dead people.

Sitting at her Yamaha keyboard, my mother, eighty-three years old, hit the keys with surprising firmness as she played the final tender notes of "Danny Boy." She laid her veined hands in her lap and said it was time for a cup of tea. I set the pot and a small pitcher of milk on her dining table, thinking how her playing had improved since Paul taught her to play "Going Home," a song from the movie *The Snake Pit* that had freaked her out when my father took her to see it on their honeymoon.

When Noam invited Laura and me to join him in Ireland, we accepted without hesitation. In two weeks we would meet him, now eighty-four, in Dublin. When we settled, I asked, "What would you like me to bring you from Cork, Ma?"

On her sixtieth birthday, my brother Paul had offered to fly our mother and a guest anywhere in the world. I suggested Cork. "Why would I go there, Beverly? Those people are all dead," she said. I was constantly stunned by these proclamations, all a part of her sparkling, sardonic personality. Travel outside the US was out of her comfort zone, but I could visit on her behalf.

When we were kids, she told stories of summers at her grand-mother Ellen's farm in Marlborough, Massachusetts, her uncles and aunts dancing, laughing, and telling stories of family back in Cork. "By the end of the night, everyone was crying, but then they'd tell my grandmother how much fun they'd had!" She would shake her head at the absurdity of it. Ellen (Nelly) Walsh—we called her Memé—was the first person at our house, a box of powdered donuts squeezed under her ample arm and the smell of talcum powder trailing her, when my mother came home with a new baby. Memé, buxom in her ample blue and white polka dot dress, her chunky-heeled black tie shoes like those the nuns wore at my mother's childhood paro-chial school signaling her arrival, died when I was twelve, my mother thirty-six.

"What would you like me to bring you from Cork, Ma?"

"I would like a ring. Pick one out for me, but not a Claddagh. Get something you think is nice." She set her jaw and sniffed the air, as if to insinuate that her reply had little emotional bearing. "You know how I love my rings," she added, smirking as if not knowing would have been ridiculous, but the shine in her blue eyes gave her away.

I had one foot out the door when she whispered, "Want to play a quick game of Scrabble before you go?" I looked at the clock and put my keys down. I could get out just before rush hour if the game was fast. We played over cups of hot milky tea. When I laid down my final tiles for a win, she asked, "Can I go one last time?"

"Sure, take a turn." This confused me. Charlotte would never sug-gest anything outside the rulebook. She made a multi-bonus move totaling forty-four points. "You beat me!" I said, mocking outrage, engraving in my mind this memory of how-it-always-was.

She gave me "that look," her blue eyes staring into mine, her mouth set sideways, daring my challenge. "Well, you said I could go, so I guess you lost! Next time you'll know better." She laughed, then her face changed. "Can you help me get back into my bedroom? I need a nap." I gathered up her oxygen tubes and held the wheelchair handle as she moved herself into her bedroom, pulling her legs up onto the bed. I covered her with a blanket and closed the drapes against the waning light.

"I'll be back on Saturday," I said, kissing her cheek. "I love you. Good game."

"You really won," she whispered from behind me in the semi-darkness.

Had I heard right? A softer side of my mother revealed itself now and then as cancer and emphysema burrowed into her lungs. I had seen glimpses of her gentler side in my life, but this softening broke my heart. I missed her edgy, argumentative self, the Charlotte who still made everyone laugh, often unintentionally.

"No, Ma. I agreed to let you take another turn, so you won the game." I heard her sigh, and I left, just before I lost it.

On Saturday I woke up thinking that Jay should visit his grandmother. We stopped at a tile store to choose samples for her kitchen backsplash. She wanted the tiles installed soon, to surprise Paul, who had bought the condo with her. She chose Jay's favorite. On our way out, she yelled from the kitchen, "Jay, what if I don't see you again?" He reminded her that we'd see her the next weekend, on Easter.

Laura asked me to go back with her an hour later. She had taken her to a pulmonologist two days before, and for the first time my mother understood that she might live only a few more months. We sipped tea in her dining room.

"I really liked that doctor yesterday. He was respectful," Laura said.

"Ya, but I'll never get off this oxygen."

"I'm sorry, Ma. But it will help you feel better," I said, not adding, "until ..." She looked down at her nearly empty cup, maybe remembering Memé reading tea leaves.

"The news was a little hard to hear."

"Yeah. How are you doing? Are you scared?" Laura asked.

"No ... well ... yes. But now at least I know what's happening, and that helps." My mother had probably embraced hard truths more than I knew.

I got up to hang photos in her hallway. She had recently asked me to finish the wall with a photo of my father in his Marine uniform, and of her father holding his prized guitar. We left with the promise of returning the next day for another Scrabble game.

Paul and Denise had each dropped by that week, and she had laughed with Ron by phone the night before about the time she accidentally put him into the bathtub wearing his brand new red shoes. Two hours after Laura and I kissed her goodbye, my mother left us, peacefully, in her own bed.

We four siblings shared stories at her funeral service, then sat in silence as "Danny Boy" played through a speaker. When it ended, Ron nudged me and pointed to the back of the room. I waved Noam and Morris toward us. Ron added levity by pointing out that he felt smarter wearing Noam's old tie, while Noam observed that he himself was also wearing one of his old ties.

Five days later, carrying the raw ache of my mother's loss, Laura and I boarded a plane to Dublin, then a train to Cork, where I hoped to feel her around me. Noam had answered some questions about mortality in an interview with Doug Morris and John Holder, on ZNet, in May of 2013, so I had some idea of how he felt about death.

Q. From a fourteen-year-old living in a world in which they are constantly surrounded by tragedies, and the reality of human mortality ... how do we make sense of dying?

NC: When I was that age I was terrified of dying. What struck me as terrifying was not that I would die but that this point of consciousness would die so the whole world would disappear. Because, after all, there is nothing out there except what I perceive and if that consciousness disappears everything disappears. What happens then? Over time you get to recognize that it is just part of life. As you get older, at least to me, it seems less of a problem.

Actually, just to illustrate, dramatically, last night I came very close to dying, closer than I realized ... I'd forgotten to turn the car off and closed the garage. The garage is under the house and carbon monoxide was seeping into the house. You can't smell it, it is odorless. Actually, I would have died except for the fact that Bev Stohl had put a battery into an alarm that I didn't even know was there, and the alarm went off. I managed to get the car off, but it was that close. So, if it had happened, it would have happened.

Noam had this near-miss days after my mother died. Laura and I looked forward to traveling with him in Ireland.

23

Dublin: And I Must Bide, April 2013

Bev suffers an Irish bout of "bursting into tears."

"Have you ever been on a pub crawl?" I guessed that it involved drinking at several pubs until one had to crawl to the next. Noam said I was more or less right. I showed him a photo of himself with Carol and Bono, the Irish musician of U2 fame who had dubbed Noam "The Elvis of Academia," taken in Dublin in 2006. He nodded wordlessly, and I wondered what he was feeling. While putting together the Dublin schedule, I learned from the Front Line Defenders talk organizers that they, Noam, and Maria, our host, would take Laura and me on our first pub crawl. Barhopping was not in our repertoire, but I figured "When in Ireland ..." I could drink an authentic Guinness, and Laura an Irish whiskey.

I was in touch with a fellow named Sami M., since he'd helped Noam manage crowds in London during a solo trip. We stopped at Sami's home for appetizers before traveling to our B&B, where Noam had already checked in. We found him sitting in the front parlor, wearing a thick gray sweater with a rolled collar, lifting a dainty porcelain teacup from a silver tray. I knew the sweater must be from Maria, who had sent him his first of many Irish knit sweaters, a simple blue cable knit, in 2000. Her sweater gifts remained his signature garb for two decades.

"Where were you?" he asked, as we hugged hello. "Weren't you due to land a few hours ago? I was getting worried." I was touched by his concern, but felt like a teenager who had broken curfew and regretted right away not letting him know our ETA. After barely a day in Dublin, Irish guilt was already permeating my thinking.

"Do you like the sweater Maria gave to me last night?" he said, holding his arms out for us to judge. I was happy for the change in subject, and also for his new sweater. I had hidden one of his originals, a blue-green pullover with a hole in it the size of a baby's head.

"It's a beauty!" I said, picking a small crust of bread from it. "Now that you have another to rotate, people might stop asking me why you're wearing the same two sweaters in all of your photos."

"Listen, tonight's talk will be boring for you—you've heard it all before. Since you've already set the schedule, why don't you relax here, or join Sami at a pub and get a taste of Dublin?" He was being generous, but I sensed another truth behind his offer. He knew I would keep an eagle eye on him, and he wanted to do it his way, to go until he was too tired to stand. This is what I always tried to prevent, and why I had come. I had read the lecture abstract, "Can civilization survive really existing capitalism?" Maria would look out for him, so we agreed to skip it. Laura was disappointed, but we would catch the next one.

Sami and his friend Gary, a barrister, boxer, and local politician, drove Laura and me to Gogarty's Pub, with Irish stew and Irish music setting the mood. When we stepped over the threshold, the duet up front was finishing the last verse of "The Foggy Dew." The notes sent primordial emotions surging through me. My legs wobbled and, of course, I burst into tears. I felt I was hovering outside myself.

"You've come home, have ye?" the lead singer called out to me. "Would you like to hear something?" I shook my head, blindly gripping chair backs as I rounded the corner, moving away from the musicians, their instruments, my beating heart. I heard Gary behind me. "Could you play 'Danny Boy,' in memory of her Mam?"

No, Gary. I couldn't handle "Danny Boy." But they were already strumming and singing. I disappeared into another realm as their deep voices pulled waves of heartache and melancholy toward me:

> Oh Danny boy, the pipes, the pipes are caw-aw-ling,
> From glen to glen, and down the mountainside.
> The summer's gone, and all the roses falling,
> It's you, it's you must go and I must bide ...

I grabbed their arms for support as the three of them guided me to a table in back. All eyes were on me when the lead singer called out, "Will you come sing with us?" Was he kidding? My emotions threatened to drop me in a heap onto the worn, beer-stained, dark wood floor. I collapsed instead onto the wooden bench at our big oak table, sinking into a silent fog while Laura ordered my lunch.

Buoyed by half of a perfect Guinness and soothed by a few innocuously beautiful songs, I walked up front to thank the duet. Close up, the lead singer/guitarist could have been my maternal grandfather, Charlie Segien, a country musician, and I told him this. He hugged and kissed me, and cautioned, "Stay away from 'Danny Boy' for a while."

The next morning at breakfast, Noam sipped black coffee and told us a story. "Around the 1950s, Carol and I took a trip to Liverpool on a tilted ship. Liverpool had flooded, and the ship we were supposed to take had sunk a few days earlier. You could tell as you walked around town which people had been on the tilted ship," he said, amused by the memory. "In fact, a lot of the world is already under water."

I looked down at my breakfast. How could I enjoy my perfectly poached eggs when death hovered. Months before, he had been leafing through a journal in his mail pile. The cover article foretold the rising sea levels. He handed it to me to read. It said our oceans are rising faster now than any time in the past 2,000 years, as if we're moving south thirty feet a day. "This decade," he told me when I handed back the journal, "is a unique time in history as we ask ourselves whether the human species will even survive." This had become a central lecture theme.

I changed the subject so as not to drown in dread. I told Noam and Laura as I picked up a Danish that as a kid, I gave up sugar for Lent each year. "Do you know what Lent is?" I asked Noam. I was sure he would know, since he often cited facts about the Church that I had never learned, or didn't remember. Like when he warned me, "Don't forget the indulgences." I had forgotten the indulgences.

"Isn't Lent when you have to return all of your overdue books to the library?" he asked, pleased with his pun. I told him that was the smart Jewish boy's version, but he got points for creativity.

•••

He left for a student discussion, and Laura and I went with Sami to view the Book of Kells exhibit at Trinity College. Afterward, I remembered that Jay's close childhood friend, Lorcan, lived in Dublin. Laura and I taxied to his house and had tea with his wife, Sorcha, an Ireland native, and met his three children for the first time. Lorcan joined us for a sweetly serendipitous visit, and we returned to our B&B to prepare for Noam's talk at the Royal Dublin Society Concert Hall.

While the three of us sat in the parlor, sipping tea and waiting for our rides, Noam asked how our pub visit was. He looked amused. Had Laura told him?

"It was fabulous. But I burst into tears when they played 'Danny Boy.'"

"We carried her around for the first few minutes," Laura added.

Noam asked, "Did you cry when you went to Africa?" I said I had, pleased that we had skipped over the detail of my "bursting into tears."

"From the destitution?"

"No, from the unspoiled beauty of it."

My trip to Africa, for an animal-viewing safari in the 1990s, with

cooks, guides, and shopping at open markets, wasn't Noam's trip to
Africa—or India, or Laos. I told him I couldn't have handled seeing
most of what he had seen. I wondered at the lives of the African
merchants selling food, fabrics, and other wares from beneath mar-
ketplace tents, or squatting on blankets, imploring us to part with
our money. How could I know how it was for them? It was difficult
enough to look at long claw marks on zebras and vultures picking
over a hyena carcass. Animals lived with the balance of nature, but
the imbalance for people was a more painful reality.

My experience on the front lines was limited to campaigning for
packaging and recycling referendums, acting as resource person for a
citywide composting project, sending political postcards, and attending rallies. I never felt that I was doing enough, aside from my work
supporting Noam.

Maria arrived, and we made a caravan to the concert hall. Noam's
inaugural lecture for Front Line Defenders of Human Rights,
"Solidarity and the Responsibility to Protect," addressed the topic of
existing support for human rights defenders and activists trying to be
heard despite the agendas of others, including the mainstream media.
His talk drew an overflow crowd, ending with a standing ovation.

My head was spinning by the end of the Q&A, and we hadn't even
hit the pubs. Noam was allowing a post-talk RTE interview to go way
over time. Neither he nor the journalist would respond to my hand
gestures or verbal pleas. Finally, Noam made eye contact. The ten of
us, chattering like birds in an acacia bush, strolled to three waiting
cars and drove to the first bar on our virgin pub crawl.

Alcohol makes my heart race, so I was drinkless as we all settled into a circle. Mary, who with Katrina had organized the Front
Line event, called out, "Christ, Beverly, can't you have one drink for
your mother's sake?" Mary's words echoed my mother's—the only
mother I knew who tried to encourage her adult children to drink.
"For Christ's sake, Beverly, loosen up and have a drink!" she'd say. I
ordered a half-pint of Guinness in Charlotte's honor.

She was eight when she traveled with Memé by boat to

In front of Dublin's Foggy Dew record store before the pub crawl: Sami Moukaddem, Bev, Gary Daly, and Laura.

Provincetown in the mid 1930s. An old photo-booth picture of them on that trip, one of the only mementoes my mother kept as an adult, shows Memé, barely fifty then, gray hair in a bun, looking seventy by present-day standards. "My grandmother ordered a beer at the bar. I had never seen her drinking a *beer!*" I once again moved through the dark hovering cloud of loss. The bar conversation was casual—recalling the Front Line event, is the Guinness made locally, is Irish whiskey better in Ireland? etc.

"It's a good thing you agreed to have your picture taken with Gary after your master class today," I said, introducing him to Gary Daly, who had attended his event at the Royal Academy, titled, "Language Use and Design: Conflicts and Their Significance." "Gary is a solicitor, *and* a boxer!" Noam took a deep sip from his whiskey, eyes wide, feigning fear.

I hedged when Mary, Katrina, and Sami offered to take us across the street to another bar. It was unlikely I would drink more, since I hadn't finished my half-pint.

"You have to go," Noam said. "Otherwise you won't be able to say you've been on a pub *crawl*!" My mother would have applauded his reasoning.

At the second pub, a group of musicians sat on the floor harmonizing, drinking, and strumming another call to home. It was rapture for me. We lasted only an hour, anticipating our morning train to Cork. Plus, my heart was racing.

I checked email before bed. Noam had questions about his Cork talk and told me he was impressed that I had given up sweets as a kid. I wrote him back, confessing that I had quit in my late teens, when I started to question Catholicism. "Probably why God once tried to choke me with a lozenge," I added.

Cork: Irish Eyes, April 2013

A simple question.

An hour after our train arrived in Cork, Laura and I dressed quickly for Noam's meeting with the former Vita Cortex workers who had staged, two years before, a 139-day sit-in at their factory when their boss threatened to lay them off, unpaid. Noam had written letters of encouragement and a statement of support via Darren O'Keefe, the group's organizer and spokesperson.

Inside the conference room, a dozen men and women silently stood as we entered. Laura and I took seats in the back to observe unobtrusively. I was glad for the distance after their powerful greeting. Noam approached the group, who surrounded him tentatively, each of them introducing themselves, speaking softly, out of our range.

I was pulling a notebook from my bag when Noam called out, "Bev, this man is a Walsh!" I rushed over and took the hand of Alan

Walsh, asking whether a woman named Ellen Walsh might be an ancestor, realizing the absurdity of my question as I asked it; I knew so few details about my Cork ancestors. He said there were many Walshes in Waterford and Cork, and he couldn't be sure. A wave of regret and ineptitude gripped me—I hadn't done my homework. I was learning to be more gentle with myself, so shook off my self-doubt and let this moment in Cork, gripping this man's hand in a county of many possible relations, be enough.

The strikers looked out of place seated in chrome and black swivel chairs around a large polished conference table. Two pitchers of water had been placed at even intervals on the rectangular tabletop, and an inverted drinking glass at each seat. We knew the group had reached a settlement since Noam's involvement, but he wanted to learn the details of their sit-in and see how they were faring with the ordeal behind them. The gaps in some of their smiles made me wonder about Cork's healthcare system. I saw gratitude in their eyes as Noam questioned them about their treatment during the sit-in and heard humility in their replies. My people.

"Mary over there," Darren said, pointing to a young woman with shoulder-length hair, "was one of the two female strikers. She slept at the plant for 130 nights, right next to her machine, the one she worked on during her shifts."

"Why were you sleeping at the plant?" Noam asked, looking over at Mary.

Darren answered for her. "To make sure [their boss] Jack Ronan's people didn't come in overnight and remove the equipment and empty the place out before paying us our redundancy."

I hadn't heard "redundancy," what we would call severance pay, used in this way before. I turned the pronunciation over in my head: re-doon-den-cee, trying to recall Memé's accent. She spoke "differently," but to my child's mind, that was just how old ladies talked. Memé must have spoken with a brogue, but I couldn't ask my mother that simple question.

"How did the people in the town react? Did they support you?"

Noam asked. The room was quiet—all eyes on Noam, and they in turn had his full attention. Their faces were solemn, their strong working hands folded on the tabletop. As Noam coaxed their stories from them I felt angry that Jack Ronan had been messing with *my* people. "Friends and neighbors supported us, even strangers. We got food from the local grocers, and pizza shops brought pizzas. A local sporting goods store brought us warm jackets, as there was no heat at night." Noam leaned forward, nodding. "People brought food and money to support our families, as we weren't bringing home any pay." I eyeballed the untouched clear glass pitchers of water on the table, trying to figure out how to move away from my welling emotions. Darren said an older woman whose husband was near death reopened her bakery to make a cake for the group on his birthday. As I thought of my great-grandmother's people, the memory of my mother plunged another blade into my heart. What *did* happen to people when they died?

I handed Laura my note pad to write down the main points and moved to the table. As I reached over to flip and fill the first glass, a set of sparkling gray-blue eyes the exact color of my mother's looked up at me. "Thank you, ma'am," he said, and as I continued to pour, each lined and lovely face looking up at me in gratitude with a version of my mother's eyes. I tried in vain to hide my pooling tears.

Afterward, outside the conference room, we hugged Noam. "You made me cry again," I said, offering to hold his papers while he took off his jacket.

In his own style of pulling away from suffering's stronghold, or maybe to ease my sorrow, he made an exaggerated frown. "I'm giving my papers to Laura. You'll only burst into tears and get tear stains all over them." My bursting into tears in Dublin hadn't been lost on him. I was comforted by his ability to witness hardship with humor and compassion, and to listen and take action without allowing the struggle to steer him off course, however emotional. Laura, who practiced listening to her clients' stories with a *boundaried compassion*, had also been teary in the conference room, she told me later. We had two hours to shop before Noam's evening talk. In town, we found four suitable rings for the women in my family, but the experience was rushed and underwhelming.

The title of the UCC talk, "The Threats to Humanity's Freedom and Existence," didn't lighten my mood. The organizer knew that Cork was my great-grandmother's ancestral home, and he offered to help me find my roots on a return trip.

On the flight home, I mourned the fact that I hadn't felt my great-grandmother or my mother around me with any certainty. What had I expected? To cheer me, Laura shared a limerick she was writing. We worked on it for a while, then wrapped a throat lozenge in the limerick and conspired with our flight attendant to pass it to him at the other end of the plane. The second stanza was an inside joke about spilling things. This was the first:

There once was a man named Noam
Who traveled from Cambridge to Rome
He told many faces
In all of those places
"We have to work hard to save home."

I sunk back into my funk, staring at the Irish tea the attendant had just handed me with a—*thing*, a dry scone-ish oval with a scant rash of raisins—exactly the kind of treat my mother would have eaten with her afternoon tea. I poured the milk into my tea, stirred, and dipped the scone into my cup. Something in my throat hitched as I realized—felt—how we stay connected to the dead through everyday living, by carrying on our daily traditions. Like drinking tea with milk. Like seeing my grandfather in the face of the musician in the Dublin pub. When I recognized how I would keep my mother close, I did, of course, burst into tears.

The attendant asked in her Irish brogue if I was OK. I blubbered, "My mother died ... her grandmother, Cork. I couldn't find her ... the tea ..." When we landed, she hugged me and gave me a bulging bag

of Irish tea bags. In the tradition of the happy Irish, I cried. Drying
tears, I saw Noam across the aisle, blue briefcase in one hand, the
other waving the limerick. "We have to keep this!" He hadn't signed
up to fill a hole for me, and he didn't know he was so important to
me, but he did, and he was.

24

Trouble in Beantown: Boston Marathon Bombings, 4/15/13

Too close to home.

We noticed a small lump on our cat Bean's head when we returned from Ireland. Our vet confirmed cancerous tumors; we would have her put down at home on the following Saturday. On Friday morning, I was scratching her neck on the bed, when Laura appeared wearing a grave expression.

"Bevy, I have to tell you something. A police officer at MIT was killed last night outside the Stata Center," she said, citing a connection to the horrific Boston Marathon bombings days earlier, on Patriot's Day. "Watertown is under lockdown, and we're being asked to 'shelter in place' with doors and windows locked."

"Shelter in place? What does that *mean*?" I asked, grasping for one brief moment the terror of wars and rebellions too many people outside of my small world lived with, some for entire lifetimes. "There was a car chase after the shooting, and one of the two men was killed a few blocks away, at School and Mount Auburn Streets. One brother was killed, and the other ran off. He may be wearing an explosive vest. The police are looking for him."

This was a hell of a way to spend one last day with our verbal and demanding cat. I turned my phone on to see that I'd missed several messages from Jay. TV footage showed camouflaged troops and tanks a half-mile away. Amid texts and calls from family and friends as the news endlessly looped, I took a break and covered Bean with a soft blanket on our guest room bed and sang the lyrics I made up when we got her eighteen years before. When my tears fell onto her head, I smoothed them over her wound in a crisscross motion, my personal blessing.

Noam was at home with a bad cough. I called to offer him a ride to his doctor via our friend Al, who could travel freely from Lincoln to Lexington. He declined, reminding us to take the Watertown commotion seriously. He had warned me to take things seriously before. Did he see me as lax, remiss? "And stay put," he said. Though we had no choice but to stay put, his concern was tender.

When police fired shots at a boat on our TV screen, we heard the faint crack-crack-crack reverberate outside our front window. The brother was soon arrested. We learned later that they had both worked at a pizza shop that delivered monthly take-out to us.

That night, our city mercifully silent, we carried Bean to her favorite places in the house. On Saturday, Jay and his veterinarian friend Pat came to put her down. Her last full day with us was, like her younger self, biting and nasty, but the love that rose from it, and the community that bonded in fear, gratefulness, and relief reflected the sweet, soft sides of our Gremlin cat.

The changes we all felt were inalterable, though all too familiar to Noam. I overheard him on one of many interviews pointing out, "There were, two days later, bombings in other countries ..." How did he handle looking despair in the face 24/7?

A Funny Thing Happened on the Way to the Podium

Awaiting a Mystery Speaker.

On the heels of the marathon bombings, I sent Noam a schedule for his May trip to Oakland, California, to present a lecture, "Palestinian Hopes, Regional Turmoil," for the Middle East Children's Alliance

(MECA), for which he was founding advisor. Holly Near, a songwriter and activist whose music I loved, would open the event with songs from her album *Peace Becomes You*. Event organizer Penny Rosenwasser, who later stayed with us while promoting her book *Hope into Practice: Jewish Women Choosing Justice Despite Our Fears*, invited Laura and me. I'll always wonder why I chose not to go.

Noam looked at the schedule. "Now all I have to do is find time to prepare talks." I jokingly suggested he make them up between his introduction and taking the mic. He said that had actually happened. I sat back and listened.

He had prepared a talk in Gaza as part of a linguistics conference. At the podium, he realized he should make adjustments considering the large number of nonlinguists in the audience of 800. "After about five minutes, the moderator/translator walked over to me and said, 'They'd really like you to talk about the Arab Spring and the problems of Palestine,' so I went ahead with that.

"Another major talk that hadn't worked out as planned was even funnier. As I was waiting to be introduced, the head of the Political Science Department tapped me on the shoulder and said that the audience would prefer that I talk on a different topic. But when I was introduced, the moderator announced the first topic. I told the audience, 'Uh, two topics have just been suggested. If you want this one, raise your hand; if you want that one raise your hand.' Kept to the majority.

"There've been even weirder cases, like Carleton College."

Noam could speak on suggested topics on demand—the US and the World Court; climate change and the possible extinction of the human race; whether we will as a species make the decision through our actions to ensure our own survival. He is a self-described sympathizer of anarcho-syndicalism (look it up). This didn't easily roll off my tongue, nor stick in my head. What kind of a brain could flawlessly recollect political facts, exact statistics of those facts, explore tangents of the details, and cite statistical sources? When I asked, he told Laura and me about Carleton College.

He was sitting in the front row of the auditorium waiting for the introduction of the main speaker. When he heard his own name announced, he thought, "Hmm, I wonder what's going to happen next?" He gleaned the topic from the last three words of the intro and prepared an entire lecture on his way to the podium amid applause. I couldn't imagine approaching such a situation with curiosity rather than panic. I suppose it shouldn't have been a problem for a man who could open buffers in his brain and retrieve neatly chronicled information.

This may be an even better example of how quickly he can prepare a lecture. Noam to me: "Do I really begin every talk with 'Uh'? I thought it was 'Well.' Got to do something while I'm trying to figure out what to talk about."

25

Pleading Computer Insanity

Technophobe seeks Technophile. Must hate computers.

The fact that Noam is a self-described technophobe was one of the first things he divulged to me. He has consistently held that all technology, in all situations, is not fixable. He insisted that if something *could* go wrong with anything, it *would* go wrong. He wanted nothing to do with finding solutions to technological problems, because to find a solution, he had to care, and he didn't care. Years before, he had been able to redirect a substantial stream of water flowing from the gravelly, rutted road above his cottage so it would bypass the property and flow downward toward the pond, which proved he was capable of solving puzzles if he focused.

When he was in what he saw as a desperate situation, he took desperate measures. He called Theresa Tobin, head of the Humanities library and curator of his papers, at her home when he couldn't access a journal in the MIT library system. Theresa helped him retrieve it. Before they hung up she asked him if he knew what time it was. He had had no idea he'd called her at 1 a.m.

Noam was convinced computers, printers, and anything technical, motorized, or battery-powered, even electric staplers (trust me, I got that one) conspired to torture him. Coffee makers, washing machines, dishwashers, elevators, garage doors, subscriptions, cars,

phones, and his GPS were also culprits. When I tried to teach him to
change the date on his watch, he walked away waving his arms and
shouting, "I don't want to know!"

He often sent me panicked emails. "My computer crashed/The
font has changed/My screen is tiny/My paragraph is magnified/My
document disappeared/It's all hopeless," insisting each time that he
had touched nothing. I'd seen him thinking, hands hovering above his
keyboard, his fingers absent-mindedly touching down until an arbi-
trary command affected his document view and his sanity.

At the office, Noam was accidentally kicked offline while answering email and became frustrated trying to figure out the logic behind
the new Outlook Express program. "You have to be crazy to understand this email system," he groused. "The people they designed it
for are insane. The people who *do* the designing are insane." I asked
him to step away from his laptop and let me figure out in peace how
to get him online. He stood and paced next to me. In less than a minute, he was back at it.

"It's hopeless. Just shut it off. Close it. Forget it. I have plenty of
other things to do. Assaf will look at it with me tonight, and we'll get
it working. This program is designed for people without any logical
sense."

I tried to throw myself offline at my own computer, with no luck.
I tried again in the afternoon but still couldn't get him back online.
Then the red x that had been sitting in the lower right-hand corner
was gone. I told him he might be back online.

"No, I don't think I am. Let's close up the computer and forget it!"

That night, his friend Assaf figured out that when the red x disappeared, he *had* been back online. Noam hadn't believed it because by
his logic, he would have had to be insane to believe it. I should have
tried then to open his email, but he was so adamantly against my
doing this that I gave up. When he was exasperated with computers,
I had to go along with his annoyance until he put the problem back
in my, or Glenn's, hands. Or until he had dinner plans with Irene and
Assaf.

I have no doubt that if he cared about technology, if he *wanted* to understand, he could, but he doesn't care. The end of an email he received bore the standard Yahoo closing: "Do you Yahoo?" Noam drew a crooked circle around the phrase, with a note to me, "Tell him I don't know what he's talking about."

It was no secret to those who knew Noam that he and computers were mortal enemies. Assaf told me years later that talking about Noam's frustration with computers "brought back many fond memories, going all the way back to my days as a graduate student, when I discovered that Professor Chomsky preferred to use his old-fashioned typewriter rather than the newly invented electronic text editors."

In October, Noam watched from his doorway as I ran into Morris's office with Morris trailing behind, the question of how he could look at pages of tiny linguistics tables and graphs still on his lips. Noam grabbed me before I fully stepped out of Morris's office to ask me about a problem he was having at home retrieving articles. He screwed up his face and asked, "Why don't you put that on your— what is it called, blog?—put down that you run from one professor to the other trying to fix things for these old guys. Or put it in your next stand-up routine."

I said, "Every day here is a stand-up routine." It was almost true. A recent quote from Jay Keyser's book *Turning Turtle* rings true:

To enjoy life to the fullest, you have to be crazy.—Don Quixote

Returning: January 2014

Black spots, white lies, and levels of gray.

Noam emailed me one morning with a question. I sent the reply right away and asked for either an "A" on my grade sheet or a gold star on my forehead.

"Better. I'll erase one of the black crosses on your tongue. Only one!" he wrote.

"What makes you think I have more than one? I've been trying to be good."

"When you're talking backwards, you open your mouth more, and I can see." I said I would learn to speak with my mouth closed, which was safer in the long run.

Noam: "If you see an extra black spot on my tongue tomorrow, they invited me for dinner afterwards. I told them I have to race off for another commitment."

Bev: "Good! I have so many black spots on my tongue from stretching the truth that I will burn in hell." My exaggerations of the truth were what the Catholics called *white lies*. His time had to be guarded. He couldn't always enjoy the luxury of a pre- or post-talk dinner, even with worthy activists, the people for whom he most often made time.

When I was seven, I prayed to my parents' God at night. In catechism class, our omnipotent Savior suffered in tattered loincloth, outstretched palms and bare feet bleeding on the crucifix. The religion of my youth was guilt- and fear-based. I stopped attending church in my late teens, after my confirmation. I recited the Hail Mary and Our Father by rote at weddings and funerals while shifting my beliefs to a more universal spirituality open to personal interpretation, putting aside the scientific questions evoked by Adam and Eve, apples, and snakes.

I walked toward MIT's medical department with Roxy to refill meds, reciting an internal Hail Mary. When stressed, I still called in these prayers of my childhood. I was anticipating our pending trip to Rome with Noam, with the possibility of meeting the seemingly more contemporary Pope Francis. But meeting the Pope wasn't the thing moving me to pray.

In late November two months before, flying home after a visit with Laura's father and sister on Kauai, chest pain spread to my shoulders and back. Laura, focused on her Italian lesson, murmured sympathetically. I put on a Woody Allen routine, animating the intensity of my pain using limbs and facial expressions, to which she responded by handing me two rainbow-colored Tums. I paced and changed positions, but my pain remained a solid eight. A Woody Allen thirteen. I pulled at her headphones. "Laura, I'm in some serious pain." Finally, she kicked into crisis mode.

A flight attendant asked (probably to avoid a lawsuit) if I had felt pain before boarding the plane. Then she called for a doctor over the intercom. In the ensuing buzz of chatter, my experience popped into full color. Passengers looked around for the patient. Suddenly self-conscious, I adjusted my t-shirt and looked around too, until a female doctor blew my cover and knelt next to me. "Are you taking any meds? Did you take them today? Can you describe the pain and tell me where it's located?"

Laura observed us with a therapist's calm concern as the plane fell silent. The doctor, a pediatric surgeon, listened to my heart with a (I'm tempted to say *tiny*) stethoscope, which she pulled, like Felix the Cat, from her bag. She gave me two antacid tablets for my elevated heart rate. What was with these people? The attendant suggested I was having an anxiety attack and pulled a big gray oxygen tank from an overhead compartment, commanding me to put it over my mouth and breathe. I never had anxiety attacks. My pain soon downgraded to a two. The antacids had probably helped. Dammit.

I took a loudly announced solo walk off the plane. At home, tests revealed a "sliding hiatal hernia." When my PCP confirmed that this could mimic a heart attack, I felt absolved of overreacting. So here I was on my way to the pharmacy, as the days to my next flight neared, reciting my childhood prayer toward the sky:

Hail Mary, full of grace,
the Lord is with thee.
Blessed art thou amongst women,
and blessed is the fruit of thy womb, Jesus.

I habitually bowed my head, ever so slightly, at the word "Jesus." I glanced up. Could anything return me to the innocence and faith of my Catholic youth—maybe bring spiritual meaning to the trip to Italy? In the funk of losing my mother, at a time when I needed an anchoring faith, I felt only loss. My biggest cheerleader, she had applauded my stories since celebrating my ninth-grade writing award. Every few months during her last years, she'd asked in her inimitable Waltham accent, "When are you gonna finish your book about you and Noam?" I hadn't been able to write since she died in March. I didn't want to disappoint myself, nor her, especially in death, but the words couldn't be summoned. I had let her down.

At MIT's medical department with Roxy, I sat on a bench to wait for my prescription, drawn to the vibrant yellows and blues of the clothing of the woman next to me. Not usual MIT attire. As I stared, she took my hand and held it firmly. I felt oddly at ease. Looking at Roxy, she said, "The spirit world knew you needed comfort, so they sent you this dog." No surprise there, as Roxy was my best friend. I thanked the woman, who radiated calm. She gripped my hand firmly as I listened in on her conversation with a blond woman, as if she wasn't finished with me.

"I'm afraid I'll fail as an artist," the blond woman lamented.

"You already are an artist," she said, and the blond woman cried.

The pharmacist called my name, and I pulled myself away. Meds in hand, I looked back to see the two women hugging. The blond stood and squeezed my arm, eyes wide, then left. This colorful, dropped-from-the-sky stranger then guided me to a spot outside, her face inches from mine. She put her mouth to my ear.

"I tell my children I won't always be this woman of full flesh and bone, but when I'm gone, I tell them, I am going to come to them as a stranger and put my eyes up to theirs and tell them something they need to hear." I felt outside of myself, floating. She put her hands on my shoulders and looked at me, then whispered loudly into my ear again, "You are worthy of this. Now get back to your writing, and don't be lazy."

I could feel my mother in the phrasing, felt her offbeat humor, her insistent push, her energy and essence. I was overcome, but composed myself enough to ask this complete stranger, "Who are you? How do you know this?" She formed an angle with her left hand and tapped her fingertips to her chest.

"God. It's God," she said. Seriously?

I remember that my response was incoherent, and that she looked directly at me before walking away. Dazed, I led Roxy back to my office. My sister and most friends would believe me if I shared my experience, but would Noam? As a kid he had feared Catholics because of "the Irish kids in the neighborhood, especially when they came out of the local Jesuit school, [who were] violently anti-Semitic." I did tell him. He said after visiting *La Carolina* in Colombia, he could believe anything.

Ready or not, we were going to the Vatican. Perhaps as a way for the universe to show its appreciation for our faith, however fleeting, I heard from Barry, a well-informed man in Portland, Oregon, who referred to himself as "homeless by choice." He called me now and then to share world news and suggest readings for Noam. He was sleeping inside, at the home of a church friend all that week. I slept better when I knew Barry was sleeping inside. I also felt the deeper meaning of our work when I arranged for Noam to make a video statement to help free jailed Egyptian activist Ahmed Maher. I bonded quickly with Ahmed's assistant, Michelle McElroy, who also understood what it was like to work at the side of a dedicated activist.

26

Rome's International Science Festival and the Vatican

The Vatican for Dummies.

The third and last time Laura and I would join Noam overseas was in January of 2014, when he was invited to Italy by His Eminence Cardinal Gianfranco Ravasi, president of the Pontifical Council for Culture, to give a lecture inside the Vatican State. Andrea Moro also invited Noam to give a lecture, "Language as a Mental Organ," at Rome's International Science Festival, with press conferences and a live TV interview on *Pane Quotidiano*. He would also participate in a video opera titled "A Conversation with Chomsky." Last minute complications prevented Valeria, the woman with whom Noam was creating a new life chapter, from joining us, to Noam's great disappointment. She had come into his life exactly when he needed her. From that moment, he wore a perpetual smile and looked years younger.

"This is how my story will begin, if we meet Pope Francis," I told Noam over eggs and coffee in Rome. "Two gay women and a Jew walk into the Vatican."

"You mean one divorced Catholic, a Protestant, and a Jew who was once baptized in secret by his Catholic nanny walk into the Vatican," Noam said, delighted by his adding to the joke, while adding that his baptism never really "took."

Our group visiting the Vatican's museum collection: Laura, Bev, Father Tomasz Trafny, our kind and patient guide (whose name escapes us), Noam, and Andrea Moro. In the front is the inimitable Franco Bottoni.

Well, two divorced Catholics, if you're counting Laura.

"Laura is Catholic?" he asked. I felt surprise every time at the depth of his memory. He had picked up that I had misspoken.

"Oh, sorry, I take that back. Laura was never Catholic. She was once married to a Catholic man, but she was brought up Protestant."

"Laura was married too? I didn't know that."

"Yes, to the second oldest of eleven kids in a big Catholic family so devout that a nun traveled everywhere with them. Their motto was 'Have nun, will travel.'"

When I told him I felt guilty for lying about our departure date in a form letter, he said, "Good news. My dentist's office gave me a little brush to clean off my tongue. I'm going to buy you one for your birthday." This led to a debate about whether Catholic or Jewish mothers instilled more guilt in their kids. We agreed that it was a toss-up.

Sadly, the Pope had another engagement, so couldn't attend Noam's

Vatican talk, "Science, Mind, and the Limits of Understanding," but we hoped to see him before we left. Laura and I were ushered like royalty to the front row of the hall, all eyes on us. We hadn't researched Vatican protocol, so as the Ambassadors to the Holy See introduced themselves to us, I thought, "Holy——!" Were we supposed to bow, curtsy, kiss a ring? This is a small exaggeration, but we did wonder how to address them—Mr. or Mrs., Madame Ambassador, or Ambassador X? We ended up chatting easily with this group of friendly and intelligent people, in cordial conversations one might expect from an ambassador and spouse.

I had organized the Vatican events with Msgr. Tomasz Trafny, executive director of the Science, Theology, and the Ontological Quest project, overseeing publications on themes connecting philosophy, theology, and the natural sciences between the Pontifical universities and the scientific community.

At a private reception following Noam's talk, I told Tomasz that I was intrigued by this modern scientific slant, considering the schism between science and religion in the Catholic lessons of my youth. He said it was assumed that, as adults Catholics would understand that stories they were told as children, for example, about Adam and Eve, were only figurative. I countered that for a Catholic child, the fear of not believing exactly what you were told carried the threat of hell. I suggested that a letter of clarification and maybe an apology to Catholics who had left the Church might, considering other issues, bring some back. He nodded, but said that wouldn't happen in the near future. I let it go for two reasons: my respect for Tomasz, and my lingering childhood intimidation by the Catholic mystique.

Knowing we had hoped to meet the Pope, Tomasz said, "Let me see what I can do tomorrow, before you leave." We were ecstatic, but alas, we slept through our alarm by two hours and called Tomasz in a panic, horrified at having left him waiting, sad that we had lost out on meeting the Pope. He was, of course, forgiving.

Blind Faith

Extra! Extra! Bev replaces a lightbulb!

One morning Noam arrived proclaiming, "My home printer is done. I'll need a new one." He showed me his hard proof of the printer's demise—lines of black print, gray print, then black, and so on. I asked questions. "Did any other document print out like this? Is your toner light flashing? Did you cut and paste the document?" He had no answers, only a story. "Did I tell you how my nephew David once fixed my home printer?" he asked.

I offered my most obvious answer. "He plugged it in?"

Noam: "Nope, easier."

Me: "Pressed the power button?"

Noam: "Nope, even easier than that."

Me: "He touched the printer?" (That had to be it.)

Noam: "You're not even trying."

Me: "OK, *Uncle*! I give up."

Noam: "He walked into the room and looked at it, and it started printing." He grinned, and I shook my head, fishing for a comeback, not to be outdone.

"I'm going to do something even more amazing the next time your printer isn't working," I said, taking his bags from him so he could remove his coat.

"What will you do? Just think about it?" he said, hanging his coat on the rack.

That was my plan—he had outsmarted me. I yelled after him as he walked away, "But I will think about it from MIT, thirteen miles away from your house!"

I fished screws and brackets from my collection and drove to Noam's house the next Monday to check out his printer and repair the window blind he had accidentally pulled down off its brackets. Valeria was traveling, and we wanted everything working by the time she returned. He eyed my toolbox and shook his head with the certainty of a pessimistic outcome. Being a more optimistic pessimist myself, I sent him into his office and went to work. In his bedroom I removed the blind's broken brackets, securing new ones with drywall screws. Screws included with most items are cheap and easily stripped, and often of the single-slot bayonet type. If a book of secret rules for a less frustrating life existed, using Phillips head drywall screws whenever possible would be item number five or six.

I slid faceplates on the brackets to keep the blinds in place and found the wand on the floor under the window, but I couldn't connect it because the ring connecting it to the turning mechanism was missing. I went next door to Noam's office looking for a next-best solution and told him we would fix the printer next.

"The printer is hopeless," he said. I ignored him and reached for a pen with a jumbo paper clip stuck through its pocket clip—probably a phone interview activity. His desk area, like his desk at MIT, was sprinkled with tight paper springs.

In his bedroom, I pulled the paper clip from the pen, opening it enough to poke it through the hole in the wand, connected it to the loop at the top of the blind, then twisted it with needle-nosed pliers. I called Noam in to demonstrate.

"Another miracle. How did you do it?" He twisted the wand left and right, intent on the connection at the top. "Ah, you used a paper clip. Just what I would have done!" I turned the wand again, revealing the front yard. He said he never looked out the window, since the blinds were always closed. This begged the question of how and why had he pulled them down in the first place. Whatever.

We turned our conversation to those with the skills to repair things, versus those without, versus those who think they have the skills, but don't. "Noam, did I tell you about the time my father put up a new pole lamp in our living room when I was a kid?" He smiled and tilted his head, listening. "The lamp was too tall, so my father cut the pole down, without measuring. Now the lamp was too short, so he jammed a wooden salad bowl under the now-too-short pole. He was proud of what he called his 'invention.'" As I told the story it occurred to me that Noam called some of his improvisations "inventions." I had once dumped throat lozenges out of a bowl on his desk to clean it, imagining the germs. In the meantime, he returned from lunch to find them heaped on his desk and scooped them into an empty cardboard tea box he found near the coffeemaker. I returned with the clean bowl and saw the box of lozenges.

"How do you like my invention? I was pretty proud of myself when I found a container for the lozenges. It was almost like cooking." Almost like cooking. This was exactly the sort of thing my father would have said. No wonder I loved this guy.

"On to the printer," I said, and he heaved another sigh of despair.

"See if you can wend your way to the printer without killing yourself," he said, admitting only then, when considering *my* safety, that his home office was a death trap. For years he wouldn't let me move anything until he'd had a chance to go through the stacks, until we had moved his computer, until we boxed up old books, until we sent the manuscripts to be archived, which had to wait till spring, till summer, till hell froze over.

Books balanced perilously on a narrow table perpendicular to his desk. Cardboard boxes bulging with papers were pushed against the baseboards beneath walls of shelves overflowing with drafts, books, journals, and awards in an alternating checkerboard pattern, much like his voluminous library and storage room back in Building 20, except that this office was one-third the size.

I walked a foot-wide pathway around the perimeter in the way I learned as a young, aspiring ballerina—one foot in front of the other. This left me wondering how Noam got to his printer without tripping. My guess was that he tripped.

Reaching the old, inverted cardboard box he had used for years as a printer "table" (I hadn't until now recognized his cardboard theme), I examined the printer. It was plugged in and had power, there was no paper jam, and it wasn't asking for toner, so I turned it off, waited, and turned it on again to clear commands.

"OK, print out the first page of the document that was streaked with the gray lines," I said. It printed out perfectly in black ink, with no gray highlighting. "This is like asking your baby to talk again when your friends show up," I said. When he looked at me blankly, I raised my voice in case his hearing aids were out. "Now print something a few pages long." When the pages printed without any problems, I laughed.

Noam's home office.

"What's wrong?" he asked, imagining the worst. If he knew the deep, dark me, he would know I *never* laugh when something does go wrong, unless it's gone so ridiculously wrong that I've become hysterical. "Laughter through tears"—that's how Noam explained the phenomenon when a situation called for a Yiddish lesson.

"Nothing is wrong. That's the problem. The printer is working perfectly."

"You've fixed it!" he said, raising a victorious fist. The fact that one of the smartest people on the planet believed I had again fixed something that was never broken would get no argument from me. We said goodbye, and I returned to MIT.

An hour later, I opened an email from Noam. "The blinds and printer are both working perfectly, thanks to your brilliant repair skills." This reminded me of an experience with another MIT professor, Ilona Karmel Zucker, whose 1969 novel *An Estate of Memory* was considered one of the most powerful accounts of the Holocaust. Ilona had been run over by a tank in a Nazi labor camp, so walked with the aid of two metal crutches for the remainder of her life. One day my friend Cindy and I arrived at Ilona's home to find her and her husband, Hans (Francis) Zucker, a physicist and science philosopher notable for his work on antennas, looking dejected.

Sections of a storm door were strewn across their back yard. They had pulled it down to fix a loose hinge, and then gave up trying to put it back together. As the four of us stood outside the doorway I felt shades of Noam: always assume such things are hopeless. I convinced them to leave me alone to study the puzzle pieces. Every few minutes a distraught face would peer out from a window, ducking when I looked up. Twenty minutes later, the door was installed and working perfectly.

"You're brilliant!" Ilona said, hugging me. Hans's moment came after lunch, when I climbed a stepladder to replace a ceiling lightbulb in his upstairs study. "It's a miracle!" he said, clapping his hands. "It's been hard to work in the dark."

Miracles, like brilliance, run along a lengthy continuum.

Settling back down to work, I shook my slightly swollen head back to normal and made a note to add paper clips to my toolbox. And a jar of fairy dust.

PART IV

Some Things Change,
Some Stay the Same

27

May Day

Bev and Laura make warm toast out of lemons.

The coming months were both fun and difficult. In February of 2014 Laura and I considered joining Noam and Valeria in Santa Barbara, where Laura's mom, Emily, lived. Noam would give a lecture titled "Security and State Policy" for the Nuclear Age Peace Foundation. We look back with regret on our decision to stay home.

In March, Noam and Valeria arrived at the office together, all smiles, waiting for my reaction to—something. After I acknowledged Noam's new shirt and fresh haircut, he grabbed my hands. "Notice anything else different?" I looked down at his hands, then Valeria's, and spied two shiny wedding rings. They had sneaked off to a B&B nearby—and married! Valeria suggested that I propose to Laura, as Noam gave an enthusiastic thumbs-up.

Dorie Ladner's afternoon visit fit the celebratory spirit of the day. Now in her seventies, Dorie had been a major player in the Mississippi civil rights movement, and in the Zinn Education Project. Before she met with Noam, she sat in the chair next to mine asking questions like "How is his heaaalth?", drawing out her words as Southerners do. On good days like this I got to shake the hand of history and learn more about the world of social justice. She said it was her dream to meet Noam, and I could see by his face when he welcomed her that

Bev and Laura, and their mothers, Charlotte and Emily.

he was equally as happy. I thought back to a Valentine's Day dinner in 2009. Laura had proposed to me just as I bit into a hot pepper, which sent me into a coughing fit. Laura says it was a five-year coughing fit. We had been living together for seven years, but I was hesitant to jump back into marriage.

On the heels of Noam and Valeria's surprise, a voice bellowed above my doubts. I invited Jay to dinner as a witness, and for support. My hope was to glide through my dreaded sixtieth birthday by wrapping it inside our wedding. "Laura, should we get married?" I asked, chattering nervously about a May backyard wedding, calculating the number of guests we could fit, rambling on about decorations and food. I looked at Laura, and then at Jay, who looked confused.

"But Laura hasn't actually accepted *your* proposal," Jay said.

"She hasn't? Look at her face," I said. Her smile exposed her back molars.

"Of course I'll marry you, Bevy," she said.

When I broke the news to Noam at work, he agreed to make a wedding toast. Our catered lunchtime wedding would take place at our house on Saturday, May 3, the day after my birthday. Emily, an energetic and upbeat eighty-two, would fly from Santa Barbara to represent herself and my mother. We had just heard that Jay Keyser had fallen in his home while exercising and was in critical condition. I was upset by the news but could only send him positive energy.

On April 30, Laura was finishing up with a client at her Watertown office, I was tying up loose ends at work, and our friends Linda and Gary were about to begin their drive from Pennsylvania when I got a call from Linnea, Laura's sister. Emily had suffered a stroke and was in a neuro ICU. A surgeon would repair her bleed and put her into an induced coma, but the prognosis wasn't good. With mechanical numbness, I called the caterer to delay, then called my brother Ron. He and Lynne would drive me from my house to Laura's office. Watching Laura's face change as we told her about her mother seemed cruel. That night I bought two plane tickets to Santa Barbara and wrote our guests to postpone the wedding.

We spent May 1 and my birthday the next day with Emily. After a hospital visit on May 3, sitting at her mother's dining table, Laura looked at her watch and then at me. "Bevy, we would have been married in twenty minutes, Boston time."

I jumped up and said, "Grab the keys to your Mom's Smart car." At Hendry's Beach minutes later, we parked the car and ran toward a small oceanfront tower which opened at the top to a wide expanse of the Pacific, with a long view across the beach where we had swum and collected stones.

We began rushing up the stairway, bumping into a couple on their way down. An intense eye-to-eye exchange with the man pulled me off guard, and I found myself blurting out our story. Without hesitation, the man said, "I've performed wedding ceremonies. I can marry you. And Lori here is a photographer."

The four of us climbed the stairs in single file. After a few words

Laura and Bev's wedding day photo.

and very little prep, Laura and I exchanged impromptu vows, each faltering as we teetered on the surreal emotional plane we had been riding, and Steve pronounced us married. Lori reached into her pocket and handed us two heart-shaped stones she'd collected from the beach. Later that afternoon we pressed the stones into Emily's hands as we relived our serendipitous ceremony with her. She never woke. We held her memorial in Santa Barbara ten days later. Back home, we settled on a new wedding date of August 2—my late father's birthday, with Jay and Denise standing up for us. At our altar we filled a blue glass bowl with shells and sand from Hendry's Beach and placed our two heart-shaped stones inside. Daisies, our mothers' favorite flowers, floated in water above.

In front of more than sixty friends and family, we were married amid bursts of Native American flute, guitars, ukulele, and harmonica. After the ceremony, Jay and Gary drove us around the neighborhood in Laura's Model A Ford, where the two brides in its rumble seat elicited double takes and cheers. Then we joined our guests for a feast. The one precaution for the caterer: *No hot peppers*.

28

Stayin' Alive

Bev gets some advice about Stayin' Alive—and cultural matters.

"Everyone is writing me about their personal problems—I don't know how to handle these letters. I'm not Miss Lonelyhearts," Noam lamented after checking email on his laptop. I had ignored his ongoing campaign to get me to read Nathanael West's *Miss Lonelyhearts*. "You ought to read it. It's a sad book, but also humorous. At least that's how I remember it from fifty-odd years ago. Read it and let me know what you think," he said. I gave in out of curiosity. Why was he being so insistent?

When I told him I had read it, he asked, "What did you think?" and chuckled.

"Why did you want me to read it?" I asked in a voice more whiney than I intended.

My synopsis to Noam: "So ... 'Miss Lonelyhearts' is a man who helps people with love-life problems via his newspaper column. He has an affair with a woman to try to shake off the depression that comes with being Miss Lonelyhearts, and in the end, the woman's husband shoots him! Not only was it a sad book, but it was not, in any way, a *humorous* book. There was no balance. I don't always expect a happy ending, but a book should make me feel occasional joy for a character."

He laughed at my take-away from the story, but I wasn't sure why. I laughed at his laughing, and I wasn't sure why. "Maybe we should write a new form letter. 'Dear *Person in Pain*, my psychiatric shingle has been retracted.'" I watched as his amusement turned to compassion, and then downright gloom.

Handing me a pile of backup correspondence the next week, he again bemoaned the increase in letters asking for personal advice. At the top was a letter with a note from him, "Any thoughts on a reply? Tell them I'm away, on Mars?" Mars was his go-to hiding place. When I warned him to be careful, he said, "I *think* I cut our notes out before I write back. If someone sends you a letter bomb, maybe I forgot." Who was joking about bombs now?

I guessed that Noam suggested I read *Miss Lonelyhearts* to point out to me the potential pitfalls of being too empathic. Kind replies ratcheted up the stakes, made us appear to be saviors. My heart was soft, to a fault. I had mailed phone cards and food gift cards to folks in need. Noam had an equally soft heart. Actor-activist Marlo Thomas once emailed him that she was writing a book about how the words of others had influenced well-known people to become who they were. Noam had shared with me a story he told in the *Manufacturing Consent* documentary. As a kid, he stood next to a boy being bullied by classmates, but did nothing to stop them. He decided then that he would never again watch this happen. In the end, he didn't want Marlo to use the story because it was about *him*.

I'm sure his family, books, and his Brooklyn newspaper stand buddies helped shape his humanitarian focus. I asked him now and then what compelled him to respond to everyone, but he'd only sigh.

Laura saw Noam's deep compassion and respect for *everyman*, the way he listened without noticing awkwardness or insecurity, no matter who they were. No wonder people sought him out.

He agreed with me that one message of the book was the pitfalls of reaching out. Hearing this, the possibility of a gunman charging in haunted me. I imagined zipping a sheet of metal into the bottom of Roxy's bed. We could crouch in a far corner under my desk and use it as a shield. Later that week, Matt from our main office told me that a bearded man was yelling about Internet security, digital security, and conspiracy theories on the seventh floor of the Gates Tower. "He referenced Professor Chomsky at least once, but disappeared before campus police arrived. They think he left the building," he said.

"They *think* he left?" I asked, laughing nervously. He suggested that I lock my door. When I talked about this later with Jay and Laura, I admitted that I didn't always feel safe in that office. Had I been lucky all these years? They convinced me to be more vigilant at work. I can't say that I was.

Close, but No *SNL!*—Late 2014

Beam me up to Pop Culture.

I loved the office's lighthearted moments. Shigeru Miyagawa, a linguistics professor who shared our suite during my last few years there, called out, "Bye, Bev! I have to meet my friend George Takei for dinner." Pause. "He's in town for a show at the Somerville Theatre." I had no clue who George Takei was. Shigeru's expression told me I had once again exposed my lack of pop culture coolness.

"He's Mr. Sulu on *Star Trek*." Silence. "Didn't you watch *Star Trek*?"

"Oh, sure, a few times," I said, remembering the first and last episode I sat through, wherein a male character becomes impregnated in his forearm. I couldn't watch shows like this because the other viewers had to put the TV on hold as I asked things like, "OK, who are these people, and why are they on this ship?" I know why this happens. While others focus on the story line, I'm checking out symbolism and word choices, noticing patterns and discrepancies. In other words, I'm watching a completely different show.

"Laura and Jay will know who George Takei is," I said lamely.

"He's well known in popular culture. He hosted *Saturday Night Live!*"

"Really? Noam was asked to host *Saturday Night Live* in the late

1990s! Or did they only want him to play himself? Anyway, I think I'll write about it on my blog."

"Oh, wait then. Maybe I should check and make sure he did host. Lots of people wanted him to." Shigeru threw down his briefcase and pulled a chair up to his computer. When he discovered that Takei had *not* hosted *Saturday Night Live*, I told him the story of the time *SNL* had asked Noam to appear on the show.

One day in the late 1990s, one of the producers of *SNL* called our office. Two of the show's writers had written a loose script for Noam, who needed only to be on the set and play along with the cast. I called Noam at home, trying to stay calm. I wanted my friends, family, and the rest of the country to see my boss appear on, and possibly host—had they said he would host?—this funny, iconic mainstream TV skit show.

"Hi, Noam, it's Bev." Breathe ... breathe ... slow ... down," I told myself. "I just got a call from a producer of *Saturday Night Live*. He would like you to go to New York next weekend to play yourself on the show." Noam was quiet. I had a fleeting image of him reading a book while listening in for key words. I tried to be convincing. "I think this would be a chance to get your voice out to millions. *Saturday Night Live* is an extremely popular show."

"*Saturday Night Live?*" he asked. "I think I've heard of it. I might have watched it with the kids when they were younger. Uh, hold on, let me talk to Carol."

Noam yelled down the stairs. "*Caroooool*! It's Bev ... *Bev*! She's asking if I want to be on *Saturday Night Live*." Pause. "It's in New York. I said *New York*! What? *What?*" Pause. "*OK, let me ask.*"

"Bev, what do they want me to do? Would I have to prepare anything?"

"No, you would just show up and play yourself—play it straight. Their script will play around you. They may also have you on the news segment."

"OK, hold on. Let me talk with Carol again. *Caarrooool*! ..." Long pause.

I was getting hopeful. Noam returned to the phone. "Uh, Bev, can it be taped somewhere closer, at a different time?" he asked. I had my work cut out for me.

"It would take place at the *Saturday Night Live* studios in New York. In New York City. It's, um, a live show. So … no." Saturday—Night—Live. Wasn't everyone familiar with the show? Didn't everyone know how it began, after an initial skit every single week: "Live, from New York, it's Saturday Night!"?

"When would they want me there?" he asked. Our conversation was beginning to feel like one of Noam's favorite skits, the *Who's on First?* baseball routine, which our shorthand conversations too often resembled, followed by the phrase "clear as mud?"

"You would arrive next Saturday at 9 p.m. and leave when the show ends, around 12:30 a.m. Let me look at the calendar and give you the exact …" I said, trying to cover all bases, as it dawned on me that he might actually have meant "what date." But he was already yelling back down the half-stairway to Carol, who was probably in the living room at her computer.

By now I was convinced Noam had never watched *SNL*, or he had watched while writing a lecture in his head. Noam repeated, loudly, "It would be next weekend … I said, *next weekend!*" I heard Carol's unintelligible voice in the background, then Noam spoke one last time.

"Uh, Bev. Carol says no."

When I posted this story on my blog years later, it was reposted on *Reddit*—where Noam had done an "Ask Me Anything" Q&A. A former *SNL* producer and the writer he had worked with both recalled their request, and sadly, our reply.

I never asked Noam if he knew George Takei's name, but I guarantee that he would have been more interested in the fact that Takei's family had lived in internment camps during World War II.

I hope to see George Takei host *SNL*. At least I would know his name as Mr. Sulu now that Jay, my pop culture expert, and Laura, a long-time Trekkie, have filled me in. This meant paying attention

Page from Jeffrey Wilson's graphic novel *The Instinct for Cooperation* depicting Noam, Roxy, and Bev.

to three partial *Star Trek* episodes and trying to believe that a crew could travel light years in a few short days. Even after Jay and Laura's guided tutorials, I still don't know who those people are, or why they are on that ship.

As for Noam, I didn't bother telling him that he, Roxy, and I had been depicted in Jeffrey Wilson's graphic novel *The Instinct for Cooperation*. He would only have given me a blank look and moved on.

29

Found Again: Early 2015

At a crossroads.

Norma was a wise soul and a grounding voice, our own Annie Dillard, writing a version of the following to her friends every year: "Spring is coming. The snowdrops in my yard opened yesterday— about a half-dozen of them. The daffodils and crocuses are beginning to bloom, and the primroses are all pushing up." I loved her optimism as much as I trusted the spring's ability to pull me back from winter's gloom.

For a few years after Carol's death in 2008, when Noam returned full time to the podium, I supervised the timing and book signings at his talks, and ensured that he wasn't mobbed for autographs or cornered for long-winded chats. On one occasion, in late 2012, I sat waiting for him to arrive for a panel discussion called "Radical Futures and Prospects for Freedom," with author, educator, and political activist Angela Davis at Boston's Berklee Performance Center. Twenty minutes past start time, the planners looked at me with open hands and raised eyebrows. I ran around the venue while calling Noam's cell phone (knowing that he wouldn't pick up).

Overtaken by something outside myself, I pushed through the front door and jogged down the street, shooting a glance down

Massachusetts Avenue before turning right to peer across a long and wide crosswalk. There I spied Noam in his beige raincoat, blue canvas briefcase in hand, worry plastered across his face. I waved like a mad woman until I caught his eye. His expression turned to relief, and I'm sure my face reflected the same. When the traffic signal changed to *Walk*, I ran to meet him halfway.

"How did you know?" he asked, squeezing my hand. His driver had let him out on the wrong corner half a mile away, and he hadn't noticed until the taxi drove away. "It's as if you knew I would be at the crosswalk." In a way, I had known when I ran out of the venue that he would be around a corner, looking for a friendly face. Maybe even mine.

Full Circle: May 2015

Bev experiences Elizabeth Kübler-Ross's stages of grief.

Roxy hadn't eaten much in a week, and things got serious when she began to pant. Following a trip to the vet, a fever and a nefarious case of pancreatitis threatening her gallbladder and liver landed her in the hospital. Laura and I turned our focus toward her as we stared down the serious possibility that Roxy, now thirteen years old, might well die. I was devastated.

We returned home a solemn couple, with little to do but wait. Our friend Gail Finnie Rundlett was hosting a concert with Arlington's United for Justice with Peace honoring the one-year anniversary of Pete Seeger's death. Aside from providing respite for my aching heart, the concert would allow me to pass on some words of thanks to Thea Paneth, our main UJP connection. So I went.

Pete Seeger's assistant had called our office in 2008, months before Carol died. "Pete is a big fan of Noam's, and would be honored to talk with him," she said. I got an adrenaline rush when public figures put a meeting with Noam on their wish lists, and there had been many.

My secret agenda was to talk with Seeger first, after checking on Carol's status. Then he would call Noam's house. When Pete called, I told him I was a fan of his activism and music, and divulged that his "Turn! Turn! Turn! (To Everything There Is a Season)" was one of my guiding principles. "What was it like to be blacklisted from singing for over a decade due to your political actions?" I asked.

He said he found comfort singing on smaller stages and playing for friends. Quite unexpectedly, he asked if I would like to hear the song he planned to sing to Carol. Pete Seeger was on the phone, singing "Circles" to me, a song written by another of my idols, Harry Chapin. Tear droplets smudged my to-do list.

> All my life's a circle;
> But I can't tell you why;
> Seasons spinning round again,
> The years keep rolling by.

> It seems like I've been here before;
> I can't remember when;
> But I have this funny feeling;
> That we'll all be together again.

I long to revisit that moment: Pete Seeger singing Chapin's lyrics suggesting this life might not be the end for us, with a young and healthy Roxy snoozing on her bed under my desk.

Inside the church, the music lulled me into moments of solace, moving me away from the heart-felt pain I carried from the accumulated losses of my mother and Laura's, and Sylvia and Danny. With Roxy sick, I needed this uplifting respite.

During the break I hugged Thea and thanked her for generously organizing UJP members' personal deliveries of home-cooked meals to the Chomskys during Carol's illness, and for her unwavering peace efforts. "I will never back down from my stand for peace. Not one inch," she said. I admired her tenacity.

Gail's rendition of Richard and Mimi Fariña's "Pack Up Your Sorrows" grabbed me by my throat and stole my breath. Thinking of Elizabeth Kübler-Ross's stages of grief, I tried to accept that Roxy might not live, while bargaining with the universe that she might live another year. Gail's words mirrored mine:

> But, if somehow you could pack up your sorrows,
> And give them all to me,
> You would lose them, I know how to use them.
> Give them all to me.

Laura and I lived much of our lives striving to ease others' pain, and this is how Noam, Pete Seeger, the UJP groups, and other activists lived theirs. By the end of the night I vowed to keep honoring and trusting the circle of life. Two days later, the day before her thirteenth birthday, Roxy, our little revolutionary, woke up, stood up, and put up a fight with the vet. We packed her up and took her home to love her back to her cheerful, energetic self for two more years.

PART V

To Everything, There Is a Season

30

January 2016: Moving
Toward Wrapping Things Up

Coming to terms with the beginning of the end.

From the time I took this job, I assumed that two decades later there would be more hope in the world—after all, weren't large numbers of committed activists working toward this goal? I wondered how Noam felt as each year passed with increased catastrophes and ongoing wars. The cities of Saint-Denis and Paris suffered a series of coordinated attacks in November of 2015, and then came the Paris shootings in January at the satirical weekly newspaper *Charlie Hebdo*. I was arranging interviews and statements on both attacks, so Noam was going nonstop. I sent a note to Michel Gondry and learned he was OK physically, but like most, feeling generally unsafe. When interviewed, Noam again brought up other killings that had been largely ignored by the press, like the assassinations of three journalists in Latin America in December.

Noam and I sat together to look at the day's schedule, chatting about politics, particularly about Bernie Sanders being the best candidate, but, we sadly concluded, probably not our next president. We agreed that a Republican president would be a disaster for many reasons, including the denial of our grave environmental situation. Moving to business at hand, I asked about two out-of-state lecture queries. He told me not to worry, that he and Valeria would take care of travel from now on. I had noticed gradual changes in my job, and maybe I should have anticipated this, but hearing him say it with such finality, I felt the nearing of the end of this amazing life chapter.

"You still have a lot to keep you busy," Noam said cheerily.

My work was divided into three major segments, beginning with managing correspondence. At first Noam sent correspondence and recommendation letters for me or my assistant to print out and sign, but when the web caught on our email load multiplied enormously due to the ease of corresponding. Planning his office schedule entailed communicating at length. Film crews added agreement forms, lighting and camera allowances, office photos, and specs.

Second was arranging talks and Q&A's on and off campus at universities, colleges, and other sites, mostly within the Cambridge/Boston area. Arranging visits with MIT's Knight Science Fellows, Neiman and Sloan Fellows, and peace action folks was energizing, even fun. I had convinced myself that I was doing my part by supporting Noam's work, by "helping greatness." Ironically, setting up these meetings saved me from the same despair their topics engendered in me.

Third was building schedules and arranging flights and hotels. I loved molding and shaping the trips' components—taxis, breaks, meals, interviews, lectures, Q&A's, visits to local attractions, from a coffee house frequented by activists, to a tour of Italy's mosaics, to fit together like a puzzle as I connected with planners globally. My goal was to avoid the usual problem: without a trusted ally present to safeguard his time, Noam was bound to return exhausted, sick, or both. To be sure, he was often responsible for the prolonging, acquiescing to constant requests for more time. This frustrated me, and even him. I was beyond grateful to those who were willing to keep to our agreed-on schedule.

"What about local talks?"

"We'll play those by ear. Don't worry, you still have *plenty* to do," he said, motioning toward my computer, folders, desk. I smiled, maybe a little weakly, and handed him a schedule I had just completed for a Helen Caldicott event in New York, telling him that I'd already put it together. It was odd to think it might be my last.

He looked down at his hands and rolled a strip of paper into a spring. "I think you've been doing a lot more than I realized."

This was a welcome acknowledgment. "I've done my best. It's been fun, and interesting. Amazing, really." Change was in the air.

My father always told me two things: "Do your best," and "Be careful." His words became my internal mantras during this time of transition.

Months later, our morning held promise in the sweet and unexpected moment when Noam gave me "the look," wordlessly conveying that he had made the catch: he had picked Morris up at his apartment. Noam left his Cambridge condo early on these days, because it took a while to get Morris to his car. Morris's speed wasn't the issue. In his ninety-second year, he wasn't slow even by an eighty-year-old's standards. The culprit was his advancing Alzheimer's; he'd forget his plan to come to the office, even with a morning reminder.

We all felt a small victory when Morris came in with Noam, wearing his ever-present red backpack and calling out husky hellos—simply being Morris. Our workday promised a flurry of visitors and activity, the way it had when Morris came in every day.

Noam and I were exchanging books and letters in his office when a loud clanging under his desk exposed a wide-eyed Roxy jabbing at his empty trashcan. Noam opened and closed his hand like a claw a foot from her face. "You're too early, Roxy. I haven't eaten lunch yet." I loved when the five of us, counting Roxy, were in synch, tucked away in our world at the end of the hallway, around the corner from the rest of the department. Me juggling emails and schedules, Glenn finding books and online articles for Noam, who sat in his office drinking watered-down coffee during meetings, poking his head into Morris's office, or vice versa, in between.

I brought a local talk request in to Noam. He took it from me, and casually mentioned that he and Valeria would be handling the local talks now, as well. Ah. This was another transition. I moved to straighten a group of books, biographies by Barsky, Sperlich, and Lyons, nudging their spines to line up, as he did the same on the shelf below. One hand was shoved into his jeans pocket, and with the other he pushed a boxed collection by Carlos Otero to the bookshelf's edge. I had always aligned things during intense times—lining up a fork and knife parallel to my plate, rearranging folders while procrastinating on a complicated schedule. I'd watched him open paper clips into the letter S during meetings, and tear narrow strips of paper while he was thinking, rolling them into springs. But I didn't know until then that he shared my penchant for alignment. At that moment we moved our focus back to the office, since his next visitor had arrived.

After work I drove to Belmont's Payson Park Reservoir near my house. My faithful Roxy's front paws balanced on the compartment between the front seats. "Roxy, do you want to go for a *walk*?" Her enthusiastic reply to my question had me upping the ante, and I replied with my own animated, *"Come on! Let's go for a walk!"*

She had lost most of her hearing, but she could read my exaggerated anticipation. I hooked her up, finding familiar comfort in her soft curls as I lowered her to the ground. She hadn't been able to jump out of the car for months, and her climb up the steep stairway, like mine, was a little slower than on our last visit.

I'm sure I was talking to myself as I walked the perimeter, gathering my thoughts, regaining my wits. I guess I had imagined helping Noam with his correspondence, getting signed books into the mail, and arranging phone interviews even after his retirement. After years of being his go-to person, his trusted gatekeeper, and eventually his "guardian angel," was I ready to let go of the reins? And if so, what did I want for *myself*?

As I walked the perimeter a second time, the nagging thought I hadn't been able to pinpoint came into focus. The way Carol and I had managed things had worked for two decades. We had been his planners, his protectors, his first line of defense. But she was gone, and Noam's routine, his life, was different now.

By the time I reached the stairway again, I could see beyond my

confusion to the simple truth: it was time for *me* to let go. Carol
would have agreed. Although I would miss the conversations, serendipitous escapades, inside jokes, and puzzles that had rounded out
our workdays, this moment of clarity was freeing.

At home, I dropped my backpack and keys onto the kitchen
counter. Roxy stood patiently by her bowl while I added a few treats
to her prescription food. "Roxy, I feel like dancing," I said loud enough
for her to hear. She looked up briefly, then returned to her food,
spraying nuggets onto the tiled floor. I lifted my arms and waved
them like tall pond grass rippling below the water's surface, as the
weight on my shoulders slid off and away.

Roxy and I would retire the following year.

Regardless of his mental status, I wanted to thank Morris for his
pragmatism, for showing me a shortcut into Cambridge, for reminding me to look through a less emotional lens. He had trusted me
enough to let me clear up a rash on his face, to thaw his frozen car
lock one winter, to remind him of doctor's appointments in later
years. Just that morning, he had called across the suite to me, "Bev,
can you show me how to get my messages?" In his office, I found
him looking at his phone as if it were unfamiliar. I pointed to the
password I had taped to it a month before, above the rectangular
digital window.

"There it is, Morris. Press the buttons in sequence where I've
taped the numbers one, two, and three, and the phone will prompt
you for your password." I stayed with him so we could do it together.

"Oh, yes, that should work," he said, after we pressed the last
button.

The next time Morris came in, I told him in private that I would
retire the next year. He said, "You're quitting? You know, when you
quit, Noam and I will probably wrap things up here." I didn't tell him
that we had already begun.

31

Time Out

A division between before and after.

In the Nick of Time

I was going up to my office from the parking garage on a rainy morning in early October months later when the elevator stopped on the first floor. A young man got in holding a pair of trendy sneakers. He looked familiar, and I figured he was one of our L&P students. More noteworthy, he was soaking wet and barefoot. He hit the 9, one floor up from my office. I asked, straight faced, "Did you swim here?"

"No—actually, I ran all the way from my apartment," he said, just as seriously.

"You don't have an umbrella?" I asked.

"You can't run with an umbrella," he said. I squinted sideways at him. I wanted to say the obvious—if he had an umbrella, he wouldn't need to run, but that didn't seem to be the point. Anyway, who was I to tell this stranger what to do?

Despite his standing in the Stata Center elevator in his bare feet, his repartee was restrained, his ironic humor surprising. I tried to figure out what to make of him. "I like your spirit," I said. "And I plan to write about you on my blog."

"Then I will have to read your blog," he said.

"It might take a month or two to post this. I write stories and not daily stuff."

"A month or two?" he asked, appalled.

Once again I heard the voice of my bff Deb, my muse and reader, urging me to post more often, even if only a paragraph. I don't know why that was so hard for me.

"I'll try to get to it sooner," I promised.

My floor pinged, and I turned to ask him his name.

"Brad. Skow." Back at my office, I opened the department's website and learned that Brad wasn't a student. He was a philosophy professor focusing on the study of time, questioning whether time actually passes. I thought, "If he thinks time doesn't pass, then what's the big deal about waiting a month or two for my blog post? I should put him in touch with Knut, the grad student with the red sweater who blew my mind with his reminder that time was always passing." I would have loved to hear them debate a question—since answered—my brother Paul had posed to his old MIT classmate, High Energy Physicist Dan Amidei, when the Higgs boson particle was discovered:

The "natural" state of matter is to be massless. If a massless particle must move at the speed of light, its internal clock must never move because of relativistic time dilation, right? But if that is true, how can photons scatter? Scattering implies a change in state, so a division between before and after. But for a particle that doesn't see time passing, how can it change in time?

When Brad came to sign his book *Objective Becoming* for me, we discovered a profound intersection of our lives. "My birth mother gave me up for adoption at seventeen. I've been reading stories of young mothers and adoption ever since, trying to figure out why women make one decision or another," he said.

"Brad, I had my son just before my eighteenth birthday." The two of us were pulled into another realm, connected with an intensity beyond time and place, as if looking at one another in alternate real-

My brother Paul and three other MIT physics and math students on campus in the mid 1970s. Leo Katzenstein, Paul Boisseau, Dan Amidei, and Alan Gluchoff.

ities. We saw what might have been had I, or his mother, made different choices, or had different choices made for us. I was sixty-two, meeting my own son for the first time, and I was also seventeen, holding my son for the first time. When Brad praised the choice I had made to raise Jay, I told him I often wondered if that choice had been selfish, even cowardly, as giving up a child could be as loving and difficult as keeping him. He told me how it felt to be a child given away by his birth mother, despite being adopted into a good family. I hope my perspective helped him find peace, as his had helped me. Our talks continued for months, and I met his three children.

My time with Brad had me feeling like an insider to the musings I had witnessed at MIT about the mind, and the passing/not passing, of time. I wanted to know more, and felt a familiar loss, the regret of not having gone to college at eighteen to explore my own musings and interests, to consider what I might want to do with the rest of my life.

The next summer would come too soon. I already missed our deep and intense connection, as if I had been missing him for all of my adult life.

Men and Their Pens: Spring 2016

> *If you want to change the world, pick up your pen and write.*
> —Martin Luther

My work life settled back into an enjoyable routine once I made the decision to retire the next summer. Noam arrived one morning looking glum. "Uh, Bev. Where can I find an extra pen?" He didn't want just any pen. He wanted a blue, medium-point retractable pen, the type of pen he had used for decades.

"Did you lose your pens again?" I asked, smiling. His shrug and sigh said that not only had he left his pen at home, but he had also misplaced his sense of humor, and yes, an entire box of pens. I searched my desk, and rifled through his blue briefcase and the crevices of his desk as he looked on. Finding no pens, I went to a place of last resort: the drawers of the hallway filing cabinet, by now a retired office supply graveyard. I found a number of things that had outlived their usefulness. Blank, notched Rolodex cards, legal-sized copy paper, business envelopes stamped with Building 20's return address. I pulled out loose packs of wet and dry screen cleaner and opened them. The wet was dry, the dry was crispy. I threw out the screen cleaners, recycled the old envelopes, and donated the boxes of copy paper to the general supply closet.

Cleaning out the clutter was a relief, because I had always imagined that if I died suddenly, someone might open those drawers and think, "How could we have trusted Bev to be Chomsky's assistant if she couldn't keep her supplies orderly?" Then I would be embarrassed (except that I would be dead), as if I had failed at my job or gone to work in my underwear, because people—whoever *they* were—would

Noam wielding his favorite pen, sitting in what would become the Crying Chair.

have assumed my overarching lack of organizing skills as evidenced in that one cabinet. That is, however, where I found, at the bottom of the last drawer, a box of blue ink, medium-point retractable pens, circa 1999. I pulled one out. The ink had dried up. When my order of two twelve-packs of pens arrived a few days later, I gave him a box and kept the other in my desk, because I knew Noam.

For six years after Carol died, I traveled to Noam's house to fix any computer or printer problems. If he were due back from a trip, I picked up groceries, brought in mail, and turned on lights. If it had snowed, I shoveled his front walk and made sure his driveway guy plowed and cleared a path to his mailbox. Lastly, I tackled the chaos on the thick oak desk near his small wooden typing table. I was convinced that he dumped the contents of his briefcases onto that desk weekly, so organizing it would be futile, but I could at least reduce the clutter. I would lift an old schedule, uncover a pen, two sheets of paper, an award, a folder, a book, another pen, a letter, a birthday card, six more folders, a pencil. Discovering a big item, like an expensive boxed pen set, felt like a casino payoff. By the end, I had usually mined a dozen pens. But Noam had sold the Lexington house a year before, and he and Valeria had moved into a Cambridge condo, so there was no going back to search that oak desk.

Two weeks after giving him a full box of pens, he handed me a sheet of paper, the words *check with me* scrawled on the top. I asked what it meant, and he squinted his eyes as if contemplating something grave. "Oh, right. Can you order me another box of pens?"

"What happened to the dozen I gave you?"

"I lost them. I put them somewhere and I don't know where," he said. I asked if he remembered a Cross pen set, a gift from a Norwegian group who *got it* that Noam Chomsky should have a decent pen. He didn't recall it. I heard my mother's voice, proclaiming whenever we opened a nice gift from her, "That wasn't cheap, ya know!" lest we neglected to appreciate its value, lest we forget to connect the dots and see how much she loved us.

I told him, "My father used a Cross pen to keep his ledger and write checks." He looked at me as if a good pen had never made his bucket list. I took the last box of pens from my desk, pulled out two for safekeeping, and handed him the rest.

More than once in my life, I had asked myself, "What is it with men and their pens?" Watching Noam walk away, pens in hand, I slipped back to 1966, and the sound of my father's voice yelling from downstairs in our living room. "Where is my *PEN*? Who borrowed my Cross pen and didn't put it back?" Put it back *to where?* I wondered. Then, the inevitable: "Everyone come and look for my pen!"

Our den, my father's hangout, boasted a black-and-white TV on a laminated wood cart with wheeled aluminum legs, a plaid sofa, and orange and yellow shag carpeting he kept groomed with a rake. There was no room for a desk, so he sometimes kept his pen on his mahogany bureau. Some mornings as I grabbed a handful of quarters from his change pile for lunch, I would spy his pen there, next to a black plastic comb, a pack of Lark cigarettes, and several matchbooks. (My parents flossed with panache at the end of each meal using the edge of a matchbook.) In the end, my father usually found his pen where he had last used it.

My favorite was a silver, fine-point classic model that opened with a ritzy twist. My handwriting was flawless, even elegant, when he let me use it. Its smooth and confident glide, the sureness of sweep and flow of ink on paper were addictive. I wondered if Noam felt this way about his cheap retractable medium-point pens as he scribbled minuscule marginal notes, commented on thesis drafts, or prepared class notes on long pads of unlined yellow paper.

As Noam left for the day, I noticed several vertical ink stripes above his shirt pocket, the result of not clicking his pen closed before slipping it in. I offered to order him a pocket protector, once a stereotypical mark of an MIT nerd. He said he had one somewhere and would look for it. In other words, No.

The End of the World

A human meteor heads toward Earth.

Noam had been interviewed about the upcoming 2016 elections before and after a month-long trip to California, Germany, and Spain. While he was away, Trump became the US president-elect. In a pre-election interview with the *Huffington Post*, Noam said that the GOP was "literally a serious danger to human survival." In a Truthout interview, he stressed that Trump's November election was possibly one of the most important dates in human history, depending upon our reaction. An article in *The Independent* quoted Noam calling this moment six years before: "If somebody comes along who is charismatic and (seems?) honest, this country is in real trouble ..."

At 10:30 a.m., hearing his hello over my desk partition, I felt like a kid whose father had come home to fix what was broken, to make her world right again. I hugged him. "Good, you're back. It feels like the end of the world."

Linda and Hallie try to get Bertrand Russell to crack a smile.

"Did you know that was the newspaper headline in Germany, in *Der Spiegel*?"

"Seriously?" I asked. He put his hand up, index and thumb scanning left to right as if to highlight the headline one word at a time. I brought it up online:

Der Spiegel depicts Trump as an asteroid headed for Earth … November 11, 2016: "German weekly news magazine portrays the US president elect as a menace."

The article went on to quote R.E.M.'s song, "It's the End of the World (as We Know It)." Everyone had been talking about strategic voting, which we agreed might have helped keep Trump out of office.

Afterward, we chatted briefly about my thoughts on retirement, and his thoughts on leaving MIT. Neither of us gave specific details; our plans were percolating. He sometimes hinted that he would move, other times he wasn't sure. It was clear that his world, and mine, teetered on the edge of a precipice, with changes and challenges on the horizon. For the rest of the day I hummed the chorus to the R.E.M. song, popular when Jay was a teen.

A French documentary crew was setting up. Producer D. Mermet asked me, "Comment vas tu?" I knew his question from years of high school French, and answered in English, "I'm OK, considering this is the end of the world as we know it." Gil, another crewman, showed me that the "Trump as asteroid" article was queued up on his phone. Me: "Mon Dieu." Mermet: "Mein Gott!" I couldn't have dreamed how horrible the next four years would be. It's always been a puzzle to me how citizens of other countries seem to see the US political situation more clearly than many US citizens. The world felt anything but fine.

A visit from my dear friend Linda, another bff, and her dog Hallie got me through that day, helping me feel grounded when the world was falling apart.

32

Looking Back

Is the dog who is animated Roxy?

During my time with Noam and Morris, I answered via my blog the much-asked question, "What is it like to work for Noam Chomsky?" Another question, "Who was your most memorable visitor?" was a harder one. I know how Noam answered this question: "If you could sit and chat with anyone, past or present, for an hour, who would that be?" His answer: David Hume (an eighteenth-century Scottish writer, philosopher, and economist).

Tied with Sufi for first place, my most memorable visitor was filmmaker and director Michel Gondry. All creativity, playful personality, and self-deprecating humor, Gondry arrived twice yearly with his 8mm camera for a four-hour marathon interview. He returned to Paris with the daunting (my projection) task of hand-drawing each frame of every dialogue to create an animated film of Noam's theory of language, called, "Is the Man Who Is Tall Happy?" Our mutual love fest (in my eyes) began in 2010.

During each subsequent visit, we all gathered behind Michel's laptop to view the most recent segment. With the hypnotic delight of childhood, we watched as Noam's voice and words morphed in animated liveliness onto the screen. The film addressed thought-provoking questions about concepts to which I—and probably others—had never given a name. Things like "mental representation" (is a book filled with drawings of images truly representing those images?) and "psychic continuity" (when the prince turns into a frog, why does even a child know that the frog is still the prince?). The term "mental representation" perplexed me at first, as it did Michel, and we both asked Noam to clarify it for us more than once.

He explained again that mental representation suggests that you have in your head a set of properties, abstract representations of a dog or an apple. The point is, it's not just a certain property, or a particular apple or dog you have in mind. You know if you see a car, it has to have wheels and seats and doors and certain other things. In a child's book, we have to choose to portray one apple, one dog, one car, but we need a more abstract notion of what they are. The three of us also traded notes about the concept of externalization of language for communication. I loved my individualized MIT education.

Between visits, Michel and Noam emailed about the French elections. Michel sent videos of his TV commercials, documentaries, and framed drawings of his animations, adding to our anticipation of the finished film. I knew Noam had been drawn in when he asked me to hang a photo in his home of him and Carol walking in a park. The film project helped Noam heal from Carol's death and prepare for his new life to come.

Early on, Michel sent me a zip drive of the rough film. Watching it, Laura and I thought the dog Gondry had drawn to illustrate psychic continuity and mental representation was identical to the animated Roxy who runs into animated Noam's office with an animated Bev (me) at the film's end. We needed to know if the dog in the film was modeled after her. We wanted to enjoy her fifteen minutes of fame.

Hi Michel, Laura and I have been wondering—the animated Roxy at the end looks a lot like the film's animated dog. Did you draw the dog in the film with Roxy in mind? —Bev

Bev, of course the dog in the film is your dog. That is why I draw it!

Big kisses, Michel

Mystery solved—Yay, Roxy! The local premier took place on February 7, 2013, at Brookline's Coolidge Corner Theater. Some of Noam's and my closest friends, family, and colleagues and MIT folks involved in the project and their guests sat in the first three long rows, with MIT affiliates and Cambridge/Boston area folks filling the rest of the auditorium. Laura and I sat with Noam and Michel in the front row as the big screen wove tapestries of spiraling, twisting, morphing color, texture, and movement, animating for us Gondry's thinking process as he interpreted Noam's words in his own, visual brain. It was intense; our friend Jan closed her eyes at times to avoid imagery overload. For me, seeing Noam's ideas play out in animation had the added benefit of his words and ideas forging memorable images in my brain. In the Q&A that followed, Gondry brought out Noam's playfulness. This fascinating project directed by this wonderfully idiosyncratic, creative person made me happy I had wholeheartedly committed to this job.

Just after the 2016 elections, I needed a lift and wrote to Gondry to ask how it was for him to meet Noam for the first time. He wrote:

[It] was April 30 2010. I was walking towards a giant ball of creased tinfoil [the Stata Center], wondering how the structured brain ... of the most intelligent man on the planet could function in this architectural mess. The foil was Frank Gehry and the brain was Noam Chomsky. Michèle Oshima, [then] director of Student & Artist-in-Residence in MIT, was holding my hand but that was my knees that were shaking. The tinfoil ball looks more friendly from inside. We swiftly reached the 8th floor. Beverly welcomed us warmly.

Here I have to make a pause to give you the tour of the whole Chomsky operation. Expectations can be misleading. There is

Noam, Beverly and Roxy, Beverly's dog. That's it. [Glenn was out that day.] In addition, a few times a day, an enigmatic old man [Morris Halle] comes out of an invisible office, speaks two words to Noam as if he was asking to go for a beer, then disappears again.

Years after I can make fun of the situation but at the time my knees had gone from shaking to wobbling. Beverly noticed them and nicely said, "Don't worry, he is very nice. He will be here soon." Then Noam came out of his office. He walked towards me ... He looked big and small at once. Not small when he was far and big when he was close but big and small at the same time ... it's as if the Rushmore mount was moving towards me. This sensation dissipated when we shaked hands ...

kisses, Michel

Two Gondry drawings: Left, Bev on a bench near the Stata Center holding Roxy; right, Noam, and Roxy as Wonderwoman.

I read his reply on Inauguration Day, as another of Bertrand Russell's quotes rolled around in my brain: *The trouble with the world is that the stupid are cocksure and the intelligent are full of doubt.* I had needed this Gondry fix. A second fix would arrive by text after my retirement, when another memorable visitor, actor Catherine Keener, sent me a selfie of her and Gondry having lunch together, reminding me again that I'd had the best job in the world.

33

A Good Friday: April 2017

Two young visitors bring out Noam's playful side.

Life resumed with a new normal when Noam returned after his now customary two-month Arizona winter escape. I brought ten-year-old Annika and eleven-year-old Declan into work with me on Good Friday to show them the MIT campus and to meet Noam while they had the chance. Also, Annika had been carrying a question for him since the January Women's March. The first thing Noam saw when he arrived was the kids and their craft projects spread out on Shigeru's worktable. "Wow, what's going on in *there?*"

"My, uh, grandchildren, Annika and Declan, are here. They're Jay's partner's kids—Lisa's kids."

"*When did this all happen?*" was written on Noam's face, or maybe he was confused by my use of so many possessives. "Whose grandchildren?" he asked.

"My grandchildren. Jay and Lisa aren't married yet, but they're committed and they may …" I introduced them. Their exchange of handshakes seemed sweetly formal.

"Annika has a question for you, when you're free." I had told them Noam was one of the smartest people on the planet. After that buildup they were shyly nervous when we all gathered later outside his library. I took some photos, then switched to videotape as Noam told the kids he hadn't watched TV at their age, but he had listened to the radio.

"I listened to the *Lone Ranger*. He was a cowboy. He said, 'Hi-ho, Silver!'" Pause. "He had a silver horse."

"Was his horse silver? I had watched the TV show decades after the radio version, and I remembered a white horse. Noam's recollection of decades-old details was always accurate, and I was sure he had simply misspoken. Mostly, I was sorry I'd interrupted.

Noam turned to face me. "Sure, it was a white horse. Silver, it was called. He called out, 'Hi-ho, Silver!' You don't remember that?" he asked, turning toward the kids, who had no clue who the Lone Ranger was. I told him I had watched the *Lone Ranger* with my brothers on Saturday mornings when we were little. The kids were quiet, listening, as he relived, with candor and delight, his childhood memories.

"Did you hear that, guys? He had no TV back then."

"No TV!" Noam repeated in a faux stern voice. His playfulness with them filled me with nostalgia. The fictional Lone Ranger wore a mask cut from his murdered brother's vest and devoted his life to fighting outlaws. This fact reminded me of a 1999 interview during which Morris's son, Tim Halle, asked Noam how he dealt with the depressing issues he addressed and challenged daily. Noam had replied: "[I don't feel] depression. It's more agitation. A lot of adrenaline flowing. It may not show, but a lot of anger." At times as I waited at his open door to interrupt him when he was alone, deep in thought, I glimpsed the expressions—frustration, worry, or irritation—flickering beneath his own mask. I observed this real-life Lone Ranger with a mix of tenderness, awe, and admiration. To Noam, we were all his brothers.

"Annika, do you have a question for Professor Chomsky?" I asked.

Instead of looking at him, she turned to me, her nervous expression saying, "I forget. Do I have a question for the smartest man on the planet?" I reminded her that she wanted to ask Professor Chomsky a question about the Boston Women's March.

"You went to the Women's March?" Noam asked.

"Yeah," she said, now looking toward Declan, her hands on her hips.

Declan and Annika take a break after helping Noam sign two cartons of books.

"Was it exciting?" Noam asked.

Declan shot Noam a furtive glance as he shifted to give his sister the stage.

"Yes, but it hurt my legs," Annika said, referring to our hours of standing and walking. She looked up at me. I reminded her that she had asked me how, and whether, marches could change things. She pivoted her head and nodded in Noam's direction, as if to insinuate, "What Bev said ..."

A week before, I had also asked Noam a question: Should we fear terrorist attacks during the march? He said they were unlikely but warned, "There will be provocateurs. I just hope [the protestors] don't fall for it." From our vantage point, all had been peaceful.

Now he answered Annika's question. "Well, I think it got a lot of people interested. So, maybe it will have an effect. You gotta keep trying," and he raised his fist in the air, smiling at each of us in turn.

His answer brought to mind something he had said that struck me during his 2003 interview with Liesbeth Koenen: "There's only one thing that always works. It has changed the world: *keep at it.* Whether it's slavery, women's rights, or the environment, slowly but surely, keep at it. You'll get there ..."

Coming back up in the elevator after picking up pizza with the kids, Declan asked if he could see a robot. Of course—he'd love that. I had blown an opportunity to engage him beyond his world of video games and apologized for not arranging it. By an extraordinary stroke of luck, the one student on the elevator said, "I have a robot. Would you guys like to see it?" Seconds later, on the fourth floor, our world sparked and colorized as we neared the larger-than-life silver robot, the one Roxy and I had spied stacking boxes through CSAIL's courtyard window.

I told Noam about our robot adventure and offered to help with two cartons of his book *Requiem for the American Dream* to be to autographed for a Harvard Square event with Arundhati Roy, Indian author and political activist. Two years before, a film of the same name had been released following four years of filming from time to time in our offices.

"Do you think one of the kids can help me sign the books?" he asked.

"Noam needs help signing fifty books. Who wants to help?" They all but trampled me in an enthusiastic run to his office, creating a system in no time. Declan lifted a book from the carton and opened it to the cover page. Noam signed it and placed it at the back of the table, where Annika collected it and put it into a new pile. She grabbed the empty carton and stacked signed books into it. I was impressed when the girl I couldn't get to clean up after our baking competitions wrote "signed books" on the flap in black marker and folded the flaps neatly down. In photos, Annika's hair swings, and Declan's body blurs with speed as they show one of the planet's smartest men what they're made of. Witnessing this, Noam said, "Who needs robots when we have *them?*"

With both cartons signed, boxed, and labeled, Noam gathered his things to go home. Annika, more at ease after competing with her brother, asked Noam as he stood by them to say goodbye, "How many books have you written?"

"About forty or fifty," he said. My head whipped around exorcist style.

"When I tallied your books sometime in the nineties, you were nearing seventy, not counting publications of lectures and discussions, and books like David Barsamian's. Are we counting interview books and published lectures?" He agreed to take a closer look later, and I thanked Annika for finally getting this project onto our agenda.

On Tuesday he and I went through the bibliographies I had printed out, deciding which of the edited selected readings, lectures, and collections to include in the count. By the end of 2016, he had written more than 80 political books and over 30 linguistics books. When we added a few books of interviews and Q&A's, there were 120 books in all, so far; more than twice his guess. After lunch I helped him sign two remaining cartons of books. "It's funny how kids love to have a task. It was as if they were having a competition. Declan seemed very serious," he said.

"They *are* competitive with one another. They're good kids. You know, they'll probably move in with me within the year."

"Is living with you a good thing or a bad thing?" he asked.

"I mean, they're not moving in *with* me, but with Jay." He had sold his condo and temporarily moved into the first floor of our two-family to help us renovate. When he reconnected with Lisa, he decided to stay. "It's a good thing. We're becoming a family." Lisa's family of three moving into our Chandler Street home would be a very good thing.

34

Noam Shares His News with Bev and Glenn: May 2017

A tapestry to feel and see, impossible to hold.—Carole King

After playing his cards close to his chest, Noam asked me to schedule an afternoon meeting for the three of us in late May. I had been unsure of how and when to share with him the retirement date I had been considering, so this would solve my dilemma. When I told Glenn about the meeting, he said he wasn't convinced it meant that Noam was leaving.

None of us—Noam, Morris, Glenn, nor myself—had wanted to face the inevitable. Each time I thought of asking about Noam's future plans, I felt awkward and hesitant. I'm pretty sure he did, too. The day finally came for "The Talk." I would call it the "Big Reveal," except that Glenn and I had an idea of what was coming. Bursting with the need to know for sure that morning, I busied myself straightening our suite. When Noam rounded the corner, I pounced. "Do you have news for us today?"

"Yes, today is the day," he said without hesitation. I knew better than to take his cheery expression at face value, considering the weight behind his words.

Sitting together with us that afternoon, he took a slow breath in. "If things go as planned, I will be moving." We said nothing. He looked at each of us in turn. "Uh, Glenn should look for another job.

Things change. There is a time to plant, and a time to uproot." His choice of the word "uproot" rather than "sow" or "reap," struck me. "Uproot" was stronger, suggesting extrication. How could it not be? He had been a fixture at MIT for sixty-five years, and I knew that as much as Arizona would embrace him as a prized acquisition, MIT would miss him sorely. I would miss him sorely. He would miss his MIT friends and colleagues, and the Institute itself. His leaving would be big news. Indeed, it already was.

"I'm mostly worried about Morris. I'm afraid that without me to pick him up, he'll stop coming in completely." He had tried for months to bring Morris to work, to keep him engaged, but Morris sometimes forgot and had walked to the library, or told Noam he would rather stay at his apartment. We were all concerned about what Morris's life would look like once our office was closed.

Noam looked at me. "What will you do?"

"Be retired," I said, unsure whether I was going for funny or sarcastic, and knowing how often I had missed past opportunities for more evocative conversation by taking those less serious routes. Our time together had laid unexpected riches at my feet. This thought made me soften, though softening to Noam was never a leap. "I'll travel, visit friends, go to writing workshops, write. Maybe I'll improve my piano, guitar, or ukulele skills. You've commented on my strong intuition. Maybe I'll become a psychic." I was doing it again.

"When will you go?" This was getting real.

"My last day will be July 31." This meant that our last day working together would be in early July, on one of his rare summer days in. So there it was. I had puzzled and fretted and dragged my feet toward this moment for a good while. I took a deep breath, as when a loved one finally passes after a painful struggle. No more denial, no more uncertainty. The words, unwavering, had been said. We were both leaving.

A sensation of deliverance hovered, along with the dying out of a long and familiar reality. When asked, "What do you do?" could I describe how it felt to leave MIT after thirty-eight years, twenty-four

Photo courtesy of Edward Manukyan and Aypoupen.com.

Edward Manukyan, meeting Noam before the performance of his musical tribute to Noam at Kresge Auditorium.

of them in this dynamic, intense place? I would live for a while in
the in-between limbo and try to savor a new sense of what-is-to-be.

"We should start clearing things out in June. Should we send form
emails letting people know you won't be accessible for a while? That
would help stem the flood." Glenn, who hated change, was quiet,
while I was revving up.

"I don't know enough yet about timing, whether I'll still have an
office in the department, and that sort of thing. You may have seen
that we're going to Uruguay in mid July." Since we opened his emails,
we did know. We also knew he was planning to look at housing in
Arizona. I had been aware of virtually all of his plans for the last
twenty-four years, and it had been odd to pretend ignorance.

Noam looked around, and sighed again. "I don't need this big
space anymore. I'll come back and visit, but I can use any office to
see people." I suggested that if he was planning to return, he should
consider sharing an office with Morris again.

"Like in Building 20!" he said, his eyes widening.

"You had offices across from each other when I came in the nineties."

"Before that," he said, suddenly animated, raising his hands to chest level, an index finger above each of his thumbs, pushing them forward until fingers and thumbs were no more than an inch apart, as if the office were the space between them. "Before you came, when we were first in Building 20, Morris and I shared this one small office. We were crammed together. It was a good way to have unplanned conversations." His face had softened. The concept of coming full circle to share an office again with Morris, whether or not it would actually happen, seemed to ease for the three of us the inevitability and the sadness of moving on. Maybe the idea, even if a fantasy, would perk Morris up, too.

Noam looked at me. "Have you driven by the Lexington house lately? The people who bought it promised not to replace it with a horrible McMansion like the ones springing up around it, but they lived in it for a year, and then tore it down. The trees I planted from little seedlings," and with this he pushed his thumbs and middle fingers into the air to demonstrate their original size, "had grown into a forest, and for the most part, they're gone. Take a drive by. The house they're building looks like a huge auditorium."

All this left me feeling melancholy. Later in the day I asked Glenn how he felt about his job ending. He said he wasn't sure it was ending—that since all of the changes were still off in the distance, and Noam seemed tentative, he wasn't going to worry about it.

"Seriously, Glenn? You didn't hear Noam say that you should look for another job?" I suggested he go back and ask Noam, but he didn't want to just yet. Even after this meeting, Noam continued to use qualifiers, like "if I move," and "depending upon where we go." Two steps forward, one back. I let it be. We each had our own way of processing, our own system of denial.

As I turned onto Noam's street to check out his old house lot that weekend, I wondered why it had never clicked that his street

shared the name my parents had first given me when I was born—
Suzanne. He was right—the shell being erected where his house had
stood looked like a concert hall. He literally could not go home again,
except maybe to lecture.

When I gave my official seven-week notice in June, I was asked if
I wanted to keep working part time until Noam's move. I declined; I
hadn't had an entire August off in forever. MIT's Human Resources
Department soon informed Glenn that his part-time job would
extend several months beyond Noam's fall departure. So the deal was
sealed. There would be no more second-guessing anything. There
would be no more *us*.

Over my thirty-eight years at MIT, I had moved steadily ahead,
at times unconsciously, working at each consecutive job to ensure
that Jay and I had a welcoming home and were both able to earn
college degrees. From the time I began working at MIT part time
for the Massachusetts Department of Energy in 1979, I had asked
myself many times if MIT was where I was meant to be. My answer
was always, "This is what I *have* to do, for the medical, tuition, and
retirement benefits."

Now I asked myself the question that scared me most. Who was
I? Who had I become? As a jack-of-all-trades, had I mastered any?
Would I regret not finishing my degree to work as a psychotherapist?
On one of our walks, Deb said, "You will be rid of the mirror that
says you're Noam Chomsky's assistant, Bif [her endearing childhood
version of Bev]. Just as I am rid of the mirror that said I was database manager or assistant registrar at Harvard Business School. I am
now Deb the knitwear designer, knitter, bookmaker. You will be Bif
the writer, traveler, pie maker [Jay and Lisa had jokingly requested
I make more pies after retirement], woodworker—whatever you
choose."

Closing up the office methodically would take about two months.
I filled boxes with photographs, materials to be archived, DVDs. I
saved files electronically and copied Noam and Valeria on a list of
projects to be completed.

Tucked in among his favorite books was a plain wooden box hold-ing Noam's Kyoto Prize medal, an award he received in Japan, in 1988, for his work in cognitive science. With a vague concern that I might be jumping ship before reaching land, I put it on his worktable with a note, hoping he and Valeria would take it with them to Arizona along with other treasures and awards not yet archived.

35

Bev's Retirement Party: June 2017

Do linguists study the spaces between the words?

In late June Roxy and I took an hour-long walk around a campus strewn with decades of memories. The quiet infinite hallway smelled of old notebooks and floor wax, denim and chicken noodle soup. I passed the building where my friend Cindy and I had spun the pottery wheel in a class in the early 1980s. I couldn't find the woodworking shop where I had learned to biscuit and miter, my body muscular and fit from games of racquetball at the old athletic center. How many times had I been tempted to apply to a woodworking school in Boston, where I would stand at a worktable rather than sitting at a desk.

A celebration of my retirement was a few days away. When I took this job at thirty-nine, it was beyond any realm of possibility that I would stay twenty-four years, and even more preposterous that I would retire before Noam or Morris said their final goodbyes to MIT. At sixty-three, I was one year younger than Noam was when I was hired. Morris had been close to seventy, and their retirement was far off.

Noam was working from home on the day of the party, and I was afraid he might have too much going on to show up. My family, and friends from my entire thirty-eight MIT years, would celebrate with

My family gathered for the occasion ... at the Russell poster.

me, but it wouldn't feel right without him. Laura spent the day at work with me, to keep my mind occupied.

Ron, Lynne, Denise, and my nephews Erik and Bobby arrived early and hung out at our suite. At party time we moved to the Red Lounge, transformed by colorful table covers, decorations, and flower arrangements, a bar area, and trays of elaborate appetizers. Paul, Jay, Lisa, Declan, and Annika arrived soon after.

My oldest friends, yoga buddies, and our Totem Mamas group drifted in like misplaced apparitions in my MIT world. The lounge was humming. Morris and his son Tim appeared over Deb's shoulder. Seeing Noam enter behind them was more of a relief than I had anticipated. Glenn stood at a table with my three previous assistants. Sheila had come from Canada with her wife and their dog. Next to her was Linda, who had been so inspired by the work of Noam and his colleagues that she left us to pursue a grad degree focusing on Middle Eastern studies. And Beth, whose offhand humor and outlook so matched mine that we immediately bonded when we had worked together at Ocean Engineering decades before.

I hovered above the scenes. Annika and Declan scribbled sentences oddly similar to the symbols and lines linguists had scrawled on the same white board to illustrate—something. In the back of the room, the rumbling laughter of Morris, Louis, Wayne, Sylvain, and Jay Keyser felt like home. Noam was nearby, laughing with Ron and Denise, their arms around one another. All of my people mingled together for the last time—the closing of a circle.

My family had met Noam and Morris before. Paul and my nephew Erik attended a political debate between Noam and Alan Dershowitz. Others joined musical homages to Noam at Kresge Auditorium, Q&A's, lectures, panel discussions, and MIT's premiere of Michel Gondry's film *Is the Man Who Is Tall Happy?* Morris and Noam had come to my mother's funeral. We had been in one another's lives.

One day in 2003 actor Danny Glover was to meet with Noam. Shaking Noam's hand, my sister Denise, who was filling in for Sheila that week, shared a scene from Glover's last movie. "He's sitting on a toilet and if he gets up, a bomb will explode," she said. I imagined Noam, a pop culture naïf, hearing her words the way a dog hears a human voice in a *Far Side* cartoon: *blah blah* toilet ... *blah* bomb ... explode! (To put this in perspective, I had given him a CD of his favorite movie, Charlie Chaplin's 1931 silent film *City Lights*, for his seventieth birthday.) As we stood there, I thought, "Did I say she was my sister?" She looked like me, and anyway, who was I to talk? I had *acted out* movie scenes to expand his mental movie archive.

Jay Keyser's voice rose. "I don't know how many of you know that Bev writes a blog," he announced, causing me discomfort as he compared my writing to that of Ira Glass and David Sedaris. Most departmental faculty had read my 2015 *Chronicle of Higher Education* piece, "What It's Like to Be Noam Chomsky's Assistant," but I had revealed my blog to very few. Jay read the piece "Elevated," in which I invited a stranger to sing with me on an elevator. In the spirit of spontaneity, he asked everyone to sing "So Long, It's Been Good to

Jay and Deb (his godmother).

Know Ya." Glenn was nearby to lead the chorus.

When dear, dog-loving Professor Judy Thompson honored Roxy's fourteen years at MIT with the award of a squeaky stuffed duck, I held her up like the *Lion King* cub, to cheers. Brad Skow, the professor I had first met soaking wet in an elevator, caught my eye from the spiral staircase at the center of the lounge. Brad and I had taken an unexpected, deep emotional dive when we discovered a serendipitous connection a year before. My heart leapt to see him there, but when I looked up again, he was gone. Feeling the loss, I wrapped up my comments and handed the mic back to Jay.

"Wait, Noam wants to say something," someone shouted. Noam. After all my worrying, I had forgotten he was there. Dressed in a checkered summer shirt and a new pair of jeans preworn at the knees, he took the mic and turned to me.

"Uh, be careful if you sing 'Danny Boy' in front of Bev. She will burst into tears, especially if you're in a pub in Dublin."

It was an inside joke, which was fine with me, because it said something about his memory of our time together. After elaborating on my tendency to burst into tears, he became serious. The room quieted.

"When you walk into our offices over there [he gestured toward our suite], you will find a warm and welcoming atmosphere. Bev created that." A short pause followed. "Difficult day-to-day things happened in that office. I know it couldn't have been easy for her, taking care of two old men. There were some very difficult times, but Bev was there, and she did it all well."

Bev and Noam share a moment.

Before he left, he held out his hands and looked directly at me. We squeezed one another's hands tightly, wordlessly, long enough for me to feel his message of silent agreement that our relationship had been significant. The inside jokes, puzzles, word games, the deaths and illnesses we had seen each other through, grueling days, lighthearted chats, and travel adventures filled my head in quick succession—a version of the Akashic records revealing meaningful scenes over twenty-four years. I would miss him. As I watched Noam leave the party, I knew it would have been too difficult to see him retire first.

My only regret that day was not taking his photo with my family. Bertrand Russell, our guardian of photos, would have been disappointed.

36

Tuesday, July 11, 2017:
Our Last Day Together

I wished I could re-create our work suite at home ...

This, a Tuesday in mid July, would be our last day working together. If Noam didn't appear to be aware of it as the day passed, I would mention it. Noam and Valeria liked to eat lunch together, so I hadn't picked up anything for him in a while, but since he was preoccupied with work, I gave it one last try. "Noam, I'll stop at the café after I walk Roxy. Have you eaten?"

"Uh, no, would you mind picking me up some sushi?"

I grabbed Roxy before he could change his mind. As we crossed Memorial Drive and walked along the Charles River, I wished I had done so more often. A half-hour later we were at Stata's café, where I would carry out my secret agenda. I passed the sushi counter and bellied up to the sandwich bar. The woman behind the counter had lost her cocker spaniel, and so made a big deal of Roxy as she reached for her bread knife. "Do you still have marble rye?" I asked. "I would like a turkey sandwich—dry, no mayo—with lettuce and tomato, on marble rye."

Today I would pick up the sandwich I had watched Noam eat for two-plus decades, the sandwich I'd requested for him in other states and countries when I was asked what he would like to eat while waiting in the "green room," or what to stock in his small hotel fridge for a late night arrival. "No mayo?" they would then repeat, puzzled.

At the office, pouring tea for him for the last time, I held his beige mug between my hands, memorizing the heft of it before handing it to him with the sandwich. "I made an executive decision. Here's your usual," I said, relieved when he laughed. Did he understand the significance of this sandwich? Did he know how often I'd asked organizers to arrange to have one at his hotel room or in a green room? Roxy took a long drink from her water bowl and settled onto her reversible bed, where I had sprinkled a few treats. She would miss the office, too. A few thoughts had come to me during our walk by the river. I took a notepad from my newly decluttered desk drawer to jot down what I wanted to tell Noam before he left Cambridge, MIT, our little world.

Bullet #1: *Should I admit that the coffee he drank for years, the coffee he assumed was fully caffeinated, had been full-strength only first thing in the morning, then decaf from lunchtime on?* His doctor had wanted him to cut down on caffeine, but he insisted on drinking coffee for most of the day, switching to tea and honey in late afternoon only when he was losing his voice. He probably thought I was being kind when I insisted on making his coffee, but I had a sneakier motive—to pop in a decaf pod from a hidden stash I kept in a copy paper cabinet, hoping the magical placebo effect would be enough to boost his energy. When he complained before an evening event that the coffee wasn't doing the trick, I visualized him asleep at the podium and made him another full-strength mug.

Bullet #2: *Should I confess that I mistakenly gave him the wrong bottle of scotch when someone sent one to each of us as thank-you gifts?* The first bottle I'd pulled out of the packaging was a single malt, I assumed the better of the two. I later noticed that the bottle I had taken home was also a single malt scotch, so I looked up the value of both bottles in a panic and was horrified when I realized I had taken the more expensive bottle. I had a vague memory of confessing this years later, but maybe I should send a nice single malt scotch to his new address when they moved.

Bullet #3: *Should I admit that I still had, hanging in the back of my closet, the green-blue Irish knit sweater he asked me to fix years before, his favorite one with a couple of holes, and rips at the cuffs where they'd been folded for a decade?* I had bought some matching yarn and asked Deb, expert knitwear designer and knitter, if she could repair it. A purist, she declared it a lost cause. When I took a closer look and saw the extent of the unraveling, I hid it. It was the first sweater Maria Baghramian had sent from Dublin two decades before. He had given a couple of sweaters to his grandsons, so each time she sent new ones, I stashed one away, presenting it to him as needed. He considered the one with the holes "all broken in." I had considered it broken, though Noam was sure I believed everything was repairable.

Trying to summon other confessions, I looked over at Sufi's robe, still hooked on the coat rack where I had draped it five years before, when Noam passed it on to me for safekeeping. If that coat rack could talk, it might reminisce about the decades of jackets, cameras, umbrellas, and sweaters it had held on its sturdy silver-gray shoulders. The robe reminded me of Sufi's words: "You were meant to be here."

In an alternate reality I would have taken everything—coat racks, desks, chairs, wall art, files, and tchotchkes—so I would never have to say goodbye to Morris and Noam, to any of it. I would hear each of their stories again, this time with popcorn and a recorder, and relive conversations like the one below, which began with me asking Noam why people so often didn't think logically:

Me: "Noam, which came first, the chicken or the egg?"

Noam: "Ah, that's a pretty deep question. I think you should ask Morris. He may tell you a story about a chicken and the Wise Men of Chelm.

Me: "Morris, Noam said you might tell me about a chicken and the Wise Men of Chelm."

Morris: "Yes, but it was not a chicken. It was a fish," he said, holding up an index finger. "A carp, to be specific …"

And then there was *the Shah and the Elephant*. When Noam asked me to agree to an event he wasn't completely sure he would attend,

scheduled for some future date, he would say, "There's always the
Shah and the Elephant. Ask Morris." The simple answer I got from
Morris was if you don't want to do a thing, there's the chance that
something might happen to get you off the hook. The Shah might
die, the elephant might die. Or *you* might die! In his early eighties
Noam said he didn't think the Shah and the Elephant reference was
funny anymore. Death was too real.

In this way I learned more about the interior lives of Morris and
Noam, and about Yiddish culture. While writing down Bullet #4,
about granting my friend Susan and a couple of activist friends short
appointments without asking, I heard his voice calling out.

"Bye, Bev, see you next month!" He gave me a wave as he neared
the door—the same door we had opened to students, activists,
authors, Sufis, political hopefuls, political prisoners, movie directors,
musicians, comedians, world champion boxers, overwhelmed fans,
international leaders, Cirque du Soleil clowns, brilliant thinkers, lost
souls. I should have taken DNA samples from that door's handle. I
sprang up and rushed over, as if I could block his exit. I couldn't let
him waltz out, just like that, as if this were an ordinary day; I would
be *gone* next month, *for good*. Even on ordinary days, I would give
Morris and Noam goodbye hugs, warning them not to get into any
trouble on their way home. Standing there, I asked the question I
knew the answer to. "Isn't this our last day together?" Could he have
forgotten, when the reality of our ending screamed full volume in
my own head? I feared that the minute he disappeared behind that
door and resurfaced fully into his new Arizona life, I would fade from
his radar and merge in his memory with the tens of thousands of
folks who had spent an average of twenty-four minutes with him,
hoping he had retained, even pondered, a nugget of their discussion.
Many had confided in me that their meeting with Noam had been
life changing. I wanted to say, *"Twenty-four minutes in his office changed
your life? Imagine twenty-four years!"*

For more than two decades, I had held a key to a magical land,
where I joined the Buddha on the mountaintop, opening the gate to

those working toward their own brand of enlightenment and walking through gates of my own by proximity. I had a front-row seat to despair, hope, and radical, revolutionary change. I met hands-on advocates re-greening Vietnam and procuring laptops for poor kids. I had seen actors use their public personas to shine lights on issues of mental health, refugees, sexual violence, women's rights, prison systems. I had talked with neuroscientists executing cool experiments, and researchers investigating real and imminent threats to the Earth. I had talked with brilliant minds, the web's creator, Morgan Spurlock after his infamous fast-food experiment, and tens of thousands of people in between. They had, with Noam, sparked my curiosity and thinking. Noam had unknowingly helped me hone my creativity and humor. I saw the Noam behind the mask and beneath his many hats as scholar and activist. As my friend Andrea Moro pointed out, I had seen, worked, and played with "The Third Chomsky."

My eyes fixated on his fingers resting on the door handle as he answered. "We won't say goodbye. Can you make arrangements to come back in late August, and we can … ?" He lifted his hand to make a flapping gesture. I gave him time to finish, but he said nothing, either because he was used to me finishing his sentences, or because he didn't know what came next. *Could* I come back in late August and check in? Check out? Share my bullet list? Had he truly been unaware of our end?

I was sorely aware that I would no longer hold his protective shield, or *be* his shield. It was as if I was about to step out onto the other side of his door and become the stranger I had been before I walked over his threshold for the first time.

My mother had passed down to me the practice of finding temporary ease in simple denial. Somewhere inside me the idea of a delayed farewell was comforting. I asked him to let me know when to come back, and with a quick hug I let him go. Just like that. For many reasons, and for no reason at all except that there were no more ways to say goodbye, nothing left unsaid, I didn't return. Soon after, he left for Arizona. He may as well have moved to Mars.

The Crying Chair/The Confessional

It was necessary to laugh, when she would rather have cried.
— Jane Austen, *Pride and Prejudice*

During my second year on the job, the department purchased an ergonomic high-backed chair to relieve the pains in my neck. By the end of its tenure, the chair's legs wobbled and the fake leather split where my elbows rested as I typed, twisted, turned, and talked, sometimes all at once. Noam's elbows had dug into those same spots during real-time online interviews, since he mostly had a computer-less office. Some chair dancing on good days, and frustrated arm gripping on difficult ones, added to its eventual demise.

The chair where Noam sat to meet with me was years newer than mine. It also rattled and shook, but for different reasons. A high school student looking for work had assembled it, and local lore (meaning that I started a rumor) had it that he tired of putting it together and threw the remaining bolts, washers, and nuts into the trash. Over my final months, as I packed up, cleared away, and emptied out, Noam's meeting chair took on a new persona as the Crying Chair.

Diminutive but mighty Diemut Strebe gave the chair its name when she came to say goodbye during my last week of work. The commotion of her black clogs and upbeat chatter, her high-pitched voice accented in a mixture of German, Dutch, and Italian, and her smattering of accessories announced her arrival. Her customary short black leather jacket and tight jeans highlighted sinewy muscles. Her signature blond hair spiked where she'd raked her hand through it in an energetic moment.

Using DNA cartilage cells from Vincent van Gogh's great-great-grandnephew Lieuwe van Gogh, and saliva and blood samples from two direct descendants of van Gogh's mother, she had re-created a model of van Gogh's severed ear, a project she called *Sugababe*. The gallery had offered to pay for flights to Germany for Laura and me to hear Noam speak into the ear the month following our initial wedding date. Noam later told me what he'd said to the ear: "So, I would like Mr. van Gogh—the original—to explain to us what he had in mind when he cut off his ear. Was it to illustrate the Platonic idea that great art has an element of madness?"

Diemut had photographed our wedding, and came to lament, "I was thinking about it, and I needed to tell you in person that you can't leave." Her emotions, and the reality of my no longer working on the other end of a table, phone, or computer from Noam, made the fact of my leaving hit me harder.

"Sit on my lap," she said, slapping her knee. I didn't, mostly because she was half my size. Diemut said to the student we had hired to help pack, "I have met many gatekeepers and assistants, and Bev is the whole package. That she is leaving—it is shit." I spurted a laugh. She told him I had welcomed many people in to see Professor Chomsky when someone else might not have.

Her words made me think of a fourteen-year-old teen who came for a half-hour meeting. I had met progressive parents dragging their kids in, hell bent on introducing them to an influential person, though to be sure, some kids were happy to visit. This would become a topic in the movie *Captain Fantastic,* in which an unconventional family celebrates Noam Chomsky Day in lieu of Christmas. In this case, the young teen had read most of Noam's political books, and could maybe toss around phrases like anarcho-syndicalism. The father, who had driven him this long distance, wanted to join in, but his son insisted on going in alone. He might have read Noam's books, but he needed a lesson in generosity, in my humble opinion. I sat him in the Crying Chair and proposed a compromise.

"Let's make a deal—I'll give you an extra ten minutes so your father can meet Professor Chomsky and sit in on the beginning of your meeting. Would that work?" He agreed. If I had any power in that office, I was grateful that my intuition and compassion could guide it.

Tom, an Armenian activist, sat in the Crying Chair and said, "Through simple kindness, we touch people in unknown ways, as you did when we met." Then Noam joined us and Tom handed him a box. "Have you ever smoked Cuban cigars?" Noam said that Fidel Castro had given him some good ones a decade ago. He couldn't bring them to the US, so he gave them to his daughter Diane in Mexico. Her husband, Guillermo, loved them.

An old advisee of Noam's, the upbeat Andrew Nevin, sat in the Crying Chair. Laura and I had eaten dinner with him during our second Rome trip. He had heard I was retiring. "I remember when we met. I was intimidated before my first official meeting with Noam, and you told me to take a seat and relax. I never forgot that moment." While waiting this time, he tested me on my backward-talking skill.

Others had sat in the Crying Chair and told me about their work feeding children of war or making fuel from garbage, holding up their fears and frailties against the super-human image they held of Noam. Judy Norsigian sat in it briefly when she and other *Our Bodies, Ourselves* creators waited to talk with Noam about stem cell research. Dr. Kiyul Chung, a global peacemaker working on relations between North and South Korea, had sat there to demonstrate his deep breathing techniques during his last visit. Kiyul offered flights to South Korea for an entourage of Noam, his granddaughter Sandi, Laura, and me, wanting so much for Noam to lecture there on peace prospects. Noam declined; it was too soon after Carol's death.

The Crying Chair was at times the Confessional. Visitors could have begun with a spin on the traditional confessional prayer: "Bless me, Bev, for I have been thinking. These are my thoughts ..." Most confessed to having not done enough, as if I could grant them absolution. I told them many of us felt that way. That chair, and that office, had satisfied my need to connect with and comfort people, to help them find peace, as I might have had I been a practicing therapist, which in many ways, I had been. I had at least become a better listener.

When Noam sat in that chair we had talked about significant political issues and personal life events, wondered how deaf Roxy was, made decisions about handling difficult people, considered moral and ethical dilemmas. I've forgotten many of our chats over time, but the feeling of sitting in my chair across from his, talking or listening while he rolled a paper spring, would stay with me.

Wrestling the Beast

> *One is silver, and the other's gold.*
> —from an old Girl Scout song

My last weeks were a microcosm of my twenty-four years in the office. Sylvain brought me butter from a Paris conference honoring him. I chatted with an old student, now a visiting professor, and shared lunch with our host in Italy, Andrea Moro. We joined Ann Farmer at the Cambridge Google offices for a Q&A on Noam's early activism and corporate responsibility. Morris cackled good-naturedly at some of Noam's remarks. Christopher Lydon interviewed me for his radio show, *Open Source*, which he had titled "Bev Stohl on Noam Chomsky's Soul." I didn't love the title, but did love the print version of the program, in which Noam's book *What Kind of Creatures Are We?*" leaned against Roxy's chest.

•••

I pulled the last items from drawers and cabinets and lay them on my desk. A ball of green-blue yarn used to repair Noam's sweater, business cards I'd had made for each of us, a Howard Zinn button, a forty-year-old film of an article in a rusty tin, a calculator, a folding magnifying glass, an eyeglass repair kit, hearing aid batteries and domes, paper springs I had collected from Noam's desk. Electronic timers blended into the chaos, while the distinct jingling of a kitchen timer pulled me back to my job as, in one visitor's words, Noam's structural temporalist. Our most recent timer, a silver square, had plenty of life left in it.

I took a small box with a hinged lid from the shelf above my computer, remembering the visitor who had gifted Noam and me with hand-carved wooden boxes a decade before. His family had filled mine with homemade stuffed dates. As we talked, he proudly laid in my hands a second box, with a warning that seventeen members of his family had been unable to open it, even after several tries. He was curious whether Noam could. I held the box in my hands for a few long seconds, took a breath, and nudged a corner. The box opened as wide as the man's now gaping mouth. My timer pinged, and he disappeared into Noam's office with the box. Afterwards he announced, "Noam Chomsky couldn't open the box!" I said that I had strong intuition. He bowed, looked at me sideways, and left. I worried that he might think I was a witch, then popped a date in my mouth and got back to work.

It saddened me to think of details that might be lost. For example: before I closed Noam's door at the start of a meeting, I knew through simple eye contact whether he might want a timely ending, or a short extension. Placing his unclasped watch on the table signified to me an on-time ending. I'm not sure he was aware of his subtle signals, but when I knocked early, he might later ask, "How did you know?" Call it intuition. Call it familiarity. Call it, "This person seems like a duck." We had other codes. A journalist from *The Guardian* framed his story around the "not-not-not" of my knuckles at the door, noting Noam's signal that I should try again in a while, his "not yet" wave the second time, and his eventual acknowledgment of my frustrated self. One crew put it this way: "It's rare to find someone who can hand out Girl Scout cookies while cracking a whip. Will you come with us to New York?" It had been a balancing act.

•••

At home, Laura, Jay, his partner Lisa, and I were clearing out the basement for the creation of a new family room. Even as I moved tools out to the garage, I tried to negotiate keeping my hefty work-

table. Since the 1970s, that table
and I had worked together to
build and repair Adirondack
chairs, cabinets, bookcases,
therapy sand trays, blanket
chests, and tarot card cases. I
had used it to transform Noam's
narrow gray in-box table into a
sliding-necked zebra, made his
two-sided doorbell sign, spread
out his boat canopy. My arguments for keeping it branded
me as sentimental and imprac-
tical. They wanted the behe-
moth destroyed. I huffed. They
puffed. Only when Jay wres-
tled the beast onto its back to
expose areas of hidden rot did
I refrain from throwing myself
on top of it in a dramatic fit, begging to let it live.

"Till we meet again ..."

Photo by Roger Leisner.

Noam must have felt nostalgic as well, going through the sixty
years of journals, papers, photos, and calendars I had boxed up for
him at MIT. I couldn't imagine starting a new life at sixty-three. How
could he at almost eighty-nine? It was good that he had Valeria with
him now; he carried too much on his shoulders to be alone at the end
of the day, even if the end of his day was at 3 a.m.

In 1979, my brother Paul had guided me in for a simple, no-ex-
pectations interview for my first MIT job. I am grateful for my unintentional education and fortuitous adventures that followed. On my
last day of work, I sat alone at Noam's desk and took in the familiar scene one last time. The plants around his desk, purchased more
than a decade before to quell his vertigo, needed TLC. We would find
them new homes, and the Crying Chair would have to find a new
identity. Lisa texted that she was bringing Declan and Annika's things

to our two-family, signaling a serendipitous transition between my work and home life. I would welcome our new extended family as I unstrapped myself from this long, wild ride with its own particular vibrancy, its unique spectrum of color and texture, its sharp turns, sudden plunges, and magical sense of "What's going to happen next?"

I wasn't sure I would see Noam again, except, I hated to think, at a memorial for one of his, our, MIT friends. Jay Keyser was the youngest at eighty-two, Wayne was eighty-five, Louis and Noam were in their late eighties, and Sylvain and Morris were ninety-four. My guys.

Of all my life decisions, some good, a few not so much, the decision to take this job was a standout. In the end, I had no regrets. My Sufi had been right.

Afterword

In April of 2018, months after Noam moved to Arizona, he returned to say goodbye to Morris, who died days later surrounded by family and friends. It was fitting that he was the final speaker at the May celebration of Morris's life. It's now summer 2022, and Noam is ninety-three and living in Arizona with his wife, Valeria. He hadn't directly answered this one question many had asked us from the beginning, so I took the chance to ask one last time as I finished writing this book. Even if he had touched upon a reply here or there, by now, looking back, his answer might have changed.

Bev to Noam: We know *how* you replied to everyone who wrote you—by exhausting yourself and staying up until the morning hours to do so ... but the question many ask is, *Why?* What propelled you to do so diligently something that almost nobody in your position has done—make sure that everyone received a reply to their query, no matter what? I've sent people to the Bertrand Russell quote: "unbearable pity for the suffering of mankind." Is this what drove you?

Noam to Bev: Why? I don't know. Arguably crazy. Just a feeling that people have a right to be taken seriously. — Noam

Reading this, I did what Noam most loved to tease me about. I burst into tears.

Acknowledgments

Laura Gimby has been my constant, offering patient counsel as I called out, a thousand times, "Which phrase sounds better?" Her choices resonated every time.

Had my childhood friend Deb Hoss (debhossknits.com), my engine, reader, photo fixer, and all-around savior, not pushed me to begin my blog, shared her tech know-how, and called me down off cliffs, this book might not exist.

My son Jay, a pop culture savant, urged me to connect Noam to a wider audience, to say yes to Reddit and to musicians' requests. He brought us Lisa, and also our fabulous grandchildren, Declan and Annika, who impressed Noam by helping him sign books at lightning speed. When my brother Paul steered me toward MIT in 1979, I felt immediately at home. He and our siblings Ron and Denise, their partners Lynne and Paul, and my nephews, Erik and Bobby, enthusiastically joined in some of these adventures.

Glenn was calm, capable, patient, and forgiving. His literal and figurative background music kept me afloat at our office.

I don't think I could have taken on this ten-plus-year project without suspending myself in a place of magic and trust. My friends Linda (my other bff) and Gary Green—the cavalry—inspire a can-do

Bev, Laura, Lisa, and Jay toast the future ...

attitude in everyone, and I'm lucky to call them friends. Connie Quinn, Mary Baker, Linda Bard, and Totems Jan Duston, Shelley Hartz, and Susan Tordella, reminded me that the universe provides. Denise Thibeault, Cindy Haverstock, Ellen Cantarow, Ann Farmer, Penny Rosenwasser, Carolyn Stack, Elizabeth MacDonald, Maria Sensale, Janet Williams, Monica Kearney, Steve Marchand, Chas and Dee McCarthy, Sheila and Wally Durkin, Dad29, Linnea Gimby, and Emily Aasted all read early blog posts and in some cases, book drafts. Your love, friendship, cheerleading, and honest critiques drowned out my doubts. I can't leave out the plethora of friends in my yoga pals, and "The Chicks of '72."

Jean Tamarin at the *Chronicle of Higher Education* discovered my blog and asked me to write an article for their "Observer" section. Writing that article, also titled "Chomsky and Me," and the posting of it by our department head, David Pesetsky, boosted my confidence. Katharine Westaway magically appeared to organize Noam's libraries. Her research and book draft reviews came, as she had, at just the right time. The ingenious Michel Gondry shined a new light for me on the art of storytelling. I was too close to my project to recognize a few stumbling blocks, but Jay Keyser, former MIT associate provost and Noam's close friend, was generous enough to gently guide me beyond them. Charngchi Way's video expertise was an invaluable lifesaver. Journalist Boris Muñoz and I had key conversations to be sure our book proj-ects didn't overlap. Editing the travel books of Priscilla and Ken Rhodes helped me remember the ways humor can hold a book up.

Immense thanks to my mentors. Ruth Spack, author and educator, read early chapters. Our discussions about the craft of writing trained and enlightened me. The unofficial tutorials of author and biographer Johann Hari, dispensed with humor and humanity (sure, show Oprah my book), were, as the British say, brilliant. Amir Amirani, activist filmmaker extraordinaire, believer, provided me with invaluable connections, insights, and opportunities to consider what I really wanted to say.

Since meeting at Grub Street in 2017, those in my treasured writing group: Laura Beretsky, Jean Duffy, Marcie Kaplan, Maggie Lowe, S. Schirl Smith, and I have lovingly and diligently critiqued, laughed, and cried over each other's stories.

Steve Hiatt, my calm and cool editor, patiently answered my rookie questions. Colin Robinson at O/R Books was moved by my stories enough to publish this book.

In memory of Norma Simon, Sylvia Corrado, and Gail McIver, for listening and laughing. Nathan McMahon, my second son. Morris Halle, the inimitable godfather of our suite. Louis Kampf, whose unending support, long lunch chats, and songfests buoyed me. Danny Holland, always with us.

In honor of every student who walked in my door, many of whom I came to adore, in Civil Engineering, Ocean Engineering, Economics, and Linguistics & Philosophy. You know who you are. Cheers to all who made up our days, and who will, I hope, appreciate—and even find themselves in—this book.

•••

A portion of this book's proceeds will be donated to Partners in Health, pih.org; RESIST, resist.org; and Greenpeace, greenpeace. org. I encourage my readers to donate as well, if possible.

About the Author

Bev Boisseau Stohl was born in 1954, the second of four children brought up in Waltham, Massachusetts, with a lot of humor, Catholic guilt, and empty threats.

She is a nonfiction writer with published essays in the *Chronicle of Higher Education*, *MIT Press*, *Stethoscopes and Pencils*, Chomsky. info, and on Reddit and other social media. Her blog, "Bev Stohl's Stata Confusion," is at bevstohl.blogspot.com. She was interviewed on NPR about her view of Noam Chomsky, the person behind the controversial icon, having worked for Chomsky and his close colleague and suitemate, Morris Halle, for twenty-four years. Her cocker spaniel Roxy, dubbed "the cat" by Noam, lent comic-relief to the office for the

Photo by Anne Mullaney.

last thirteen of those years. Noam, Bev, and Roxy were featured in articles and graphic novels, and animated in Michel Gondry's 2013 film *Is the Man Who Is Tall Happy?* Bev has performed stand-up and improvisation, and appeared on TV news shows talking backward and performing one of her skits. She has dabbled in woodworking, and is mediocre at piano, ukulele, guitar, and waiting her turn to speak. An active member of Boston's Grub Street writing community, Bev lives in Watertown, Massachusetts with her wife, Laura, their rescued dogs Indiana Jones and Tres, and Lily the cat.